Returning the Gift

VOLUME 29

SUN TRACKS

An American Indian Literary Series

Series Editor

Ofelia Zepeda

Editorial Committee

Vine Deloria, Jr.

Larry Evers

Joy Harjo

N. Scott Momaday

Emory Sekaquaptewa

Leslie Marmon Silko

Returning the Gift

Poetry and Prose from the First North American Native Writers' Festival

JOSEPH BRUCHAC, EDITOR

with the support of the

Association for the Study of American Indian Literatures

THE UNIVERSITY OF ARIZONA PRESS / Tucson

Second printing 1997
The University of Arizona Press
Copyright © 1994
Arizona Board of Regents
All Rights Reserved
♾ This book is printed on acid-free, archival-quality paper.
Manufactured in the United States of America.

99 98 97   6 5 4 3 2

Library of Congress Cataloging-in-Publication Data
North American Native Writers' Festival (1st : 1992 :
Norman, Okla.)

  Returning the gift : poetry and prose from the First North
American Native Writers' Festival / Joseph Bruchac, editor,
with the support of the Association for the Study of
American Indian Literatures.

      p. cm. — (Sun tracks ; v. 29)
    Festival held 1992, Norman, Okla.
    ISBN 0-8165-1376-7 (acid-free, archival-quality paper). —
    ISBN 0-8165-1486-0 (acid-free, archival-quality paper)
    1. American literature — Indian authors — Congresses. 2.
Indians of North America — Literary collections —
Congresses. I. Bruchac, Joseph, 1942–   . II. Association for
Study of American Indian Literatures (U.S.) III. Title. IV.
Series.
PS501.S85 vol.29 1994
[PS508.I5]   94-4845
810.9'897 — dc20   CIP

British Library Cataloguing-in-Publication Data
A catalogue record for this book is available from the British
Library.

Production of this volume was supported by a grant from the National Endowment for the Arts.

The following donors contributed to the grant matching fund—

Association for the Study of American Indian Literatures

Charles Brashear

Laura Coltelli

Larry Evers

Firebrand Books

Helen Jaskoski

Karl Kroeber

Robert M. Nelson

A. LaVonne Brown Ruoff

Robert F. Sayre

Studies in American Indian Literature

University College of the University of Cincinnati

University of Richmond

Virginia Commonwealth University

Department of English, Western Washington University

This volume is dedicated

to those who went before us

and those yet to come

Contents

Returning the Gift: An Introduction

Joseph Bruchac

Although what has been happening in the last few decades in North American Native writing has been termed a "renaissance," that word may be both inadequate and inaccurate in describing what has been occurring. A renaissance is a sort of reawakening, but contemporary Native writing is both something old emerging in new forms and something that has never been asleep.

I choose deliberately to use the term "Native" rather than "Native American" for several reasons, among them the preference of many indigenous writers on this continent, especially those in the area now called Canada, not to be labeled as "Native Americans." Also, though designed to replace the inaccurate term "American Indian," there is a certain trendy artificiality about "Native American." Like "Indian," it still vastly simplifies matters by lumping together people from literally hundreds of originally different cultures. Further, many Natives in North America are quite happy being called "Indians," a term which, though inaccurate and artificial, has become familiar over centuries of use, even more familiar than some of the tribal names people are now stuck with, names that were not in their own languages but were spoken in the tongues of other adjoining nations — making the Lakota into Sioux, the Haudenosaunee into Iroquois, the Alnonbak into Abenaki, the Dineh into Navajo. Short of referring to each individual writer by specific tribal origin, in terms of "ethnicity," more directly descriptive words such as "native," "indigenous," or "aboriginal" may be a better way of making it clear that these writers are descendants of the original natives of this hemisphere.

I also refer to *North American* Native writing because, if we are to lump Indians (and Inuits and Aleuts) together, there are more reasons to include the indigenous writers of those areas now called Canada, the United States, Mexico, and Central America than there are to include together the American writers with primarily European roots who have dominated the literatures of those new nations for the last two centuries.

The domination of "American" literatures written in English, French, and Spanish by writers with European roots is both understandable and, I feel, coming to an end. Some critics have described Native writers of the United States and Canada as "marginal," their work as a literature at the edge of the so-called "mainstream." But such descriptions are a matter of perspective. Native literature has much in common with the work of Asian Americans, African Americans, and Spanish-speaking Americans, many of whom have strong Native roots themselves. The "mainstream" in America is being turned back by a tide of multiculturalism. The growing popularity of North American Native writers in Europe, ironically enough, is one indication that the vitality of indigenous voices is more attractive to a great many in the community of world literature than many of the American writers described as established and mainstream. European domination — literary, political, cultural, and military to the point of genocide — and the responses to it have been central in much Native writing. Also, the Native writer has often been a person in the unique and far from marginal position of experiencing — or even being descended from — both the Native and the European world. One of the first Native writers in North America was "The Inca," a man whose mother was Quechuan and whose father was Spanish. In the 1500s he wrote the history of a Spanish expedition to Florida.

This "half-breed perspective," however, so central to the vision of such powerful contemporary Native writers as Wendy Rose, has neither made irrelevant nor silenced the voices of those writers who find themselves balanced between cultures. Nor has it resulted — at least in those writers who are producing significant literature — in their choosing their European heritage over their Native one. Instead, it has given them a vision that I find more interesting and clear than many of their non-Native contemporaries. That clarity of vision can be seen not only in the writers of the last half of the twentieth century but also in such nineteenth-century authors as William Apess. His 1836 *Eulogy on King Phillip* is marked by a strikingly modern awareness of the hypocrisy of an American democratic state built on slavery and the destruction of the Indian, as well as a bitingly satiric sense of humor — as in his lines referring to Increase Mather's speech about God answering the prayer that a bullet should strike the heart of King Phillip, the Wampanoag chief. "If this is the way they pray," Apess wrote, "that is bullets through people's hearts, I hope they will not pray for me; I should rather be excused."

Like the ideas of the "New Criticism," the relegating of indigenous voices to the margins is predicated on the belief that there is one simple empirical (or imperial!) truth in literature and that all writing can be measured by the yardstick of the great works of English literature. To say that literature can be viewed in a subjective vacuum, that one should not consider the biography of the author, the author's cultural milieu, or the place in which the work was written, is, in fact, an absurdity. If no specific context was allowed for a poem being discussed in a university classroom, then the context that actually was used to measure the work became the very much established general context of Western literature itself. It is a monocultural view that is, I believe, eventually as barren and as unsustainable (without continual pruning, clear-cutting, and pest-control) as a tree farm with only one commercially favored species.

When contemporary Native writing—the writing included in this anthology, for example—is placed outside that artificial and limiting context of "European masterworks" and viewed in the larger compass of multiculturalism and world literature, it not only stands up, it stands out. Native writers are bringing as much literary technique and verbal skill, as much pure imagination to their work as any of their contemporaries. They are also adding to it the bicultural awareness that is an antidote for ethnocentrism; the heritage of living and deeply meaningful oral traditions; the survivors' instincts conditioned by more than four centuries of various sorts of resistance with its concomitant sense of humor (like that found in the works of Isaac Bashevis Singer, another writer from a threatened people and a "marginalized " language); and a rooted spirituality at once so simple and so strikingly deep as to move and astonish readers accustomed to a world empty of the power of spiritual meaning.

The July 1992 Returning the Gift Festival brought more Native writers together in one place than at any other time in history. In choosing the Native writers to be invited to the Returning the Gift Festival, the question of defining just *who is* a Native writer came up. The Steering Committee of Returning the Gift finally decided that enrollment in a tribe recognized by the United States government was one accepted way, but not the only way, someone might be defined as a Native writer. Many of the contemporary writers recognized as American Indian do not have tribal enrollments. Criteria for tribal enrollments vary widely, not only between the United States and Canada, but even within the United States.

Among the Cherokee, for example, only those whose ancestors were listed at the time of land allotment can enroll in the nation; yet it is widely known that, as a matter of principle, many full-blooded Cherokee refused to be listed. Further, a few people with no Native ancestry (Cherokee or otherwise) bribed their way onto those rolls in order to get Cherokee land. In some cases, the use of tribal rolls as they are now constituted — as the only definition of who is and is not really Indian — may result within a generation or two in the extinction (on paper) of certain tribal nations. The recent United States Arts and Crafts legislation concerning who is and who is *not* an Indian points in the direction of allowing the individual tribal nations (and not the federal government's mandate) to make such decisions. Yet, as currently written, the law appears to say that Native people north and south of the borders of the United States are forbidden to sell their arts and crafts in the United States as "Indian made." Thus, the only "real Indians" are from the United States.

Returning the Gift finally set up the following guidelines. In order for authors to *be invited* to the festival as Native writers, they were asked to fill out forms stating their tribal heritage, indicating their relationship to and involvement with that tribal community, and assuring us that they were recognized by their tribal community. Provable Native heritage, self-identification as a Native person, and affiliation with the tribal community, therefore, were our criteria. We accepted affiliation not only with tribal nations recognized by the United States Bureau of Indian Affairs, but also such unrecognized but highly visible Native nations within the United States as the Wampanoag of Mashpee and the Vermont Abenaki, and the Native nations north and south of the United States border.

Those who could not answer those questions, whether they were of Native ancestry or not, were welcome to attend the festival but without an invitation and without being subsidized. In selecting material for inclusion in this anthology, only work of those writers invited as Native participants was accepted.

Hundreds of writers attended from dozens of tribal nations, spanning the continent from Alaska to Florida, from Maine to southern California, from the Arctic circle to the highlands of Mexico and Guatemala. Also included were representatives from South America and even Hawaii. If one experience could sum up a gathering as rich and exciting as those four days in Oklahoma were, it would be the experience shared with me by one of the younger Cherokee writers from Oklahoma:

"Seeing all those different Indian faces, all of them writers," she said, "made me realize that I was not alone." Returning the Gift both demonstrated and validated our literature and our devotion to it, not just to the public, but to ourselves.

This anthology was put together by asking every Native writer who had been invited and had attended the festival to send work for possible inclusion. Further, it was stipulated that only new, unpublished work could be considered for inclusion in the anthology. Our aim was to give a picture of Native writing as it is today and to echo some of the energy from that once-in-a-lifetime experience. Because of the enthusiastic response I received — more than two hundred submissions — not everyone could be included, and difficult choices had to be made. I selected what I felt was the best of the work submitted, even though it meant not accepting some work that was both promising and publishable. The result is a collection that not only includes such established writers as Duane Niatum, Simon Ortiz, Lance Henson, Elizabeth Woody, Linda Hogan, and Jeannette Armstrong but also introduces such lesser-known or new voices as Tracy Bonneau, Jeanetta Calhoun, Kim Blaeser, and Chris Fleet. Furthermore, Native Canadian writers are represented in about the same proportion as their attendance at the festival. This anthology demonstrates clearly the strength and the diversity of contemporary Native writing.

I would be remiss, however, if I did not point out that this anthology is not as fully representative as it would have been could we have included work in languages other than English. Significant Native writers are using French as a primary means of expression. Further, a whole contingent of Mayan writers who were at our festival is representative not only of Native voices using Spanish but of Native writers producing a steady flow of work in their original indigenous languages. I apologize for any impression this anthology might give that contemporary Native literature is only being written in English or in languages of European origin. It can be said that contemporary Native literatures are truly multilingual and multicultural, and those who attended the Returning the Gift Festival are living proof of that wonderful diversity, like a forest filled with trees of many kinds, each one different, yet all of them rooted in the earth.

On a Festival Called Returning the Gift

Geary Hobson, Festival Historian

The Returning the Gift Festival was a long time coming, with its actual origins likely as diverse as the beginnings of our nations, with perhaps not a single guiding force, or point, of origin, but rather instead a widely dispersed number of places. At any rate, it probably began at any given time whenever Native writers, in however few numbers, came together and began to wonder if there could ever be a really big meeting.

In October 1981 about a dozen Native American writers found themselves congregated at a chaotic and directionless American Writers Congress in New York. I was there, one of a group of writers who had been asked to take part in a workshop on Indian literature. Our panel was relegated to a suite in a remote wing of the hotel and scheduled at 4:00 in the afternoon, at the same time, in fact, as the Chicano literature session was slated. Not surprisingly, the turnout for our weary pre-cocktail-hour session was predictable: picture, if you will, a large half-moon-shaped table facing an assemblage of metal folding chairs, and the dozen of us making up the panel behind that table (Maurice Kenny, Paula Gunn Allen, Joseph Bruchac, Simon Ortiz, Joy Harjo, Linda Hogan, Rayna Green, Peter Jemison, Wendy Rose, Hanay Geoigamah, Diane Burns, and myself) outnumbering the scattered audience. A question or two from the audience, asking what we thought of Marxism and recent political turmoil in Africa, of whether we recognized a sense of solidarity with the struggles of African people, and so forth, made it fairly apparent that few of our listeners were there to hear a discussion of Native American literature. Except for a heavily attended, marathon poetry reading later that evening at the American Indian Community house — which in-cluded most of us panel members and was organized by Peter Jemison and Maurice Kenny — and a series of talk sessions among our little delegation of Indians, the American Writers Congress was a vast waste of our time.

Later, at a Vancouver meeting in 1986 or 1987, several Canadian Native women writers, including Jeannette Armstrong and Lee Maracle, and a few U.S. Native women writers, among them Anna Lee Walters, Joy Harjo, and Janet Campbell Hale, speculated among themselves about the possibility of an international gathering of Native writers. Then in November 1987 Jeannette Armstrong and Anna Lee Walters were in Albuquerque at the same time as Maurice Kenny, Ted Jojola, and I. We all met informally to discuss how to plan a conference, but again we came away without making any firm decisions.

Then, in the mid-1980s, Oklahomans Carroll Arnett, Louis Oliver, Lance Henson, and Barney Bush went to Joe Bruchac's home in New York State for the purpose of giving readings and to inaugurate the Cross-Cultural Communications series of publications that soon after issued bilingual works of poetry by most of this small group. That get-together prompted, among many things, more talk of an eventual Native writers' meeting. Over the years and more than once there was talk of a conference, or festival, one which would be organized and planned by Native writers themselves. While some white scholars involved with the Native American literature portion of MLA, most notably A. Lavonne Ruoff and Larry Evers, had often urged Native writers to take active roles in the organization, as a rule we did not. But all the time, the call for an all Indian-planned, Indian-run, meeting was voiced.

Soon after I moved to Oklahoma in 1988, I began getting calls and letters from Tim Troy and Joe Bruchac about planning of the 1992 Native writers meeting to correspond to the Columbus Quincentennial. I had about as much interest in fitting myself into anything associated with the Columbus hoopla as I did in fitting Donald Duck into a pair of Reeboks. Tim and Joe wanted me to be on the planning committee. It would be the gathering that various folks had talked of having for years, they said, and we would all come together and voice our responses to the Quincentennial, and so forth. I declined. As much as I felt that a meeting of Indian writers could be a good thing, I also believed that for all of us to get together and respond on cue to Christopher Columbus, even to protest and raise hell, was tantamount to a group of good little Indians in Colonial America being trotted out to hymn the praises of Jesus Christ. However, in a later phone call from Joe, I became intrigued about the festival's possibilities, especially when Joe mentioned that such a meeting could be an opportunity to address all sorts of other matters relating to Indian writing and publishing, and that, in his opinion, the celebration of Columbus was quite decidedly not at the top of his list of priorities.

Over the next few months, particularly after a planning meeting of the Steering Committee in Saranac Lake, New York, I became even more sold on the idea of what a Native writers' festival could actually accomplish. At a meeting in late September of 1990 in the Adirondacks, one of the largest get-togethers ever of Native writers, a dozen of the fifteen Steering Committee members met together, and the actual purpose of what a festival could and would be came into focus. My wife Barbara had already been hired as project coordinator to carry forth the administrative stewardship of the festival. Not a writer, but rather an administrator, Barbara's selection was fortuitous for the direction we needed to have charted for us. Rather than leaving it to all-too-often impractical writers to organize and bring into being, her efforts actually caused the thing to happen. It was also at this early planning meeting that the name of the organization came into being. Maurice Kenny, the host of the Saranac Lake meeting, had invited Chief Tom Porter of the Akwesasne Mohawk Nation to come by and greet us and, if he would, inspire us with his wisdom. He did just that. He remarked that in our avocation as Native writers, involved as we are in taking our peoples' literature back to them in the form of stories and songs, we were actually returning the gift — the gift of storytelling, culture, continuance — to the people, the source from whence it had come. We then immediately decided that we now had a name for our 1992 gathering.

Early on, Joe Bruchac and Tim Troy successfully obtained financial backing from the Bay Foundation, based in New York City. Equally important, the foundation sent along Dick Margolis as a planner and adviser to our group. Dick's initial activities in Returning the Gift's organization and development set the stage for other foundations to bestow their support. Following the lead of the Bay Foundation, the Kellogg Foundation, the Geraldine R. Dodge Foundation, the New York Times Foundation, the Josephine Bay Paul and Michael Paul Foundation, the Witter Bynner Foundation, the Poetry Society of America, the State Arts Council of Oklahoma, the Wingspread Foundation, and the College of Arts and Sciences of the University of Oklahoma made considerable monetary contributions to the festival. Dick Margolis's untimely death in

April of 1991 was felt deeply by the organizers of Returning the Gift. This generous, hard-working man had been the project historian of our organization.

Finally, the festival happened on the campus of the University of Oklahoma in July 1992. It was scheduled for July 7 through 10, but some people actually arrived two to three days early, and some even stayed over two or more days afterwards, so for those of us living in the Norman area, it was a week-long grand round-up of a time. Returning the Gift paid the way to the conference of 220 invited Native writers and 47 Native student writers who were awarded scholarships. Another 101 Native writers came on their own (a partial list of those in attendance is included at the end of the text). Quite a number of non-Native writers and scholars also attended, including Jim Ruppert, A. Lavonne Ruoff, Susan Scarberry-García, James W. Parins, Daniel F. Littlefield, Jr., Denise Low, and Hartmut Lutz. Several publishers, or their representatives, from universities and small presses came and set up shop in the Book Fair portion of the festival. Translators, notably for French, Spanish, and German, were on hand. Months later, I am still learning of people who were at Returning the Gift Festival, people I did not see at all at the time. Like the Battle of Gettysburg, or the 1968 Democratic Convention in Chicago, in retrospect it has taken many months for all the fields of vision to be recognized. Even now, disparate portions of the entire scene at Returning the Gift are still vying for focus, so that the complete picture of all the who and what of it is yet to be grasped.

Through the endeavors of Steering Committee member Victor Montejo, a Tzutujil Mayan writer resident in the United States since 1982, a contingent of six other Mayan writers representing various dialects throughout Guatemala and Chiapas were invited as well. Their presence was, by all accounts, one of the more successful aspects of the festival. Two Quechuas from Peru, and other Latin American Indians, residents in the United States but representing tribes in Panama, Mexico, and Cuba, were also present.

If anyone has ever wondered about how American Indian people (Native Americans, Natives, indigenes, whatever term one cares to use) have thought about the Johnny-come-lately Europeanized boundaries between what are today called the United States and Canada, the United States and Mexico, Guatemala and Belize, and so on, the presence of all the Native writers in attendance at the festival, from various places throughout this Red Peoples' hemisphere, should have underscored the fiction of enforced, superimposed nationality that characterizes the so-called American democracies.

Returning the Gift is a showcase of Native American literature. We all knew that too many non-Native people and, surprisingly, some Indian writers themselves, think of Indian literature as being only two or three writers who have been published by the large Eastern presses. Most of us on the Steering Committee were acutely aware that there were actually hundreds of Indian writers. *Returning the Gift* would be a way to publicize something of who these writers are and what they have to say. The festival also could be an opportunity to forge various sorts of publishing, performance, and teaching networks, and along with this, a good opportunity for writers to meet one another, to contact publishers, translators, and scholars. The festival was viewed additionally as a place to welcome apprentice writers — age not being a factor here, but rather the emphasis being placed on one as a "beginning" writer — and for them to mingle with more established writers and to give, quite probably, their first public readings. Some came hoping to forge an international Native writers' group — either an International Native American Institute of Arts and Letters, a Native American P.E.N., or other similar organizations. Some came to voice political concerns, such as issues of tribal sovereignty and education. Some were here to read their works, period; some only to listen and learn; and some came just to have fun. Whatever the reason, all the writers came, first of all, because they each had some sort of belief in themselves as Native American writers and a hope of being around others who would value that ideal as much as they did.

In the four main days of the festival, approximately 23 plenary sessions and workshops, 20 panel discussions, and between 125 and 135 poetry readings and performances were offered. Workshop and panel discussion topics ranged from "Writing in Native Languages" and "Using History in Native Writing" to "Teaching Native Literature in Colleges and Universities" and "Native Gay and Lesbian Writing." If I had the narrative and descriptive skills of Homer, I could render a complete catalogue of all the panel and workshop activities one after the other, a full listing of all who read their works and how they did, but I would have also had to be three different people, since most of the time events were going on simultaneously in different places.

Also emerging from the festival was the Native Writers Circle of the Americas, an international organization of writers, to supplant the Returning the Gift designation. NWCA will organize future festivals, bestow literary prizes and an annual Lifetime Achievement Award, and help coordinate literary events and contacts for Native writers.

I believe, though, that Returning the Gift came to mean many things to many people, with each person going away with his or her own view or set of memories. I was pleased to find that I had my own series of vivid images, of lasting impressions, moments caught, of the festival, that I know will be with me forever. I'm sure that others have their own memories, equally as valuable as mine, but here are a few of mine I want to share:

Drew Hayden Taylor, satirizing in his own inimitable fashion the tired questions as to whether he is a white or red person, calling himself instead a Pink person. That answer, he said, makes people stop and stare.

N. Scott Momaday's wonderfully told anecdote, on receiving the Returning the Gift Lifetime Achievement Award, of visiting the famed painter Georgia O'Keeffe and of how Ms. O'Keeffe insisted on serving him a refreshment — Ms. O'Keeffe even going to the extent of removing the liquor cabinet's door with a hammer and screwdriver in order to get it open.

Leslie Marmon Silko and her impassioned and eloquent talk in place of the standard reading, in which she summarized 500 years of colonialism in the Western Hemisphere, surprising most of her audience except those of us who had already read her recent *Almanac of the Dead*.

Vickie Sears, during the Gay and Lesbian Writing panel, telling of her grown daughter's rejection of her on learning of her lesbianism, and how despite that, Vickie continues to love the daughter.

Humberto Ak'abal singing a song in his K'iche Mayan language to Luci Tapahonso, very quietly in a crowded bar, while a band is playing in the background, and then Luci singing one in Navajo for him, neither understanding the words of the other, but understanding nonetheless.

I didn't see this, I heard about it, but it's as if I did see it. Late one evening, the seven Mayan writers — Victor Montejo, Humberto Ak'abal, José Balvino Camposeco Mateo, Mario Perfecto Tema

Bautista, Gaspar González, Jacinto Arias Pérez, and Antonio Cota García — wandering around lost while returning to their rooms, were stopped by the OU Campus Police. After moments of great dread, and making known who they were to the police, the police then drove them several blocks to their rooms. Police in Guatemala and Chiapas are often a different story.

And, finally, at the Sac & Fox Powwow on the Saturday after the festival had ended, which many of the writers, staying over the weekend, attended. The scene I have in mind is several American Indian women urging Miryam Yataco to join them in a women's dance portion of the powwow. Miryam, a Quechua from Peru, had never taken part in a powwow. Charlotte DeClue and my wife Barbara gave her some quick lessons as to dance steps and then Dorothy Thorsen of the Yukon helped Miryam adjust the requisite shawl before the start of the dance. Miryam then danced, doing it like she had been doing it all her life, and later said this made her feel she was being made one of the group, which of course she was.

So, what did the festival accomplish? That will obviously depend on whom you ask. But, in keeping with the subjective viewpoint I have employed in this report, I will say that for me, it proved that there is, without a doubt, a great international Native American literature out there. And this literature is a multifaceted spectrum of expression as various as the nations represented — Quechua, Cree, Mohawk, Cherokee, Q'anjob'ol, Tohono O'odham, Lakota, Quapaw, Creek, Metis, Huron, Rappahannock, and the list could go on into the scores. These writers are expressing themselves, representing their people and times, without wondering what John Updike would think of their efforts, or whether Carlos Fuentes would approve, not bothering to ask for Robertson Davies's blessing, and totally without the green light and supervision of the *New York Times Book Review* or the Norton anthology. Hasn't it always been like this?

Returning the Gift

Sherman Alexie

Red Blues

"Mom always said life with a poet would be rough."

K. L. CEDERBLOM

1

Music. Then, more music. Does it matter what kind? Let's say it is bagpipes.
Or a grade school orchestra practicing *Roll on, Columbia, Roll on*. Or the blues.
Or just a drum that sounds like the blues. I have heard that kind of drum at three
in the morning when I pull myself from bed and my ordinary nightmares. Listen.

2

Listen, listen, the Cat is pissing. Where? Where? On the chair. Where's the chair?
Cousin, that chair is three-legged and dangerous. Place it at the inherited
piano and you'll fall when you reach for the farthest chord. It happens that
way. A white woman loves you so much that seeds fall from the cuffs of your
pants and grow into orange trees. She tells you *Don't ever underestimate the
importance of Vitamin C,* but she meant to say *Don't want everything so much.*

3

So much to say tonight but the only pay-phone on the reservation is OUT OF
ORDER. Last week, I tried to call and two teenage Indian girls sent their dogs
after me when I told them I needed the phone. Once, an operator put me on
hold and left me there, halfway between touching and becoming. I didn't
have enough strength or quarters left to hang up. Then, your voice. Your
voice, again. Or is it just neon beer signs buzzing outside The Trading Post?
Or is it a car thumping over a cattle guard? Or is it this silence so brilliant I
can hear my deaf father's television from a mile away?

4

The television was always too loud, until every conversation was distorted, fragmented. *Come out with your hands up* sounded like *You will never have a dream come true. The aliens are coming! The aliens are coming!* sounded like *Just one more beer, sweetheart, and then we'll go home. I love you* sounded like *You've got so much to lose.*

5

I lost my wallet outside the 7-11 that summer and all I worried about was my photograph of you. My last twenty-dollar bill, social security card, driver's license, tribal I.D. could never be introduced as evidence. I spent hours digging through the dumpster, but there was nothing.

6

There is nothing as white as the white girl an Indian boy loves.

7

Indian boy, can you hear that music? Then, more music? No, it's only a pebble rolling down to strike a small stone, rolling down to strike a larger stone, rolling down to strike a boulder, bringing down a mountain. This late in the twentieth century, we still make the unknown ours by destroying it. There is nothing strange about a dead body or a lumber mill. I read in the newspaper that motorists kill over a thousand deer a year on the fifteen-mile stretch of highway between Colville and Chewelah. No one wrote a letter to the editor. Now, I think of her white hands, how dissonant they look against my brown skin, how together we can easily destroy our worlds.

Circularity

8

Spin the globe, faster and faster, revolution after revolution, until you stop it with a fingertip. Where are you now? YOU ARE HERE. Nothing has changed. Black Elk said *Everything tries to be round.* Van Gogh said *Life is probably round.* We're all just trying to find our way back home.

9

Touch home. I'm driving my car up the switchbacks so familiar I close my eyes. *Touch home.* Your hands on that piano almost too large for the room. *Touch home.* My best friend passed out next to the dumpster outside the Trading Post. *Touch home.* Your house older than the trees that surround it. *Touch home.* Blue Creek, Turtle Lake, so close to our uranium mine the water drives a Geiger counter crazy. *Touch home.* Your mirrors that don't hold my reflection. *Touch home.* My family portraits that don't carry a white face. *Touch home.* We don't have keys for the same doors.

10

The door opens and closes again quickly. I hear the lock click. I knock at midnight, miles from my reservation and years from forgiveness. What can I tell you? What treaties can I sign now? *I'd hold you to all your promises if I could find just one I know you'd keep.* America, I can see you outside my window, just beyond my doorstep, fading past the battered lawn. America, I hear your voice, your song every night before I fall asleep, *at the end of another broadcasting day.* America, I played Little League baseball. But I should have learned to dance. America, I have memorized the Pledge of Allegiance. But I should have learned to dance. America, I know the capitals of all fifty states. But I should have learned to dance. America, I follow your footprints, glowing in the dark. I followed them through grass, up walls and across ceilings. But I should have learned to dance.

11

During the owldance, the woman asks the man to dance. If he refuses, he must pay the woman what she wishes and he must also stand before the entire crowd and tell them why he refused. Let's change the rules, reverse the world for a moment: *Will you dance with me?*

12

Hello, you. Hello, me. Can you hear the music, Indian boy? Maybe it's a car radio. Maybe it's Bill Ford's Chevy cruising past the house. He's got just enough gas money to always be in the car. *Hello people we used to be.* Can you feel that bass, Indian boy, that treble and tremble? Maybe it's the last song at the reservation high school dance. Maybe it's the lead singer with braids who doesn't know how to read. He never learned to play guitar. *Isn't it strange? We never changed. We've been through it all yet we're still the same.* Can you recognize the tune, Indian boy? Can you hum a few bars? Maybe it's that song you heard in the middle of the night years ago. Maybe you were half-asleep and thought it was the most beautiful song you ever heard. Maybe it was drums. *And I know it's a miracle that we still go, for all we know, we might still have a way to go.* Can you hear that voice, Indian boy, like an echo, like a divining rod? Maybe it's a *Rock and Roll Fantasy.* Maybe it's a summer flood rushing down the hill toward your future. Maybe it was the blues.

13

Robert Johnson, Robert Johnson, where is that missing song? Someone told me it was hidden at Sand Creek. Someone told me it was buried near Wounded Knee. Someone told me Crazy Horse never died; he just picked up a slide guitar. Here I am, in the reservation of my mind and I don't even have a drum.

14

If you listen close, if you listen tight, you can hear drums twenty-four hours a day. Someone told me once that a drum means *I love you;* someone told me later it means *Tradition is repetition.* Late at night, I take inventory of what I have lost, make plans for the future, but there's only so much I know about survival. The television is white noise, and the midnight movie is just another western where the Indians lose. Nothing changes. So, I keep counting, *one little, two little, three little Indians,* all the way up to ten little Indian boys, stop, then start again, until I count the entire world. These small measurements are all I have as defense against inertia. Believe me, I can never call the reservation home. I don't have keys to any doors here; *I never learned to dance.* Listen, sweetheart. Can you hear that music? Then, more music? It's just me and my blues.

Annette Arkeketa

Quincentennial Ghostdance Song

For all participants who attended "Returning the Gift," Norman, Oklahoma, 500 A.C.

indigenous nations
daughters and sons
dance
the web of words
swelling the
"heart of the hemisphere"

spiritually
pure inherent
blood songs
saturate the earth!

we are what has happened here
we are what has happened here
the nations are here
the nations are here

our children will be what has happened here
our children will be what has happened here

the earth has always been here
the earth has always been here

we have always been here
we have always been here

thank God and Mother Earth
we are here
we are here

so strong!

The Wolf Is Howling

We teach our children

"to cut your hair
is only done when
you show bereavement

for one cradled
in your heart
who has recently
passed on

as time
heals your sorrow
your hair will grow
to mend the pain
you feel"

So a superintendent
at our child's school
uneducated to our indian child's
braid

sends a note home
pinned beneath this
boy's braid

"your child will not be let
back in school
if he does not
cut his hair!"

his mother protecting
this "education"

cuts her son's hair

the wolf is howling

Jeannette Armstrong

Before the Long Night

the sun dropped across the wind
flaring brick orange streamers
the dusk red of mars' scorched skin
in passing
fearful eyes implored each other
chanting
chanting
mouthings of sound ascending into a crescendo
into a dry droning of the hornet's last dance
retracing honey and pollen trails
in the late fall's bronzing of earth's green
in that late day we called forth the saints and the sinners alike
to utter the myths
and we watched the hole ballooning out
over the seas
burning bright green algae

> your first breath is when it happens
> the moment you fuse with the mother

RETURNING TO THAT GIFT IS WHERE THE BEGINNING IS

> "I'm sure you realize that science is the study of HOW THINGS
> HAPPENED"

watching winds blow
across high country

stark clear glacier voices speak without uncertainty
of meticulously chronicling
the direction of footprints crossing windswept plain
the Ayamara
the Kogi
the Inuuk
the Leduc
many others
the long roots
gripping deep the nurturing sweet thick liquid
feasting the story

    all knowledge is seeing rhythm

I SAW COYOTE

    "We concern ourselves solely with logic or truth becomes
        precarious."

below
long night moves across the land
blue-white shafts slice outward and up
and last light glints off
steel
glass
moving refractions crisscrossing
over the dull droning of camocoptors and phantoms
retracing scarlet mirage trails and the flaring orange blossoms
of patriot and scuds scorching a deep red path
in the days of earth's browning

    winding through twilight the clicking of the gnarled cane
    against stone ahead traces a slow sure pathway in the dark

SPIDER INVENTED THE DREAM CATCHER AND WE GOT CAUGHT

    "The difficulty is to pinpoint WITH EXACTNESS how the
    molecules combine causing such phenomena."

we gathered to watch the story unraveling
the strands were multicolored
smooth as ribbons they undulated
on wind currents

and she turned
and turned
a spindle
streaming silvery threads
away into night

> does someone remember the hole opened up once and that a
> woman fell through

SOMEBODY SHOULD SING A SONG
> "It seems that a pivot point has been reached in ascertaining that
> everything that exists is a synergistic process of thrust, the origin
> of which we know nothing other than that it continues."

the stars come out at night
to sing together
and somewhere the black widow
begins a new web
leaping the void
carried by wind
trailing a silver-blue thread
vibrating only very lightly under the stars

Gogisgi / Carroll Arnett

Mecosta Corner Bar

It could just as well be
in Albuquerque or Gallup,
Rapid City or Winner,
Shawnee or El Reno — go in
one, you been in them all.

Last time I was ever in
there this big good ole boy
down at the end of the bar
hollered up to me, "Hey chief,
I'm gonna cut your hair."

Back then I wore a ponytail
that touched my belt, and I
suggested something he could do
in his hat or up a rope. That
didn't set too well with him,

and he started toward me with
the neck of a beer bottle in his
fist, so I cocked my thumb and
pointed right between his eyes
and said pretty loud, "Now look,

pilgrim, if you're serious come
ahead on, but one of us is goin'
to the hospital, that's a fact."

By then the bouncer was between
us holding his sawed-off pool cue

at port arms. "Awww shoot,"
grinned the pilgrim, "I's just
teasin'." I nodded, "Sure
am glad — for both of us."
Turned out a real nice night.

> *Okay. Who remembers*
> *the original meaning*
> *of the word nice?*

Three Okie Coyotes

Not four, only three
for the Trinity,
stretched upright and
nailed to tall posts
along the highway
outside of Coweta,
each with a Miller
beer bottle shoved into
her mouth.

Deepest
regret is that I had
no camera to record it
except the one in my head.

There is no peace there.

My heart is on the ground.

Marilou Awiakta

Dying Back

On the mountain
the standing people are dying back —
hemlock, spruce and pine
turn brown in the head.
The hardwood shrivels in new leaf.
Unnatural death
from acid greed
that takes the form of rain
and fog and cloud.

In the valley
the walking people are blank-eyed.
Elders mouth vacant thought.
Youth grow spindly, wan
from sap too drugged to rise.
Pushers drain it off —
sap is gold to them.
The walking people are dying back
as all species do
that kill their own seed.

A bulldozer slashed the breast
of the Indian mound—
    back and forth
    back and forth
scraping ancient soil
bone/pottery/prayer
into a dump truck
until the land was flat

            except

for one hip bone.
It stood upright—
a periscope from Mother Earth—
and drew into its dark socket
    the wide open wound
    with its ragged edge of grass,
    trees standing nearby
    drooped in dust and shock,
    machines receding . . .

A monarch butterfly
drifted over the site.
She lit on the bone,
slowly flexed her wings.
"When I move my wings
energies change around the world
    round and round and
    up . . . up . . . up . . .
    into the sky.
I may cause storm/hurricane/tornado
when I move my wings."

"I know," said the bone.
"Now men have moved me."

Lorenzo Baca

she had picked coyote up
just west of flagstaff
as he held
his right hand out hitchhiking
and gripped with his left
his old suitcase
filled with fresh love letters
said he was headed out
to second mesa
to see a pregnant lady
he knew

she laughed too much
talked the same
and referred always
to her car
as prince
as it happens the old heap
was a plymouth four-door valiant
so he also called it prince
(though he thought it rather silly)

the girl
claimed to be
an apache movie star
but he already knew

she was just from mescalero
after all
he did recall
having met her at a recent cocktail party
out in hollywood
in california

that's when he overheard her
tell some bald guy
that she'd be heading
back home
when she got her unemployment
so he knew
just where and when to be
on highway 40
going east

after sleeping several hours
(while she talked)
coyote awoke to ask her
why she'd picked him up
she continued rattling on
but what she really said was
i'm attracted always
to bald men
or to young men whose hair
has turned white too early
and of course
to great big furry tails
(she had a fantasy-on-her-mind look)

by winslow
she was feeding him 'bout anything he wanted
(and taking care of tips)
as he laughed and flirted
with all the ladies
waitresses and customers alike

as they drove north
out towards the highway
she slowed the prince

to let a couple of rednecks
in their white new pickup truck
pull out in front of them
they heard the insult echo
you goddamn indians
she drove on
about a mile down the road
then coyote made her stop the prince
he jumped out
howlin' and shouting out
in clear pure english
why don't you all go back to europe

now it was dark
except for
full-moon light
and she was driving him
to his destination in exchange
for a look and feel
of his pair of
solid turquoise dice
which had been carved
(he claimed)
by a navajo medicine man
in exchange for
some love potion

on that lonely
northbound road
inside the diné reservation boundaries
coyote saw a big McDonald's hamburger sign
he didn't like
he thought
how do these indians here
allow it

he requested
that she turn around and stop
coyote left her singing
to her radio on the roadside

he climbed off
slammed the prince's door
made his way through
barbed wire
sand and brush
and came upon
(or underneath)
the sign
(it looked four times smaller from the road)
so he said a little prayer

he began to pull and shake
the huge posts holding up
the McDonald's hamburger sign
until he heard it crack out loud
he kept on
a-shaking and a-pulling
'til it came a-crashing down
to his own size

once on the sand-ground
he ripped it all apart
then hesitated for a moment
shaking off the sweat
and smiling at the moon
and quickly did a fast war dance
complete with song
he howled to himself
while looking at the big moon
and pissing on the sign

he found the woman
back at the prince
still singing at the radio
he asked her to drive on
then leaned over and whispered
just had to take a piss

Marie Annharte Baker

In the Picture I Don't See

In the home of a pink lady
with a pink & gray decor
I sit on a Mexican blanket
draped over a gray love seat
a blue & black geometric offsets
a thin rosy pink stripe
intersecting with the blue lines
divides my ass in two
to my right derriere
pink ruffled curtains
match with the pink carpet
in which I plant my toes
the gray bottoms of my feet
go with the gray couch
the gray end tables coordinated
with the flower-print mirror
hung above my head
on the pink wall with pictures

I should be more pink
a shade of blush overtakes
my welfare blues, gray undertone
of shame at the sharp contrast
I bring to this ostentatious
maybe typical Mohawk warrior residence
I've got wigwam wonder

wonder who lives here &
am I at all related to them?

I explore a Chinese ceramic vase
on the window ledge & discover
it is a huge porcelain egg
ready to birth
another color scheme
a more pretentious decor
concoct a life-style
the kind I might one day achieve
but not if anyone notices
the small gray tipi ring deposit
on the sides of the pink bathtub

it's safer outside the pink lady's house
the weeds grow tall
shade under the umbrella
invites the wanderer to rest
sit on one of the chairs
by the table in the unoccupied zone
the sun deck's strange ambience
comes from the wild backyard
providing the most excellent camouflage
SQ combat might easily occur
among the foxtails soldiers jumped
a lost safari might bump into herds
of buffalo or find conquistadors

The backyard is big as a continent
the pink lady recently returned
from Pocano, a neo-rococo lovers' hideaway
she shows me a souvenir photo
she posed in a champagne glass
complete with pink husband
they hug tight together with bubbles
in a heart-shaped whirlpool tub
both in bed smile awkward
the honeymoon camera is voyeur
part of a threesome caught in the act

The pink husband reassures me
painted Indian babies on plates
are reproductions of a little squaw:
this papoose has a teary eye
yet I'm the one who suffered unrest
woke up at 3 A.M. by drunk drivers
yelling & pointing at bumpers
like Kateri the saint or church lady
next morning whatever disturbs me
I forgive and forget without trouble

I notice how warriors are organized
in kitchens where both men & women talk
sip coffee, talk to mothers
sisters, brothers, other Indians
the terrorism of my hosts is amazing
during the blockade people sobered up
put up with a shortage of bologna,
fast foods, cheap cigarettes, contraband
every cupboard drawer became neat
& organized like Mercier Bridge

The pink lady will keep up her house
until she is invaded again by troops
the honeymoon will be over soon enough
she will have kids & chaos & closetfuls
& a different color scheme to blend all
but she will be finicky in minding
reserve demonstrations & community
on my next visit I'll do my part
sun-deck surveillance is within my scope
check out the foxtail detail
for unplanned excursions or clashes
I'll look for the gray linings
my inquiring mind wants to know
what's behind pink socialist clouds
The identity problem is 100,000 Indians
do not know tribes of origin
I see how other Indians make up lies

better than I do but I do care
if they pretend a past

I have tattooed Indian status
on my big toe, band number
without the photo to show
if I am asked when I sneak
behind the lines in disguise
I am provable in the event
of siege, demo or protest

Even those who know the truth
of their identity say something
different, unusual, unbelievable
I want them to keep stories simple
not everyone works for CSIS or CIA
I don't want everyone to be an Indian
when my identity is made questionable

Them wannabes might have exciting decor
interesting bric-a-brac or pristine
backyards but the right to being Indian
is not a pretty picture
I don't always want to be fighting
for a home & fight my own relations
to give me sanctuary or recognize
my status is not improved economics
every Indian who wants a better life
better fight, be comfortable with protest

José Barreiro / Hatuey

A Chapter from *The Indian Chronicles*

One hundred eight. *My loss of innocence . . .*

It has been three weeks and I pick up this pen. This pen I hold that opens forth so much hurt, arousing memories of a more innocent time, of my own elders and what happened to them. I sit to write and the mere act provides picture after picture, as in those painted *cuadros* that I saw at the Cathedral of Seville, Christ being flogged, Christ being stabbed, Christ bleeding in the agony of crucifixion. I remember real crucifixions; I remember beheadings upon beheadings; I remember wanton injuries to child and mother, wanton, wanton, the boot of the soldier applied to the neck, the torch of the Inquisition to the pyre of Taino. But of all that my mind can hold, I most dread the memory of my own innocence, my Taino goodwill upon which I have gathered so much hatred.

One hundred nine. *A devilish bout with the grape . . .*

The result of memories brought on by this task of writing, plus a touch of deviltry, an incident occurred on New Year's Eve. It has cost me dearly with the monks and even puts in jeopardy how much I can do in the Enriquillo negotiations. I am so bothered with myself I will write it here, as confession.

In agony I had finished writing on Caréy and my elders when a bottle Fray Remigio offered, an error in judgment for both him and me. A bottle of wine we passed back and forth, the young monk and I, as we weeded my patch of onions and peas. The wine we drank in the late afternoon as the sun cooked my brain. By dinnertime, a holiday affair that day, I was deep in my spine, or I should say, my spleen. For one thing, I sat at the abbot's table without care, waiting as the younger monks served me. As wine was passed, I drank a glass and then another. His Eminence, Abbot Enrique Mendoza, sat at the head chair. He is a calm man, old and a bit frail for his many duties, though he walks steadily through his day and his sharp eye misses little.

"Master Diego has had his pleasure in the wine today," he said, with a glance at Fray Remigio, who immediately felt the scrutiny.

"My mind is clear, Your Eminence" I said. "Fear not unreason from this humble guaxeri." It was true: I had just entered that place that wine can bring you where everything gets starkly clear. It had been a long time, nearly five years since the last time I succumbed, though I admit I have had my long days of inebriation.

"I fear not," the Abbot said. "Tonight is the eve of the New Year. We shall eat well and enjoy good company. Among others, Oidor Suazo himself will soon join us, and I believe he brings along that noted intellect, don Gonzalo, who I am sure will prove highly entertaining."

A worse combination could not have been joined by the devil himself. Don Gonzalo, of course, was Oviedo. I felt my whole body stiffen — anticipation and loathing quickly stirring my senses.

"Fernandez de Oviedo y Valdés," I said with loose tongue, pronouncing fully the Castilian sounds I have learned too well. "It is a good thing don Bartolomé is not present."

Several monks laughed a bit too heartily and the Abbot smiled, mischievously, knowing don Bartolomé and Oviedo are bitter enemies. Abbot Mendoza has a sense of strategy. He supports the positions of don Bartolomé, but the two men are often at odds on daily matters. The Good Friar's reputation and authority can at times suffocate all other volition and the old Abbot is often overshadowed by las Casas. So, in his absence, the Abbot courts the same high office holders of Santo Domingo, including Suazo, who have approached the Good Friar.

Minutes later, Oidor Suazo and Oviedo were the first guests to arrive. Oviedo recognized me at once. I remained in my chair as he took his seat and in his face I could see some wonderment at my presence at the table. "Our great Admiral's Dieguillo-boy has grown into quite the personage," he said. "Now he sits as a guest of abbots."

"Properly, sir," I responded. "It is you who are my guests, as the islands are my natural home."

Food and wine were presented promptly by monks who hurried in the silence following my remark. But I was feeling good. Besides, custom was on my side. Governor Diego Columbus himself it was, legitimate son of the admiral and former governor of the Española Island, who in his father's own memory, granted me the right to join a Castilian table, sitting me near him many times at official gatherings in the final weeks before leaving his governorship.

"The Indian is a notable one," Suazo joined in, as always speaking of Indians only in the third person. "Truly, he can say he was with the first admiral, may his grand soul rest in eternal peace."

"Thank you, sir," I replied, reminding them: "It was by order of the Columbus family that I have this privilege . . ."

"Very well, Dieguillo," the Abbot interrupted me. But I continued,

". . . to sit in the company of such esteemed intellect and authority as the present company."

The meal began quietly at that juncture, and I was silent as the young monks serving plates of fish, fowl and pork, rice and beans, scurried about. I knew a reproach was likely from the Abbot if I persisted, and though my nerve to push the conversation was taut, I naturally backed off. In my mind I have been contemplating the work ahead with Enriquillo and the Good Friar and have wanted to avoid, now least of all times, any public altercation whatsoever.

In my silence, as always with a guaxeri like me, I was totally ignored. Perhaps I am that good at dissimulation by now, after years of surviving by blending into my own trance. But it was not hard, really, as the company quite readily ceased to see me altogether, even the Abbot (thus I continued sipping).

As they do on this island on New Year's Eve, other gentlemen dropped by and the table grew to more than ten important men. Only I, and young Silverio, who was helping to serve dinner, were Indians in the room. The convent cook had prepared four large *brazos gitanos,* a common sweet cake of Valencia, and the wine cellar key the Abbot turned over to the serving monks, who kept pouring the wine. The company conversed about many subjects, from the preparations for planting of new sugarcane to the variety of accommodation and experience of the ocean passage, but finally, as always, their conversation ranged to the life of the people who had been encountered on our islands, how they did this or that, subjects acutely painful to me.

Of course, Oviedo dominated in this regard. He liked speaking about my people, as he is also writing a history of the Indies, talking of Tainos and *nitainos,* this cacique and that one, about villages of the large islands and of the *lucayas*, speaking even of my long-lost home of Guanahani. I sipped as he explained who we were and how we acted in the times before the Castilla. For nearly two hours, the wine, rather than excite me to violence, distanced me from Oviedo's words.

At one point, while drinking steadily, Oviedo talked about the marriages of my people and how they were accustomed to making love. He went on and on, as I had heard him years before (and precisely at don Diego Columbus, the second admiral's table), about the caciques having many wives and how upon a cacique's death, sometimes one or more wives would be buried with him.

Everyone laughed. "A hard lot on wives," said an *ascendado* sitting to my left. "Of course, the Indians did many barbaric things."

I twisted inside myself, not because what he said about caciques' wives was totally untrue, but because in my mind, it was not cause for such ridicule. In my mind the Castilla did much more barbaric things. "It is of interest," I said, "that more often than not, a wife's devotion and love compelled her voluntary journey to the spirit island, what we call Coabay."

"Even so, a barbaric custom it is," Oviedo answered, quickly.

"Yet, I wonder if a Christian lady would ever consider doing so, that is, out of devotion?"

I got a laugh out of most of the men, including Oidor Suazo.

"The Indian is clever," said the Oidor.

"So observed the most revered Queen Isabel, the Catholic, at Barcelona, when she met me in 1493," I said.

I realized I was being boorish to speak so much, interjecting myself like this, but as I sat in my chair and looked upon their persons, they all became smaller and smaller and I felt the superiority of my knowledge.

"The Dieguillo is clever," said the Abbot, "but tonight his tongue rides the nectar of the vine. He forgets our Spanish ladies, whole convents of nuns, are devoted to the one true Lord."

I raised my glass to him with a nod, both in deference and mockery. But it was a table gesture I had seen in the nobility and it ingratiated me somewhat (or so I thought) to the group.

Oviedo continued more calmly, now about our abilities. "It is true that here and there a clever Indian is found. Witness our natural companion this evening. But overall the Indians were a sorry lot before our coming. Most were imbeciles, made by nature to serve."

About our holy people, he said: "Blindly, the Indians believed their

26

witch-men, *brujos* they called *behiques,* who fooled everyone by bab-
bling with their little *cemi* idols. Of course, our priests discovered immediately an assistant of the brujo who would hide behind the altar of cemi
and emit sounds, so as to frighten the people."

Oviedo lifted his wine glass and pretended to hide behind it, making
phantasmal sounds, then feigning a witch's voice: "I am your master, give
me your tribute!"

He might have gotten applause for his drama, but at that very moment I interceded. "We never had tribute; it was always exchange, trade."

It was my mistake. He had had enough of me. Quietly, a blotchy redness flushed Oviedo's oval face. "Idolaters!" he spat. "The true Indians
from those days worshiped images of the devil himself!"

"Never mind this diablillo know-it-all," the Abbot interfered, to calm
him down. He looked at me sternly, then turned with a smile to Oviedo.

"I understand from don Bartolomé that they were an obstinate people about coitus," the Abbot goaded him deftly, by way of deviating his
anger.

Oviedo snapped forward. "Nonsense. They did as snakes, wrapped
up under the leg, men with women, men with men. Anti-*natura,* in the
wrong hole!"

I gestured to speak and spilled my glass of wine.

"Diego might consider a retreat," the Abbot said quietly.

I shook my head and he did not insist. "Father las Casas is a truthful
man," I said. "Of all Castilla, he understands our people best."

"Only in going after gold did they abstain," Oviedo said loudly, talking over me as if to ignore me. He glanced around the table and laughed
loudly at the group. "Did you know that? Before going to gather gold,
the Indians abstained from coitus. It was the only time. Every other time
they plugged everything in sight, mothers excluded." He laughed again.
"But they abstained when they went after gold. Ha, and las Casas the
Great Defender says the Indians didn't put value on gold!"

Of course, he was all wrong, but for the moment, my head swirled
and my heart raced. Twice, my elbow slipped on the table as I tried to
keep a silent composure. The love I do feel for the Good Friar was suddenly high in my breast, mixing in with the many emotions.

Oviedo spoke on of sodomy now, in a torrent of words that pierced
me deeply, though he ignored my face. "Repulsion and shame," he kept
repeating, calling our people "irredeemable liars, lazy, dumb, a people
who would rather kill themselves than work hard. The pestilence," he

said, "was only to be thanked for wiping nine out of ten Indians off of the Caribbean islands.

"It was divine intervention directly worked to deny a place on the earth to such savage and bestial peoples, abominable and vicious. It fits them well, and it is most convenient, the frightful sentence carried out against them by an eternal and sovereign God!"

My head in a fog, his words pierced my breast, again and again. It was another half-hour before my head calmed enough to formulate words. This is where the wine lifts all caution.

"Only the blacks of Africa are more bestial than were our own natives," Oviedo was claiming, recalling Governor Diego Columbus's acts of swift violence in 1522, while suppressing a slave rebellion in his own sugar mill. Then he made a mistake, as he wound down to stop. "Your own benefactor, Dieguillo," he said, pointing at me. "He hung them by the dozen, including many Indians who joined in."

"The second admiral, who saved my life twice, was only a man," I retorted. "And a Castilla."

I saw young Silverio jump in a corner. He was the only other Indian in the room.

The Abbot sized me up. As I only held him in check with the potential for greater scandal, I continued quickly, by way of explanation.

"In the case of the Negro rebellion, exactly ten years ago, the second admiral acted swiftly and brutally, it is true. More than twenty blacks had gotten away and word was spreading to other sugarmills. He sought to . . ."

"Everyone knows he feared a general rebellion," Oviedo had caught my challenge. "But why do you say, a Castilla, by what meaning?"

"The way of your punishment has been to hang and burn our elders," I said. "Or is this strange to your learned ears?"

"Only rebellious ones," Oidor Zuaso intervened. I think he tried to change the conversation. "What say you, don Gonzalo, of the efforts to deal with Enriquillo?"

"If done properly, he would be hanged," Oviedo replied quickly, looking at me, and spoke slowly. "He is a brigand, Indian or not, and has committed acts of theft and cruel violence."

"He fights only for a justice denied him," I said.

"He is an outlaw, a rebel and a murderer, regardless of . . ."

I interrupted. "He is a man of conviction, not a fingery gold-counter!"

Oviedo stood, making as if to reach for his dagger. "This Indian must go," he yelled. "Insult I will not tolerate."

Oviedo, now turned historian, came to these islands to count the King's gold. Everyone knows that, and there are many stories on the depths of his pockets. Two monks stepped behind him, I think to prevent violence, as he stood erectly facing me, hand on the hilt of his dagger.

"Las Casas knows these things," I said, with deadly calm. "He writes the truth about us."

The Abbot stood. "Dieguillo must retire," he said, as Oviedo, facing me, yelled: "Las Casas is another lying fool!"

I stood, too, wanting to insult him again, but more words were not forthcoming. I was ready to kill that Oviedo, to yank out his lying tongue. Leaning on the table, my hand clasped a serving knife, a gesture noticed by the Abbot. "Go at once, Dieguillo," he commanded. "You are dangerously close to illegality. Do not threaten an officer of the King."

Thus did I retire to my cloistered cell, in the early hours of this new year, marking now 1,533 since the birth of the Christ.

Diane E. Benson

Coming Back I Heard Mother Earth

The body of my son
Cried from the ground
the sound, the sound . . .

Heartbeat, heart attack
The stress of the day
Conventions, Resolutions
no solutions

Land claimed
Land bare
ancient footsteps
hands and arms reach out
pleading

In the villages
young dying
Boasting transition
Only cultural confusion
two worlds colliding

They wail before the
burial as the young
body is lowered into
the ground
the sound, the sound . . .

And he's so young.

Mother Earth cries
with each stab
as her children
are brought back to her

The tears sting her eyes
as do the lies
that massage the
savage governmental rhetoric
into her wounds

Into the darkness,
the plateau of peace
sought by all
I fall, I fall

Rocking, rock, the
drum beats — the
girls they dance with
knowledge of old

Beating, beat, to
be again to be
I am Athabascan,
Tlingit, Inupiat, Haida,
Yupik, Aleut!!
And more . . .

The shores are covered
with cultural decay
as scavengers of this century
thirsty with greed
drink heavily of the
polluted bay
But —
From the waves
I hear her cry . . .
Come back my children
come back

The sound I hear
The old I hear
and I see, I see

My Spirit Raised Its Hands

(From the play-in-progress, "My Spirit Raised Its Hands," the story of Equal Rights advocates Elizabeth and Roy Peratrovich of the Tlingit nation and the timeless fight for fair and equal treatment regardless of race, in Alaska. Set in the 1940s, the story is also about contact, impact, and transition.)

The Russian Orthodox messenger has just left, and center stage is a Tlingit man stripped of his Chilkat Robe. He stands as we hear the man's mourning speech in Tlingit, and simultaneously in English.

Look, honored people of the Eagle,
my people of the Raven,
a drum sings no more,
the drum, it sinks to the
ocean floor like ancient rocks
covered with seaweed.
Eeshaan!
My heart is sinking,
beats only with the sound
of the dead.
A drum that sings
no more.
Children,
I am crying.
Can you hear?
Grandchildren, can you hear
your heartbeat?

Duane Big Eagle

New York Times in the Supermarket

I'll probably get old and ramble
like George Looks Quick
standing there next to shelves of tomatoes,
almost invisible among the scurrying tourists.
Sometimes so much anger gets lodged inside me
day after day,
I wonder if I'll ever make it to old.
Why do "they" have to take it away
from Indian people
in order to make it their own.
Saying See-ahth* didn't say
what he said.
Doesn't matter what Indian orator said it,
what matters is the message:
the interconnectedness
of all things,
and the responsibility
that comes of seeing it.
The way our fate is connected
to the birds, animals, and fish.
The way the exhaust pipes of our cars
are connected to the air
going into our great-granddaughters' mouths.
It makes you think
about what you do
and how you do it.

I drive slowly out to the beach
and watch the sun and clouds
paint the silver image of a bird,
over and over all afternoon
on the gray sea.
As evening comes,
I hear in my head
an old Southern Plains song,
the kind singers save
for a special moment in the dancing,
the kind that makes
your hair stand on end.
Like in midwinter
when the bluffs are frozen masks of ice
and you get a glimpse in the brilliant haze
of the old ones in heavy robes
standing among shadows of trees,
smoking their pipes and talking
in rays of slanting sun.
This is the way the People will survive,
this is how we will all survive:
to live the interconnectedness so deeply
that we disappear into the land,
leaving it renewed and unmarked.

*A front-page article in the April 21, 1992, *New York Times* called into question what See-ahth, Chief Seattle, said in his famous 1854 speech but did not offer information as to what he did say.

Washashe Airlines

Once I died in a plane crash
and when I got up, no one could see me.
It was a free flight
(Dad worked for the company)
but I tried asking for my money back anyway.
It didn't work, they couldn't hear me either.

I decided to catch the reservation taxi
and spend my French leather gloves
on a ride out to the bar on Eagle Creek.
The Indian bartender was off that night
and I had no money for a drink.
Only other Indian there
was Leroy Stands Tall;
he could see the shape I was in
so he bought me a beer
but he drank half of it
before he slid it down the bar.
I sat down in the corner
to write an autobiography
of my early years:

I was poor as dirt and my mother
was in love with a hitchhiker.
I'm blind in one eye
where my sister hit me with a park swing —
she didn't mean to, her little legs pumping
as she ran away from the neighborhood goat.
My legs are crooked
from a deficiency of early nourishment —
my parents fed me from a book.
My skull is flat in places,
we weren't allowed cradleboards then
so I fell down between the bed and the wall.
I'm long because my father
just caught me by the heels.
I'm named after a paratrooper.
He was killed at the Battle of the Bulge,
which is why I'm so skinny.
I'm deaf in one ear and always turn to the left.
My lungs are immense
from carrying dead Indians around.
My ribs ache from laughing
at my reflection in the mirror
(I don't give back much reflection,
my girl says I suck blood).

My eyeballs got turned around
in the birth canal and stare
inward into a space defined
by superstitions of a summer night,
by dark birds against stars.
(I don't know why I'm so alone,
I don't think I was born that way.)
I have two sons —
both almost as old as I am.
All my first three wives
left me on the same night.
Being Eagle clan, I dream of fancydancing —
I've got the legs for it
from chasing girls across the prairie —
but my memory of the old songs
is drowned out by a century
of gunshots and car horns.
I love to travel: Pawhuska, Tulsa,
Flagstaff, Paris, Venice;
but I always come home.
Hon-monin, old Walks-in-the-Night,
follows me everywhere I go;
he has even less of a chance
than I do.
Someday my dad and I
will build an airplane so light
that it'll float.
We'll take my mother and sister,
all my wives, kids, relatives,
and all the People
and we'll fly back up to the stars
where we used to live.
All those holes up there in the sky —
that's where we're meant to be.

"Osage" is an English word; in our language it's pronounced "wa-sha-shay," Washa-
she. Also, in one part of the origin story of our tribe, the People flew down out of the sky
and landed in red oak trees.

Stolen velocity, snared energy.
I rocket past gravity's orbit,
elastic as string on a bent bow.
"Wa nombly cue-ay!"
"Come and eat," they call to me,
the Old Ones
and they mean it — welcome!
Pointing with their lips* in dreams,
they stand under waterfalls;
their singing is muffled by the roar.
Arms uncurl into wings
as they swing around on the beat.
Voices carry me up;
the drum moves my feet
to touch dry earth.
Dust floats up around us,
beneath my eyelids,
under my tongue.
What's in the blood
boils and forgets,
mocks me, catches me out,
freezes into skeleton memory
and tears my skin red.
For years, nothing,
not a sign, the barest image —
until I realize there'll be no sign,
no great revelation.
Only the precise movement
of brown fingers, brown eyes,
a love of living with distance,
the act of generosity,
whirl of storms, feathered winds,
the return of rain
falling to earth in the night.

*Osage people point with their lips; it's considered impolite to point with a finger.

Gloria Bird

History

Dog smell from the blind mutt at his feet envelops him as he shuffles the deck once more. Solitaire and the traps fall one by one as he questions whether a man's destiny is cast before the hand is played out, before the dog will actually die in the house of dust and dim lamps before the man. Or as one day the dog might enter the kitchen pulled by a string of instinct turned dependency to nose the aluminum pie plate set on the floor for him and find it empty. How many hours or days will it take him, the dog, to discover the flimsy shell of the man, his leg stretched out, his foot nosing into the brown gaping mouth of his slipper? Will the dog recognize his master's unmistakable stench of urine and drying feces before howling his hunger others will misconstrue as compassion for the man who fed him but who had often kicked him awake and aside on his way through? The man looks up at nothing, his world a thin caul of yellowing skin filtering the screen of shapes both dark and light and imperceptible movement. He can smell the distinct sourness of his life, the aching bones of his hands as they lose their limber and his voice-cracking past. In his thirties a man named Camille had offered to read him his fortune, swift motions and expectancy fanned out: great wealth, fame, his name kept within the history books. All lies, of course, but he had believed them then. All the stories bound up in one flip of a card Camille had identified as Death, but then he always knew it would come to this. The great mystery of his life thereafter hinged upon a name Camille had called him by as he left the room, had hissed over his shoulder already dismissing him. Colón. And until this moment the memory of spittle flying from those curled lips had been long forgotten. He reshuffles the now softer cards admitting that over the past, say, twenty, thirty years he has not won one hand. And that lately he dreams of beautiful, scantily dressed people baring gifts, but just as he reaches out to receive them they spill blood-soaked into his bed, thud like severed hands. And there are moments when, like now, he rejects the impossible possibilities. Clearly, madness and reality, lies and truth are the same thing, the way his world is now a pantheon of monotonous repetition like commercials or his frightened prayer mastered through all this prickling slowed-down time. He is thinking he might believe again if only he could read if only he could muster the energy it takes to get up to sluff to the door to retrieve the morning paper to skim the obituaries for his name to attach to his image this driving thought of the cumbersome Other which would explain his disturbed sleep, to put to rest his overwhelming fear, to discover for sure, to have proof and, finally, to know with any certainty at all: were there any survivors?

The Heart's Resilience

Morning sun skims through the cool, dry air
sears the sleepy eyes torn from the rim of dream
as spiders build their webs across our doorways, crickets
come in through cracks of windowsill, and mice dance boldly
in the hallway predicting the coming of an early winter.
A field of chamisal in the foreground tempers
the impoverished memory of the desert's withholding hand,
feeds my hungry spirit. The arroyo empty of rainwater wakes
alive with good luck lizards leaving their imprint in swirled
sand. Cactus plants guard the parameters of our resistance, run
the fenceline. The pinnacles of earth formations rise eye level
in the distance, shift our senses. As easily as morning
it happens, a comic bird flaps its wings, madly chasing
the tail of a white cat, both crossing the highway
in front of us in some parallel universe of inversion
they can't help but respond to.

I am returned here twenty years later with two young sons
not yet a part of the memory of my daughter's birth in this land

whose presence we feel still as native wildflowers bloom freely
occupying each field of vision in variegated yellows
against the sienna earth, the color of their skins.
In the early morning we sit on our veranda on freezing benches
facing a rising sun, the powdered air rough with pollens.
At our backs the western slope is streaked by dark rains
and slow cloud shadows. Revived, a fly as large as a bee comes
to tell. Somewhere on the edge of hearing a lonely puppy yaps
to be let in. Whiffs of burning trash trail in on the living
wind. I plant myself, a toughened yucca to this miraculous land.
My sons like shoots lean into the morning sun to grow, blessed
with youth enough to take the path of the heart's resilience.

September 1992
Arroyo Seco

The Graverobbers and the Oldest Word

"Every word is directed toward an *answer* and cannot escape the profound influence of the answering word that it anticipates."   M. M. BAKHTIN

This they say, once the First Lexicon, the Word, the older sacred language was buried with the Old Ones, two events were let loose on the land: common speech took precedence, and the distant metallic beings threw their ominous shadows over the earth's surface. They wrote their ominous shadows over the earth's surface. They wrote it down so as to dominate all discourse that might follow.

At the First Word's transformation, a Second Lexicon appeared as the Old Ones merged into a single being, the Per, a being both male and female. The Per receded into the womb of the earth; a circle of ordinary stones marked the place of wombing; and the tiny indigenous horses of the continent moved in to guard the place. In time, wild grasses covered the spot, and over generations, the small hooves displaced the stones.

Among the metallic beings, a humming rumor spread of buried treasures more valuable than anything known. The rumor itself was the consequence of bad translation by the metallic beings unused to the elemental language of the people in which the place of wombing was called "holds underground." Two more events were set into motion: the mysterious disappearance of the indigenous horses and the transformation of the Per into water and motes of dust that signaled the disturbance to come.

In a burst of euphemism the digging began. Spades and shovels required the import of metalsmiths whose foul breath infected the metalworks, and whose wretched turns of phrases became a thing created, the first major breach of order that altered the universal tone. The metallic beings, their eyes unaccustomed to sacred places, could not discern the spirits of the Old Ones in the forms of water and motes of dust in what they uncovered. Neither could they hear the consummate tonality of the speaking Per. They regarded the guttural sounds emitted by the people as nonsensical as the motion of their hands. They continued to disturb the earth frantically searching for a transferable sign. Unable to find one, they designed to negate the people, naming them "Others" and blamed their alterity for the failure. The people were now gathered at the edges of the precipice of anguished earth in the descent of the comprehending and glorious Per. The metallic beings, caught off guard by the beauty of the Others, became confused by the attraction they felt for them. In a cacophony of spades and shovels and fear they proceeded to throw them over the edge. They conspired the story of the Others, a weak and inarticulate few, who had thrown themselves away. The metallic beings, unable to feel for their surroundings, neglected to notice the formation of voluminous clouds overhead as witnesses who would carry away another version of the story in direct opposition to the one written in books.

Then began the ritual absorption of the people into the body of the Per which in turn began a fourth series of events. They became an inflection of the Per, the part of the Word that is contained in the many voices of water which, in turn, comes first in many human rituals: raging rivers, shining lakes, waterfalls, lapping oceans, murky ponds, storms, male and female rain. They are the consonance and dissonance in the responsive acts of creation, in the transformation of rituals, and in the opulence of dreams.

The progeny of the metallic beings inherited an avarice for a sounding in memory associated with the frantic reverberation of digging and its instinct transposed upon a bone-gathering event, a disguised search for the missing Word. The now overtly awakened and speaking Per — whose name contains equally all things elemental and organic, dialectic and dichotomous — are equally and potentially lethal and panacean, virulent and benign, heard and unheard.

Kimberly M. Blaeser

Where I Was That Day

It wasn't just the pill bugs
gray, many-legged and pulling that stunt
like they always did
closing in on themselves
contracting into the tiny round mass
like an image of the origin circle
And it wasn't the turtle alone either
who became so neatly one half of the earth's sphere

It was partly that day when I stopped at the little creek
and noticed the funny bumps on that floating log
and how they seemed to be looking at me
and how they were really little heads with beady bulging eyes
and how when I came back a half an hour later
the bumps had been rearranged on that log

It was partly the butterflies that would materialize
out of the flower blossoms
and the deer that appeared and disappeared into the forest
while standing stalk still
whose shape would be invisible one minute
and would stand out clearly the next
like the image in one of the connect-the-dot puzzles

It was the stick bugs, the chameleon
the snakes that became branches
the opossum who was dead then suddenly alive

And it was I who fit and saw one minute so clearly
and then stumbled blind the next
that made me think we are all always finding our place
in the great sphere of creation
that made me know I could learn a way
to pull the world around me too
to color myself with earth and air and water
and so become indistinguishable
to match my breath to the one
to pulse in and out with the mystery
to be both still and wildly alive in the same moment
to be strangely absent from myself
and yet feel large as all creation
to know
to know
to know and to belong
while the spell holds
learning to hold it a little longer each time

That's where I was that day
I watched you from the arbor
never blinking
while you looked all about for me
and then turned back home
thinking to find me in another place
when I was there everywhere you looked

I knew then the stories about Geronimo were true
and that he did turn to stone
while the cavalries passed him by
mistook him for just a part of the mountain
when he had really become the whole mountain
and all the air they breathed
and even the dust beneath their horse's hooves

I walk about trying to find the place I was that day
but getting there seems harder now
I feel heavier, my spirit weighted down
and I'm thinking I must shed something
like the animals shed their hair or skin
lose even their antlers annually

while I hold on to everything
and I'm thinking I must change my colors
like the rabbit, the ptarmigan, the weasel
and I'm thinking I must spin a cocoon
grow wings and learn to fly
and I'm thinking I must hibernate and fast
feed off my own excess for a season
and then perhaps emerge
in the place I was that day
and stay there longer this time

And I walk about and watch the creatures
the tree toads becoming and unbecoming a part of the trunk
the rocks in my path that crack open into grasshoppers and fly away
the spider who hangs suspended before me
and then disappears into thin air
and I feel comforted
knowing we are all
in this puzzle together
knowing we are all just learning
to hold the spell
a little longer
each time

Living History

Walked into Pinehurst, sunburned, smelling of fish,
Big Indian man paying for some gas and a six-pack,
Looking at me hard.
Dreamer, I think. Too old for me.
Heads right toward me.
"Jeez," he says, "You look just like your mom
You must be Marlene's girl."
Pinches my arm, but I guess it's yours
he touches.
Hell, wasn't even looking at me.
Wonder if I'm what they call living history?

"Native Americans" vs. "The Poets"

Some thoughts I had while reading *Poetry East*

You know that solitary Indian
sitting in his fringed leathers
on his horse at the rise of the hill
face painted, holding a lance
there just at the horizon?
That guy's got a Ph.D.
He's *the* Indian for Mankato State or Carroll College

Indian professors at universities throughout the country
Exhibit A,
No B, no C, just solitary romanticized A
Not much of a threat that way

Real trouble is
America
still doesn't know what to do with Indians

Looked for your books lately in Powell's
or 57th St. Books?
Check first in folklore or anthropology
Found Louis' *Wolfsong* in black literature
Hell, no wonder we all got an identity crisis

You a poet?
No, I just write Indian stuff.

Trailing You

For Ike

Trailing you in stories
and then in the dreams
that come just before morning
so that I wake listening for you to finish
what you were saying
or I sit up, swinging my legs to the side of the bed

rushing until my feet feel the carpet
and the rest of what I was expecting
becomes a dream too.
Those mornings I won't talk until
I go over it all the way I remember it
waking up because my nose is so cold
and the fire has gone out in the bedroom stove
lying under the crazy quilt
peeking out of the blankets that cover the window to see
who is out in the yard
what kind of day it is
what's hanging on the clothesline
feeling the last warmth of the flannel sheets
before I swing my legs out and my bare feet touch
not carpet
but ice-cold linoleum covered with bits of gritty sand
that stick to my feet
as I run into the kitchen
where a fire is going in the cook stove
where you have been sitting drinking coffee.
Sometimes I see your face when you turn.
Other times it won't come clear
but I refuse to look at the pictures.
I want you more real than that
not to cry over as if you aren't still here.
If I could tell you the things I'm doing
bring them to you over smoked fish and coffee
you'd make them over for me with your talk and teasing
link with your eyes my past and present.
So I trail you waking and sleeping
hear you laughing as you splash cold water on my face
when I've slept too long
see your hands and hear the water
trickle into the wash basin as you pour for me
smell the side pork and hot biscuits
listen to you call "Kim-a-dill, Kim-a-dill"
as if I were a bird
and in these memories and dreams and stories of you
I find the places you sat and rested while cutting wood

I see the hole you broke in the ice when you fell through
and the path of broken ice as you kept heaving yourself up
over and over with your gun ahead of you all the way to shore
and I wonder if these poems are the path I make and I wonder
how far it is
to shore.

Tracey Bonneau

Sig Elm

This poem is dedicated to the Liliwat peoples movement.

Tall cottonwood
trees
surrounded
sacred fires
as Liliwat
hearts
echoed in desperation

a whirlwind
of mounties
jerking
sisters and gramas
off an imaginary
line
that was drawn
so carefully
so gently

sixty-four brothers and sisters
coiled inside
rings of a lifeline
embedded in a pine tree

like fireflies the mounties
painted the sky
with colorful hell i cop ters

looking through their
electronic eyelids
waiting . . .

sixty-four brothers and sisters
singing good medicine
until the mountain awoke
and beamed
into a landslide
that no one understood
except the moccasin telegraph
of sixty-four brothers and sisters.

I Saw Charlie

This poem is dedicated to Geraldine Manossa after reading "I know who Charlie is" in the Gatherings II Anthology (Theytus Books Ltd.).

He shuffled by me with gray-stained pants exposing evidence of many concrete battles. Carrying a rolled-up sleeping bag snuggled underneath his yellow-stained armpit he picked a butt up from the pavement and proceeded to savor the recycled cigarette. Muggy air surfaced layers of brown sweat that created an alcoholic reddish tinge, showing a scarlet ring around his neck. He glanced at me for a moment and stared away from me. I froze with lamentable pity that punched me right in the throat . . . finally . . . I smelt the sewer channels of this city for the first time. I goggled at the paved walls and the smelly, shit-stained alleyways, the neon jungles filled with affluent people, marching by with their four-hundred-dollar suits saluting a dead processed tree carcass measured with enough value and power to kill a nation . . . while . . . my Native brother walked by confused, lonely, preserved not by his culture but capped in ethnostress that choked him into oppression. My eyes leaked bitter droplets because this man is a warrior fighting the dusty bureaucratic walls of terror encased in concrete. I picked a buttercup from the velvety manicured lawn and looked up into the distance . . . . Slowly, I watched him carry his beat-up brown blanket as he disappeared somewhere on the skyline between the lake and time.

Beth Brant

Telling

For Celeste who told me to tell   and for Vickie

Her face is wide, innocent, clear.
She tells me things.
They are secrets. "He did this to me. He told me not to tell. I never told until now."
Her face twists for an instant, then returns to its rightful beauty.
I listen.
She doesn't cry, but my eyes feel the familiar moisture seeping out, dropping on my hand that holds hers. How dare these tears appear when she — who has the courage to tell — doesn't weep.

She gives me this.
Secrets.

*

I receive a package in the mail.
When I open it, a diary falls into my hands.
How she got my name, my address, she doesn't say.
Her letter says — "I needed to show this to you. You can throw the diary away if you want. I just needed to tell."
The diary is pink. There are gold words stamped on the cover —
Dear Diary.
I am afraid to open you, Dear Diary.
Afraid of the secrets I have to keep.
"He did this to me. My father did this to me. They did this to me. They did this."

50

I think the pages should weep as I do when I read her life.
Who turned away from her need to tell?
Who could throw away the pink vinyl book of a life — a life
thrown away by others? By others' need to throw away a life?
What do I do with this, Dear Diary?

A writer can read. She can hear. She can write.
What does she do with the need of someone to tell?

*

Our foster child comes to live with us.
One leg is crippled, the burn marks shriveling the skin.
This is his fifth foster home. He is three years old. He is
difficult.
He burns with anger — the scars we cannot see.
He can't talk. He points to things and grunts. In three years has
no one noticed he can't speak words?
My anger burns me. I feel as if I have swallowed hot grease.
What does his anger feel like?
We enroll him in a preschool for a few hours of the day, hoping
the exchange with other children will help him heal. I take him
to school and explain that he will be playing with other kids for
a while and I will be back to get him.
When I return, he comes out into the hall, a look of surprise on
his little, dark face.
He smiles with delight at me.
I realize he thought I wasn't coming back.
And he accepted it as normal — as right.
My precious throw-away boy.

We taught you how to talk.
You were innocent. You were difficult.
Innocent.

*

I write.
I wonder what difference it makes — this writing, this scribble
on paper.
The secrets I am told grow in my stomach. They make me want to
vomit. They stay in me and my stomach twists — like her lovely
face — and my hands reach for a pen, a typewriter to calm the

rage and violence that make a home in me.

I write.

I sit in this room, away from my own, yellow legal pad beneath my hand, pen gripped tight in my fingers — the writer who no longer writes directly on paper. The writer who uses machines to say the words.

This pen feels like a knife in my hand.

The paper should bleed, like my people's bodies.

*

I have a dream about Betty Osborne.

The last secrets of her life.

Stabbed and stabbed fifty-six times with a screwdriver to keep the secrets of whitemen.

Betty, your crime was being a woman, an Indian. Your punishment, mutilation and death.

The town kept the secret of who killed you.

Seventeen years before the names were said out loud.

They keep secrets to protect whitemen.

Who do I protect with the secrets given me?

My pen is a knife.

I carve the letters B E T T Y   O S B O R N E on this yellow page.

Surely the paper must bleed from your name.

Why doesn't it bleed for you, my throw-away sister?

The sister I never met except in my dream, my obscene nightmare.

Betty, do I betray you by writing your name for people to see who will not love you?

"What good is a poet . . ." Chrystos

I think about those words today and they hang like a knife or screwdriver over my head, ready to pierce me and render me speechless.

My speech that reveals itself on paper.

"What good is a poet?"

What good is this pen, this yellow paper if I can't fashion them into tools or weapons to change our lives?

How do I use this weapon when I must hold the secrets safe?

This is not safe — being a writer.

"We are the paint for their palette." Salli Benedict

What kind of picture is painted with the ink I commit to paper?
How will they use it against us?
Will I be the same as them?

I love. They do not.
Will love make the difference?

*

Today I woke bleeding from my vagina.
My menses ended days ago.
Is this where the blood goes?
Running out of my womb instead of onto the page, into the words,
the weapon.
The words.
Ugly words.
RAPE. MURDER. TORTURE. SPEECHLESSNESS.
I write and make words that are not beautiful.
RAPE. MURDER. TORTURE. SPEECHLESSNESS.

Dear Diary, did you give her what she needs?
Do I give what she needs?
A friend. A secret-keeper.

Love.
If love could be made visible, something to hold in the hand,
would it be this pen, this weapon, these words I cannot stop
writing?
What were Betty's words?
Where did our foster child's words go?
Do words dissipate, or do they linger behind like ghosts?
Do they float like spirits?
Do they cut through to a place I can barely imagine?
When I expose words, who do I betray?

"If you hide the stories in the bureau drawer, they become Bad
Medicine." Maria Campbell

Are some stories meant to be hidden?
What we do to each other.
What we do between us — the secret, ugly things we do to each
other.

How do I show the blood of them? The ink of our own palette?
Medicine.
Who will heal the writer who uses her ink and blood to tell?
Telling.

Who hears?

Our foster child is with us one year. In that time, he speaks, he
cries, he points to his leg and asks, "What happened? Who did
this?"
A judge gives him back to his mother — the same mother they say
has burned him.
And I wonder if the mother has kept a secret of her own.
Her man's secret.
Has she lost her child for three years because of another's
secret?
What lengths and depths do we go — to protect our own?
The depth of losing a child.
The length of being branded as the torturer of an infant.
Secrets to protect.

These pages should bleed.

Dear Diary, did you give her what she needs?
Can I give what she needs?
Medicine.
I want my words to be Medicine.
Will the same Medicine heal the writer who carries these stories
inside her like knives?
"He did this to me."
"They did this to me."

I BELIEVE HER.

Does she tell me so *I* can tell? The me that shapes words into
weapons.
What can heal the writer who dreams of Betty Osborne and can only
imagine her words?
Her last words. NO. NO. NO.
What can heal the writer who struggles to say the words for a
little boy? A child who cannot speak until he has been loved.

Dear Diary, did your blank pages absorb the shock of the words
written on you?
Dear Diary, did you give her what she needs?
The need to tell and be believed.

*

I need to tell.
Carving letters on yellow paper to understand the violence
committed against us, by us.

What can heal the writer who feels the screwdriver in her dreams?
Who can heal the writer that feels the burning of a child's leg?
What will heal the writer who feels like a traitor as she writes
these words, this language of our enemy, on these yellow pages?
She said to me, "I need to tell you this. You will believe me."
She wrote, "You can throw away this diary, but I needed you to
know."
He said to me, pointing to his leg, "Who did this?"
We did this.
And *they* told us to be speechless.
But they taught us new words that do not occur in our own
language.
RAPE. MURDER. TORTURE. SPEECHLESSNESS. INCEST. POVERTY.
ADDICTION.
These obscene words that do not appear in our own language.

What good is a poet who doesn't remember the language her
Grandfather taught her?
What good is a poet who sees the power of those words manifested
on us and in us?
They stole our speech and raped our minds.
If love could be made visible, would it be in the enemy's
language?
It is the only weapon I hold — this pen, this knife, this tool,
this language.
The writer has to tell. It is the weapon I know how to use.

Dear Diary, did you give her what she needs? Did you back away in
horror at the pain of her life? Did you open beneath her to
receive the blows of her testimony? Did you wrap your pages

around her incest-battered body? Did you make her feel clean
again, innocent?
Yellow paper, please give me what I need.
Pen, be my strength.
If love can be made visible, would it be on the skins of trees,
this paper spread out beneath my hands?

*

"Who will heal the healer?" Dennis Maracle

Love as piercing as the screwdriver's thrust.
Love as searing as the marks on an infant's leg.
Love as clear as her face.
Love as clean as a sheet of yellow paper.
Love as honest as a poem.

I have to tell.

It is the only thing I know to do.

November, 1989
Toronto

Charles Brashear

Grandfather Visions

As if to ask some question, or
Assign me some yet-secret task,
He almost took form from the air —
A wrinkled, gnarled-prune, red-clay face
Transparent still and hesitant;
His turquoise eyes as alive as mine;
His glances needling here and there
As if to test me before he talked.

Was it clairvoyance? Telepathy?
Some measurable aura I know
I send, and therefore should receive?
Some contact, with logic all its own?
Some sense I've yet to learn to use?
"Here am I, your ready servant,"
My silent, opened mind declared.

He was not surprised, though I was — and am —
I, who depend upon *this world* for knowing;
A skeptic, scoffer since my youth,
Who calls metaphysics
So much self- (or mass-) hypnosis;
I, content to live with questions
Until my sense supplies the truth.

But here I was, in a ghost-room
Made of small, plank doors, the sort you close

An attic with — or a basement —
Except these doors sloped up curved walls.
I yanked one, tore it loose, grabbed another.
The nothing behind was earth.

"Wait," I said, "let's not destroy the world;
The grandfathers tell us what they want —
And what we need to know."
The visions nodded their specter heads,
My hands became the land again,
His face dissolved and lost its form,
And my grandfathers flowed back to their river.

William Bray

A Horse Called Tradition

I dreamed of a man who could
ride two horses at the same time
one foot in either saddle
he circled the arena
horses in tandem
a single man on a double animal
Nothing diverging
Man and animal flowing together
rider becoming ridden becoming rider
blended, until my eyes see nothing but movement
watch for small years with no breath

one horse bolts

My blood rides the back of two horses
one the color of night
sings old songs and dances
always counterclockwise
a mane that floats in the air snapping like flags in the
hot Oklahoma wind
This horse knows his way around
and drags main on a slow Saturday night
This is a horse called tradition.

Now the other horse
This immortal horse
walks the streets of New York, L.A., London

drinks water from a crystal trough
and dances till morning in a smoky bar
with smoky people
people so thin you can reach for them
and feel nothing but cool air.
The name of this horse is change

I dreamed I was a man who could
ride two horses at the same time
one foot in either saddle
I circled the arena
horses in tandem a single
man on a double animal
Nothing diverging
Man and animal flowing together
rider becoming ridden becoming rider
lightning striking the earth
from the ground up
current flowing into me up eight legs moving in time
Moving in space.
        one horse bolts

Consider If You Will

consider if you will
the cultural bones
that lay hidden in the
comforting arms of a
fractured and impatient earth
and the mouths that open in golden
expertise to tell their story

consider if you are willing
the battles and brutals
who set the rules for what we might say and when
and where

I am in need of a new way of speaking
allowing that their words if they are words at all
jump and leap to different purpose
and leave the speaker *hadje*
which in Indian means more than crazy

Saturday, April 20, 1991

Silvester Brito

Ute Delta

Ancient, Indian delta
those spirit
river waters
still protect you,
sustaining your strength
to hold up that
old, gnarled
Ute — Peace — Tree.

In center of
your South port
I have used a
Cross Fire Place
to pray and
reach your
deep thoughts —
that they may
whisper forth
through dark breath
of green, Oak leaf
smoke of my tobacco.

I have danced
upon you, by way
of the West
and known

age-old secrets
in life and death
of a blue
painted warrior.

Now I dance
to you, by way
of the East
to learn of the
Red-south,
where lives you
have saved and
sorrows you
have absolved
are in mind of
Northern white one.

But speak to me,
if you may, of
Red-White battles
which are yet
to come, before
our people
can be free.

Meta-Charm

So they are
going to transform you
into a
meta-bionic woman?

They really
do not know
that they may
turn you into
one of those
characters, like

in the old
tribal tales that
tell of people
who fall off
of star plane,
finding it
necessary to adjust
their walk
so as not to
run into cars
or away from
earthlings. They
are said to
follow in
astral path of
celestial sent beings.

Barney Bush

Recollecting the Gift

Riding home through the muggy
night with my honeymooning mother and
her new husband who raises roosters for
fighting and has married into
the appropriate clan   i am riding the air
of a silence stunned by the
gathering of native writers   whose
time has come   that good feeling
after a powwow when you know you have
been in the blood   and the dreams
are from Turtle Island

Back here in this "holler"   my dogs are
covered with dirt and ticks — an almost
full moon's light that elongates massive walnut
limbs like black tentacles gripping the sky
Tree frogs and cicadas sing like stompdance
shakers outside Tahlequah

I draw a bucket of cold springwater from
the well   the deep of our mothers heart
and drink   drench my nakedness   bathe with
cedarsmoke   and sing a song for all those
Indians   those brothers and sisters on the
journey   this strength that brings light to
the confusions among the dark

Nya'weh — Thank you — for this journey
Thank you   Dorothy   fiery soul from Whitehorse
in the Yukon
Thank you   Chehalis Bobbi Bush   who   to set
the record straight is not my wife   but a
possible relative   to account in the
blood   rumors from long ago
And to you   Ed Edmo   the old dreamer who
awakens with new medicine — the oldest power —
and   Louis Gray   i send this invisible
embrace to you and your family
Hoh   brother Lance who clenches tightly to
the brotherhood of warriors   and Jeanetta
who keeps the fire burning in the blood
like that Liz Woody who scouts
each angle with precision . . . aiee
like Bill Yellowrobe who makes his words in
the company of unseen chiefs
And we heard you   Haunani Kay Trask   warrior
nationalist for the mainland of Hawaii — Hawaii
Nya'weh   Mr. Francis   gentle potter of young
people   Thank you for bringing those strong
voices into this hardest journey   I still hear
Hershman Johns exquisite poems   his Tuba City
silence all the way to Tahlequah   all the
way past Little Coons grave   and
how Granddad must have for a moment   heard
Eddie Webb play the flute   and
James May   Hiso Kiniwa   dream crossing his
Cherokee homeland   and Kathy Peltier
has some strange art deco plan that we will
surely hear when her dad comes home

And   Lord   how do i speak about Charlotte
that satin blooded keeper of the moon   and
Helen Chalakee Burgess   whose old Creek voice
takes the point to the heart
Thank you   Julie Moss   for bringing the
spirit of the hills with you   and your son

who calls the oldest songs from the core of
Turtle Island
And Billy O   the prince of Laguna Beach   and
nila northSun   whose poetry can "stop on a dime"
like her fancy-dancing brother — and bleeds the
ego   And electric Diane Burns
doesn't look so "punk" anymore toting that new
little New York Anishinabe   Naturally Diane
has to get sick   Maybe the fresh Oklahoma air

Thank you Geary and Barbara Hobson — You guys are
getting that tribal council look   and
Joe and Carol Bruchac rushing like elders at
a giveaway feast   where every relative
and his cousin show up   and Maurice
the guru of summer clouds   floating over brush
arbors on hot days when only the flies buzz
Thank you
and to all the grantors   Your gift is duly
noted   and will be remembered long after
our country is free again
And there are more to remember   to thank
like THAT Laguna woman who publicly returned
my sweat pants from some roadside Creek woman's
hovel   and all those cooks and
young Mid-East assistants   more patient
than fishermen   and for those who
gave blessings   for compassion
                        for wisdom
                        for respect
                        for the returning.

On Gene Rose Calling Me About Granddad Little Coon
taken to hospital with profuse bleeding from his nose

from Lawton, OK
2/20–21/91

Reality strikes again   how much i need
you   the breathing human being whose
familiar voice whispers through chimes of
silver conchos to my ears
inside whose Muskoke imagination i have
sat and gathered seed stored for late
plantings   that sprout into memories of
spoon-bill ducks   antlered heads
furry-tailed creatures and other effigies of
Mississippi and Ohio River muds

I long for you   the old men in my blood
old men in the midst of baying dogs   night
hunting in the hollows   or atop river
mounds and strings of fish   or evenings
hazed by mosquitoes and smudge pots   and
the rasp of brush arbor leaves   long before
horses returned home
You smell like an old man   an old man's
sweaty neck where my child longs to burrow his
face and smell the tobacco   listen to damp
murmurs comfort his heart with song   the
remaining youth that never wants to let go

Inside the invisible   there is an absence of
graves   but a mirage of Ohio River forest and
drives   long drives   across this Oklahoma
landscape   no state lines on Indian journeys
but what time we have left

Misho   send me your song on the night winds
that i might catch its motion   ride its
blessed melody into the glaze of winter stars
the softest doeskins smoked for our feet   the
journey over the Milky Way where grandmothers
sound the conches   the calls to come home.

Another Road for Creek Sounds and for Smoke

It is a springtime road to
Tulsa   lined with
redbuds   redtailed spirits
the blossoms of white thunder
but no rain this time

It is red earth   traveling with
Gogisgi (Smoke)   who reads the
median warning and loudly shouts
"Damn right! Do NOT drive into
SMOKE"

It is a journey to Coweta   to
Little Coons grave   to leave
gifts from Jelle in the Nederlands
and from other grandchildren

We stand beside his grave   and
bend in low whispers   when the
rain broke upon us
Smoke says "It is right that it should
do this"

On to Tahlequah   and at the same
time   we saw you   Coyote   and
your two brothers on either side
crucified again   the holy trinity
skewered on the crosses of america
whose dark breath unfurls its side

winds through the souls of our
homeland
We catch your reflections   like the
shadows of Golgotha   stretching into
the pond   beer bottles of manifest
destiny wedged into your throats

Among the familiar trances of Tahlequah
we visit with Ethel and her
granddaughter   three snapping
dogs and the remains of a Sunday dinner.

Bobbie Bush

Visitations 7-2-92

I felt your spirit near me,
I was scared.
Last time I felt spirits, I felt
three spirits;
and Uncle died.

Maybe you just came to see what I was doing.

During our life together we shared
many joyous, many terrible things.
We were separated.

Recovering from the trauma of childhood
I received "Indian Money" at age 21.
That's how you found me, through the FEDS.

You returned, calling me "Wheezie" and telling
big stories about hunting and fishing.
We talked, but not real.
You couldn't look me in the eye.

Huh! I thought and nodded my head.
It was true.
All those terrible things did happen;
Rape, Drugs, Alcohol, Theft.
You stole and you couldn't face me.

So we were separated again.

I heard one day the Sheriffs
were looking for me;
something about wrongful death.
I knew.
I felt you were gone.

The loss was terrible —
we didn't make amends —
we didn't heal together.

Maybe that's why you visited me,
to see that I am healing.
I remember you and how you taught me
to be proud of who and what I am;
before the holocaust that blew us apart.

E. K. Caldwell

You Know Who You Are

government green blurs vision
    lines the pockets with illusion
        and the same lies
            the white men always tell.

coyote wears designer clothes
        and struts around
           surrounding himself with fancy words
    knows all the catch phrases
        sounds radical enough
            in word
        acts token enough
           to assuage the white man's guilt.

coyote only prays in public
        in private the spirits are too close
           still fears what might be real.

      easier to live in the comfort zone
   when the denomination of the bills gets too large
      it's hard to make change.

Round Women

Round women
  taught to hate our bodies
Bodies that don't fit
  the ideal
of sticks and lines
  and angles
with a few curves
  thrown in

Have never cared much
   for men
who will make love
  only to bony women
Figure they must be afraid
  of the power in roundness
   power of the circle
    power of women.

Throughout time
  round women
   signify
   earth
   mother
   power

And man mistakes the power
   and rapes it
in back rooms and bedrooms
   on reservations
   and plantations
Owners
  thinking they draw
   the power into them
  while poisoning us
   with their seed.

Round women
　　told always
Look like a line.
Think in a line.
Stand in a line.
　　waiting
　　　　　laughed at
　　　　　　　　receiver of snide remarks
　　　　　　　　and open jeering.

Full moon shines
　　Round is woman
she chides us gently
　　You are woman
　　　　earth
　　　　water
　　　　knowing

Roundness of Grandmother
　　bringing healing to the hearts
　　and strength to the souls
　　of Round Women.

Jeanetta Calhoun

roll call

shawn: dead
valerie: dead
and katie joined the army
jimmy went to prison for molesting the banker's girl

only the SOB's survive intact in this town

tucker's got a ranch house that looks just like Northfork
he breeds buffalo with brahmas so he can eat gentile meat

travis was the only Indian guy the white girls went for
i heard he killed a man at the "Y"
bar over a dollar pool game

the store fronts are empty and the factories
are all gone
even the sonic at the end of the drag
closed up but weed's still the number one cash crop

the cheerleaders and BMOC's look like
twenty miles of bad road
the wear and tear of being big fish in a small pond

i escaped thirteen years ago
and never looked back 'til today

there's a "sold" sign on the smiths' house
i heard the new owners moved down from The City
this dream of raising kids in a small town
just never goes away

another saturday night . . .

1
a hawk hurtled itself into a plate-glass window
i took his wings and tail feathers
offered tobacco for his spirit

you were on an airplane flying east

2
on 42nd street in New York City and 10th street
in Oklahoma City and on a thousand other bitter streets
your dark eyes gaze into the rancid air aching
with regrets and mourning for yesterdays

the bottle of thunderbird in your hand an irony
an anesthesia
for the hungry belly and the screaming heart

3
in a clear star field in western Oklahoma
a tipi rises from a red dust whirlwind
the moon grows luminous in song
hawk feathers carry blessings across the
empty cup of america

listen
they are calling you home

Chrystos

She Said They Say

Especially for Winona LaDuke

you've sold out
I roared laughing even though I only know you from brilliant articles
& gossip about your embarrassing relative
I want to be shown
the unlikely one person who
given our lives
hasn't sold something to get by
one time or another
Even if it's grandma's turquoise necklace or
a story or some kisses or
days of nine-to-five drudge or
polishing copper pots or pretending to teach
angry children who don't want to know about it or
cleaning up after the lazy rich or
the starving poor or
dancing topless to get through college
This is the united states   This is capitalism
even when we have other ideas
We're all selling out to stay alive
I've been in the rumor factory before
uselessly trying to wash my name clean
No escaping it: a powerful, articulate, ethical woman
doesn't sell well
Where we live
insults are how you know

you've got them where it hurts
Myself I'll definitely buy
any words you'd care to put on the table

Zenith Supplies

Smashed into the corner of a glued sawdust bookcase
next to the incense charcoal
are Sweet Grass Braids
for $3.50 with a blue label saying "Native Scents" & a computer code
I can't catch my breath
All night I'm angry as I dream of selling eucharists on street corners
This sacred gift is never to be sold
but hippies don't care as they give themselves new names for the
    same old
rip off of everybody to get some kulture just like their parents
Posters of Chinese workers, clothes from India & coffee from Brazil
don't make you one with the people
Still trying to buy your way to innocence & more
Grow your snarly hair into fake dreads
We don't want you anymore than we wanted your grandparents &
    their mission schools
Leave us alone   Find your kulture & your spirituality in our
    mutual history
Stop selling out ours
Cut your knotty hair off   Leave Rasta to Rasta
Leave the Drum & Sweat Lodge & Sundance to those whose heart
    beats it
This roar of old sorrow whirls hot from my shoulders as I wash
the cooking pots of the dead
We aren't here to entertain you excuse you explain reality to you
enter your names in our lives or soothe you
Exploitation has many servants
Pick up your own socks
Live in this world your ancestors made until you feel it
until we change it

Robert J. Conley

Dlanusi

Gog'ski, or Smoker, was having a big feed at Rocky Ford in the Goingsnake District of the Cherokee Nation. Rocky Ford was not a place anyone would recognize while passing through, but it was a place the Cherokees who lived there recognized as a community. The homes of the residents of Rocky Ford were scattered throughout the hills, and even when two or three families might be located within easy walking distance or even within shouting distance, they were still not within view of each other. A near neighbor's home was always obscured from sight by the thick growth of trees, the winding roads and the ups and downs of the Ozark foothills. What made Rocky Ford a community was purely and simply the sense of community of its inhabitants. They attended the same church, a Cherokee language Baptist church, and they got together frequently for community gatherings. They also knew and minded each other's business as if it were their own.

Anyway, Gog'ski was having a big feed at his home. Perhaps there was an occasion for this feed, perhaps not. That information has been obscured by the passing of a century and perhaps a decade. Hogs had been slaughtered, much food had been prepared, and a large and jovial crowd had gathered around Gog'ski's log cabin. The crowd consisted mostly of full-blood Cherokees, and the conversation was all in the Cherokee language. Gog'ski was running around acting busy, playing the host, but he finally slowed down a bit to catch his breath, stopping in a small cluster of men who had been engaged in idle chatter.

"This is a good gathering," said Walkingstick to Gog'ski.

"Everyone should get plenty to eat," said Gog'ski. "There's lots of food. I killed three hogs."

"That might not be enough if Dlanusi was here," said Yudi, and his comment was answered by a round of good-natured laughter.

"Yeah," said Gog'ski, "old Leech could really put away the hog meat. Well, I guess he still can."

"He could if he could get to it," said Walkingstick. "I bet that's the worst part of jail for Dlanusi. They don't feed them much hog meat in there, I bet. Ask Shell."

"More like hog slop," said Shell, or Uyasga.

"Say," said Yudi. "You were over there in that Fort Smith jail with Leech, weren't you?"

"Uh huh," said Shell. "For too long."

"At least they let you out," said Gog'ski. "They won't ever let Dlanusi out. Not until they hang him, I guess."

"When will they do that?" asked Yudi.

"I'm not sure," said Gog'ski, wrinkling his brow as if in deep thought. There was a pause, and then Shell spoke again.

"Today," he said.

Everyone looked at him.

"They're supposed to do it today," he said.

The awkward silence continued until Gog'ski stood up and paced nervously.

"Today," he repeated. "I guess we shouldn't be here having such a good time. Not if they're going to hang Leech today. He could be hanging right now."

Yudi shivered, and Walkingstick looked at the ground. Gog'ski's right hand went instinctively to his own throat. He looked at Shell.

"You've only been home about a week," he said. "You were in the same cell with Dlanusi, weren't you?"

"Yes, I was," said Shell.

"Did he know then when it would be his last day?"

"Yes. He knew."

"How was he?" said Gog'ski.

"What do you mean?"

"Well," said Gog'ski, "was he sad? Was he afraid?"

"No" said Shell. "He was cheerful. He joked. He seemed happier than I, even though I knew I was getting out."

Everyone was quiet then, listening to hear what more Shell might have to say. The group had gotten a little larger since the discussion of Dlanusi, the Leech, had begun.

"It was maybe seven days before I got out," said Shell. "Sgili equa, the Big Witch, came to visit Dlanusi, and he brought some soap, the kind we make at home. There was never enough soap in the stinking jail, and the guards let Dlanusi keep it. After that, he washed every day, maybe two, three times a day. He was so clean.

"The day before they let me out, Dlanusi dipped his hands in the water bucket, and he was holding his soap. Then he stood up, and he started rubbing the soap, and he lay back on his cot. He was making a lot of bubbles, and pretty soon the bubbles started to rise up and float, and Dlanusi started to laugh, a happy sounding laugh. The bubbles were floating up and going out the window between the bars and just floating away. Dlanusi stopped laughing, but he still had a big smile on his face, and he said to me, 'You see that?' He was watching the bubbles float out the window between the bars. 'You see that?' he said. 'I can get out of here just that easy.' Then I looked closer, and inside each bubble I could see a tiny little man sitting and smiling at me as his bubble rose up slowly and floated out the window, between the bars and away, carrying him with it. That's what I saw while I was there in jail with Dlanusi."

Shell stopped talking, and the others just sat there as if stunned. At last Gog'ski got up and clapped his hands together.

"Well," he said, "does anyone want to go over there and toss some marbles with me?"

The group broke up, some following Gog'ski to play marbles, the old Cherokee game of marbles, more closely resembling lawn bowling than what white men call marbles, some others wandering until they found someone else to talk to, perhaps to repeat the strange story Shell had just told them. Shell stayed right where he had been all along. He just sat there. Later the women called out that the food was ready, and the men all lined up to be served. They were just sitting down when a horseman came riding toward the house. All watched to see who was coming, and when he got close enough to recognize, Shell was the first one to speak.

"Dlanusi," he said.

Dlanusi rode right up close. He was sitting on a shiny saddle on the back of a big, black stallion that pranced and snorted, and he was dressed flashy, like a cowboy, in black leather boots and a black vest over a clean white shirt. His long black hair folded on his shoulders, and he wore a black, flat-brimmed hat on his head. His broad grin showed his white teeth flashing out of his dark face.

"Hey," he said, in a loud and cheerful voice, "did you leave me anything to eat here?"

Elizabeth Cook-Lynn

City Games of Life and Death

Walking the Mission District of San Francisco

I can see why Indians come here
and never go home again
vast splendorous glittering glass panes
reflect someone else's shadow
and swift cars people every curve
slanting streets which are the cemeteries
of conscious thought numbly forecast that tomorrow
the wolves will finally come. But,
no one hears beyond the primal call of the flesh.

Thus, winos and scholars and horsemen
and gods gathered in for the
astonishing ritual go for the stars. For them there is no
homeland and they are doomed. They lead each other
in the heavenly dance. Colonial revivalists on
city reservations hum, again, the Flood Control Act
of Nineteen Thirty-Six in waist-deep monotone
and say, finally:
They have changed their ways.

— political statement [handwritten annotation]

83

Visiting Professor and the Yellow Sky

Davis, California, 1991

Yesterday afternoon
I woke and heard them again
raucous and loud
harsh in the dim sky

the sleek crows trailing me into the southern
winds toward the warmth of the Bay
flapping above my window
angry and out of place
too large for these dainty trees

what do you think of crows, I ask
and without hesitation
answer:
they belong up north
along the Platte
the Little Big Horn
the Cheyenne River
the creek named for them that swung past
my grandmother's house
along those mythical North Country
waters or the hills
of the West

I know they have followed me here
but I don't know why
blue-black is the carnivore
yellow the sky

I turned to the door and the
evening shade
and heard it differently
this time
it sounded like the drippings
from the hanging plant
just watered

instead it was a moth
stuck between folded papers
blue-black is the carnivore
yellow is the sky.

Kateri Damm

poem without an end

Nanabush is an English professor
sitting in an ivory tower
looking down upon the masses who go herdlike to their classes
writing books that no one looks at
reading poetry on money

Nanabush is a landlord who turns off the heat in winter
and a tenant who throws parties
while the babies are fast sleeping
the one who keeps you laughing even when your heart is breaking
and the one who tells you stories when it's wisdom you've been seeking

Nanabush is a singer
she's a heavy metal drummer
she cheats and swears and talks of death
then lets you meet her children
she throws pearls onto Parliament Hill
and dresses men in clothes of sheepskin
then she sits alone and drinks cheap wine and cries into the table
and she prays for god's forgiveness because she can't forget the sabbath
she's a lonely wooden goddess on a path into damnation

Nanabush knows Jesus
she plays tricks on Paul and Peter
he unlocks the gates and steals a peek

and cannot keep the secret
he will shit in darkened hallways
pull your pants down to your ankles
he will take your love and steal your life
and give you dreams and laughter

Nanabush is a trapper who wears sealskin pajamas
he eats fish that have been poisoned
speaks a language now forgotten
and when he jumps into the river
half crazy with survival
he tries to touch the bottom to create a new religion
but he floats up to the surface and his hands are cold and empty
so the animals give him shelter though he knows the winter's coming
and when he wakes they wait together for the storm quietly approaching
silent, nearly frozen they turn into a monument of stone

sturgeon

i twist and gasp
open and close my mouth
searching for air
whenever a sturgeon is caught in the rainy river
i know
the feel of strange hands touching my body
the struggle
to be free
the longing
to go where i want to go
i feel
the impact of stick or rock on bone
the splash of color
then the emptiness that is my head
my head like a midnight sky if the stars and moon
were captured by another heaven
i know

even when i am awake again
sitting at the kitchen table
staring at my plate with its bramble design
and rough chipped edges
i know

that is why i do not eat sturgeon
because i know
when a sturgeon is caught in the rainy river that
i am a sturgeon
and i dangle on hooks

Nora Marks Dauenhauer

Ernestine's House, Hoonah, Alaska, 6 A.M.

I woke to smell of smoke
of fresh wood crackling
from the stove
mingled with
the feel of Brown Bear Den Clan House
radiating families' care,
the taste of smoked deer meat
coming out of a container
of seal oil:
caverns of
memory.

February 18, 1991

At Grand Canyon II

For Joanne Townsend

All my senses are alive
out on the edge
from my toes to my fingertips,
but they play tricks,
become Raven circling over me.
Every hair on my head

seems to reach for him
ready to pull me over
from Maricopa Point
to Pre-Cambrian.

Arizona, October 1991

Ninety-eighter Creek

We no sooner landed
and climbed the bank when:
the huge brown bear stood,
a quivering mass of fur,
her cub quivering beside her:
my mother's beaded Brown Bear Shirt,
shimmering glass beads.

August 19, 1989

Charlotte DeClue

Blanket Poem #2

The Pox

      The women keen
songs that I hear
as if they were late winter wind
coming down from cedars
biting my face
my hands
clutching the small infant
zhin-ga zhin-ga
tiny little one.
I won't let go of him
they tell me "let go of him"
he has melted into my breasts
part of me that way
he is my hand
holding his
his tiny fingers
"let go" they say
and fold his arm inside the shroud
and wrap him tight
like mama taught *me* to do
and then put him in the babyboard
she would tie him
big brother dangling tiny bells
above baby brother's head

"hang them high" mama would say
"make him reach for them
with his eyes
with his ears
soon he will walk."
        The women lick their fingertips
dip them in red dye
paint red spots on the white linen
mama wails like wind coming up
cries and sways
wind through willow.
        The men lower him
quickly
ground loosens
folds over him like mama's arms
quickly
quickly
as if burying a secret
"he is still contagious, sister"
they say
"you don't want to be sick."
        My face in auntie's shoulder
rain
rain coming down
sweetwater rain
coming down
earth water rain
coming down
swelling
mama's belly
rising
water
sweet water flowing
mama's voice covering my ears
closing my eyes
"let go now, sister
let him sleep."

Blanket Poem #4

Visiting Day
Joe Harp Correctional Center, Lexington, OK

Big Ole Sky Woman breathes life
into open thighs. Breasts rise like circling clouds
on hot summer afternoon, dropping moisture
on blanket flowers that grow wild in prison yard.

At home we would pick them, put 'em
in a pop can and set 'em on the table.
I would knead dough with my knuckles
while he felt for my belly
beneath folds of cotton skirt. It would be
that way "at home."

Once he would have cut me burden straps
from side of buffalo calf. I would have pounded
out fat, and juice from berries.
We would lie on some creekbed
listening to locusts sing in cottonwood trees.

La Raza couple share table with friends
from the outside who talk about El Conquistador
and his new BMW, and the time Cristobal Colon
had a flat and had to hitch a ride to the Pueblo.

The guard laughs about us "suckin' face."
He knows who we have to thank for all this . . .
the Quakers and Oprah Winfrey,
thank you to Anaconda for razor wire,
thanks to the technocrats for video equipment,
and thanks to a dead warden
for the name on the place.

THERE IS A ROAN HORSE GRAZING behind
barbed wire that is not as free
as he would want to be.

THERE IS A YOUNG MAN SEARCHING midtown streets
for loose change, while another rolls pencils
across a desk. They are not as free
as they would want to be.

THERE IS A YOUNG WOMAN DISAPPOINTED with life
who pouts through a Rabbit Dance,
while her sister eyes another woman's husband.
They are not as free
as they would want to be.

Couples swear that if Columbus
had landed in another place
they would still be in love.

I think about THESE THINGS the 30 minutes
it takes to drive for Visiting Days . . .
the horse, the lips wrapped around a bottle,
the sad-eyed woman . . . the wait
that seems forever,
#88935, Unit C,
the maze of doors slamming behind me.

A tongue searches the place inside me
that keeps repeating "I miss you, I miss you."
Sky Woman opens her strong arms,
breathes life into tired eyes.
Aha! it will be a damn good day.

Ed Edmo

Indian Education Blues

I sit in your
crowded classrooms
& learn how to
read about dick,
jane & spot
but

> I remember
> how to get a deer

> I remember
> how to do beadwork

> I remember
how to fish

I remember
the stories told by the old

but

> spot keeps
> showing up
> &

> > my report card
> > is bad

Hunting Sequence

hunting in portland u.s. of a.
is a

    samsonite attache case
    parker pen
    notebook
            morning cup
            of coffee

running towards
the door

      grabbing
      tri-met bus pass
      typewriter
      melting

           in the corner

Melissa Fawcett *Mohegan*

On Loosing My Language

Dedicated to Djits Bodernasha (Flying Bird) 1827–1908,
Last Speaker of the Mohegan-Pequot Language

The green-eyed viper licks the inner corners of my mouth.
His gluey venom seeps upon my tongue
Like sticky needle and thread,
Binding up, what might have freely run from these lips —
Songs, Prayers, Lies, Words of Love
And Hope.
Voices of my heart begin to choke on pasty ooze
As Jeebi-Shkook* near silences their breath,
But they will not die.
Great Ones, Old Ones, Little Ones
All, together, piteously chirping:
"What to do now, the girl is mute, she cannot pass on The Story?"
So, I, within my living tomb, need help them, *(ancestors)*
And swallow this clotty poison deep inside my throat
That I may speak to them in Mundunog†

Where I will finally learn The Story.

This poem was inspired by Vi Hilbert, Jeanette Armstrong, Ellen White, and all the
other Turtle Islanders who spoke to us in their Native languages at the Returning the Gift
Festival.

*Jeebi-Shkook means "Evil Snake Spirit."
†Mundunog means "The Spirit Land."

Connie Fife

Resistance

resistance is a woman
whose land is all on fire
perseverance and determination
are her daughters
she is a palestinian mother who
hands her children a legacy of
war together with the
weapons to fight in it
she is a black woman draped
in purple satin who strolls
down a runway allowing only
the clothes she wears to be sold
resistance is the absent native woman
who died at the hands of
a white artist
who lives inside herself
while thriving inside of me
resistance is a girl child
who witnesses her mothers death and
swears to survive no matter
where the hiding place
she is a woman beaten with hate
by the man she loves who
decides to escape to a world
where touch is sacred

she is a woman torn apart by
the barbed wire surrounding her home
who plots a way out
despite the consequences
resistance is every woman who
has ever considered taking up
arms   writing a story   leaving the abuse
saving her children or saving herself
she is every woman who dares
to stage a revolution   complete a novel
be loved or change the world
resistance walks across a landscape
of fire accompanied by her daughters
perseverance and determination

Chris Fleet

A White Friend

Last November I drove a white friend —
I had one once you know —
down to the Res.
He wondered what real Indians
did on Thanksgiving.
So I drove him down to the Res
first thing he needs to do is piss.
Where's all the Indians? he asks with a piss grin.
I thought you were showing me INDIANS.

Well, sitting at home waiting
for the phone to ring
or dreaming of thank you notes in the mail
since some still go cordless.

What? I don't get it, he said. What do you mean?

I know, I tell him with tears of pain and laughter.

But George Washington! George Washington! he screams.
What about Washington?

George Washington? Another whiteboy with wet dreams.
Look around here real hard and you'll see him
stealing corn or shooting cars.
Every now and then I swear I see him
leaving the scene of a house fire

always when I'm convinced for the last time
that he's dead.

Wow, said my friend with a laugh,
even you wahoos have an Elvis.

Friend. Friend, I said,
listen.
When will they ever discover white isn't a color?
It's a mental disease.
And I sent him walking up the dirt road
back to his wilderness.

You'll always be a fucking wahoo, he yelled.

Watch out for the attack buffalo, I yelled back.
Got in my crumpled Escort and drove into the heart of sanity
while somewhere in the distance I heard the crack
of gunfire and saw in my rearview mirror
the white soiled locks of George Washington
disappearing into the corn.

Lax

The game of lacrosse
up home we call it Baggataway.
This game Baggataway
is given to us by the creator.
It is his game
and by playing it we become closer to him.
We become one with him.
Before playing we will say a prayer
and when we're through praying
we should see a feathered creature
carrying our prayer to the creator.
It is good that we play.
And we give thanks.
That is all.

Jack D. Forbes

The Book of Deeds

The hand fondling the martini
    manicured nails
    they clutch the mask
    polished perfect teeth
    of smiling self-deception
    as the deeds
    the acts
    the testimony
    claw out with broken fingers
    from the dust
    ripping away
    ruling-class images
    and the image
    is a mask
    not flesh
    and it hides
    a snarl
    and the deeds are true
    and the gracious face
    is made in Hollywood
    of dirty clay.

Sophisticated gentlemen
    sophistry-created ladies
    of London and Paris
    of Miami and Virginia suburbs

beneath the clay
can one find flesh
beneath the mask
a heart
or only hollow places
filled with bank notes
stocks and bonds
stuffed in
by orgasms
of deposit and withdrawal?

Beauty parlors arrange the hair
but can Paris fashions
hide the fact
oh ladies of the Great
that your husbands
are murderers
is it exciting to sleep
with one who has
caused 200 Quiché
throats to be slit
that day?

The strings around your necks
of cattle ranches
and tin mines
and uranium pits
and coaleries
are killing people
and you know it don't you —
the strings of pearls around your necks
a noose with
shiny knots for each
atrocity, do you
proudly wear the people's tears?

Someday you shall be known
exploiters of the earth,
as True Barbarians
and French philosophers

shall write books about
the Savage Minds of
New York and Buenos Aires
Washington and São Paulo —
yes, and even
Paris.

It is true, you see,
        they don't believe in God,
        some of those called Christians
        it is said
        and God, the Great Spirit,
        is recording
        on quipu knots
        their deeds
        not their words
        their deeds,
        it is said.

And the Indian
        peering from the forest
        bending between the rows
                of plantation plantings
        sweating beneath heavy loads
        crouching in a cardboard shacalli
        looks up and
        records, I will tell you,
        each deed
        on his body
        on her back
        it is said
        each deed.

And in Brazil and Guatemala
        they try
        you see
        to burn and hack up each body
        so that their deeds
        cannot be known
        but the suffering of the Indian

is already
it is said
in the Creator's thought
the deed
is known
the deed
is alive
it grows
each hour
larger it becomes.

And some of these murderers pray,
it is said,
but they pray to dead concrete,
to silence
they pray to death
to Babylon they pray
their deeds
the mutilated bodies
stand like a carcassed wall
a blasphemy
around them.

Each Indian dying in the snow
each deed
each Indian dying in the *selva*
each deed
each Indian dying in the *cafetales*
each deed
each Indian dying in the slums
each deed,
it is recorded,
it grows,
it swells
rises like a mountain of corpses
of deeds
cutting them off
by their deeds
erecting around them
the walls of Hell

by their deeds
and concrete silence
by their deeds
to which they pray.

And they throw their coins
at God
but they are not
coins of that realm
these coins
their deeds
they throw
at God
dead bodies
mutilated babies
they throw
at God
tortured women
they throw
at God
their coins
their deeds.

In vaults beneath Rockefeller Center
it is said
the lips
of corpses
still testify
to the growth
of Standard Oil
and they toss money
at culture
but it is
when seen
clearly filth
torn from the bowels
of victims
all colors, yes,
even white,

the money given to charity
smells of
old murders.

The people of the Americas
the Middle Continent
always were
Indians
and it is not true then
that those who suffer
and die and live just lives
although victims
must in the embrace of
Mother Earth be transformed
into Her brownness
Her redness
Her Indians.

Can it be that the good white people,
the suffering Blacks,
the Red-Blacks,
the White-Blacks
shall come to us
as Indians
after death
after hunger
after suffering
after seeing
they shall be deeds
is it said?
they shall be Indians
is it true?
they shall be Acts?

Those lips without flesh
will testify
it is said
before judges in eagle feathers
and quetzal plumes

it is recorded
their lips of broken bone
shall speak
become deeds
become acts
become testimony
unsilenced will be their cries
unblocked those choked throats
tongueless
hurling truths stone-hard
chiseled by their screams.

And the deed is the Indian
the Indian is the deed
Great Spirit-created
these Indians
God's generations
now deeds
now acts
the Indian
the deed
it is recorded, and
there is no escape
from the deed
from the Indian.

And it is recorded
the United States of Deeds
the Commonwealth of Deeds
the Federal Republic of Deeds
this Republic of Deeds
that Republic of Deeds
republics of Indians
republics of Deeds
like rivers swollen
with bodies, their deeds,
flow
to the sea which rises
and rises
in waves of pounding

dollars
to choke
on their deeds,
spitting up Indians.

The green dollar bills
shielding their eyes
from the sun
and they glue them on
Mary and Jesus
covering
eyes and
mouths
and ears even
dollar bills
glued on the tips
of their pricks
and missiles
dollar bills
pasted on their
lips as they kiss
their wives
with discharge
coming up
from deeds
rising inside
as corpses
float bloated
to the surface
amid the waves of pounding dollars.

And the poison, yes
the disease
of exploitation
embraced with fingers of iron
even
the children
of the exploiters
this we see.

And it shall come, yes,
    the day
    when those who still
    believe in the Creator,
    the Indians,
    the day,
    it shall come
    surely
    when the Native People
    the Middle Continent People
    will no longer know Hell
    will no longer see Devils
    and the waves of dollar bills
    will grind to dust
    and the tears will be the salt
    of new bright oceans.

Della Frank

I Feel

I am a feeling person.

I feel for the distant planets
    the bright stars the lonely moon the traveling sun
And most of all,   I feel for the much-tired Mother Earth.

I feel for the trees
    the soft flowers   the moist air   the sedimentary rocks:
They are children of Mother Earth.

I feel for land animals
    for dogs that herd sheep and goats
    for cats that run freely through meadows and forests
    for rabbits that twitch their tails and hop about
    for lizards that "bop" their heads during hot summer days
And for snakes that slither slowly and leisurely through
    brushes and rivers.

I feel for them all.

I feel for sea animals
    for dolphins that swim about uttering beautiful high-pitched
        sounds
    for sharks that glide through currents and ripples
        of ocean-blue seas
    for seals that rest upon sheets of ice under the warm sun:
May they always feel reassured of their survival.

I feel for them.

I feel for birds
    for various fowl that continue to soar over open plains
        without restraints
            singing their special songs as they migrate pole to pole:
May they always find the cosmic space to roam.

I feel for them all.

I feel for people: young and old:
    I feel for grandpa: who passed on in the sixties
    I feel for grandma: she still walks her miles
    I feel for mom and dad: mom's still on earth
I feel for my brothers and sisters:
May they always have hope and strength despite their endless struggles
    just to survive!

I feel for their feelings

I feel for them.

I feel for people
    who are left behind
when loved ones must pass to the other side
    going over gently through thin veils
and letting go of silver threads that connected them to life
    on earth:
May their loved ones weave through the mourning stages with enough courage
    to survive!

I feel for them all.

I feel for young men
    who must go to war because of oil crisis: May they find love
and compassion in that world; however long or short — they must stay
    while loved ones pray for their safe return to this side of the world.

I feel for them.

I feel for handicapped people
    I feel for the way they must struggle
    to get back on the road to life

I feel for the way they have to shuffle out into the empty streets
    and relearn to communicate with those around
I feel for the way they have to again understand using knives and
    forks.
May they always have the courage and perseverance to know that they can do
    it!

I feel for them all.

I feel for homeless people
    I feel for the way they must wrap blankets around thin shoulders
        just to make it through another winter
    I feel for the way they must sit around angry streets
        just to ask for handouts:
May they find friends who will share a bit of themselves.

I feel for them.

And most of all
    I feel for the many different churches
        that dot the face of this planet
    and for the people that go to these churches in order
        to express their desires for a "better" world . . .
    I feel for the symbols that must represent these religions
and the ideas behind "spiritualism."

I feel for them all.

There are the things and ideas I feel for   the most   in this world
in this time   in this moment.

I feel.

José L. Garza / Blue Heron

Seneca Snakeroot

For Faye Lone & family,
5 days before the powwow

Green-white the flowers bloom May and June,
twist and turn thick rootstock beneath the fertile
soil and moon. Carried to protect from
white man viper bite so common in the city.
In your eyes I see your purple dress flash
against the red-blue day. I see the long
journey we have traveled together, long
days and restless nights; your courageous
dignity, the sparkle in the eyes of your
beautiful children. I know how you have
struggled but soon time will be eclipsed,
a lapsing Long House shadow shifting the
seasons over deer track, easing into our
ancestral past. We will become the elders
soon enough. We will guide our children
along the path of Tashunka Witko, Dancing
Crazy Horse. You have done well and must
allow the Shawl Dance to protect you. The
old ways are not forgotten. Often we are
forced to grow up too quickly.

Soon our neighbors the Iroquois, Mohawk,
Zuni, Azteca, Cherokee and Winnebago will
be dancing, drawn by the truth of the

Medicine Wheel and Quinto Sol. Ancient
bones will rattle yellow gourds. White
Buffalo dreams will come to life, stomp
and snort blue autumn breaths.

                        Hawk
will circle the encampment and be pleased
by the Bird People singing on the ground.
Mother Earth will be glad to see us.
Mother Earth will be glad to see us.
Her light will shine within us.
Her light will shine before us and behind.
Her light will shine above us and below.
Her light will shine around Her children.

                    Traditional Dancers will
tie sinew strings to the cosmos. The
Blooming Tree of Life will stir up Indian
pride to complicated turns and joyful
steps of the Snake Dance, shed its old
skin, feed on the new, grow large then
turn green, fresh complex avenues for us
to follow. New people and new beginnings.
Same as life. Same as life.

Wander-lust sister, fluid orphan of the
"rez," it will be good to see you again.

There Must Be a Poem Here Somewhere

Little River, Oklahoma

Walked through the woods this morning looking for a poem,
a scrap to construct a piece of epic proportions, searched
the dry underbrush and red sand, surveyed the leaf-covered trail,
poked a finger into the hole in the Stone shaped like a nest.
Asked the Stone with a pinch of Tobacco to release Its secrets.

Walked through the blank halls of the university this day,
journal and pen in hand, following the sound of laughter
of brothers and sisters gathering their poems and hope;
some more lost than others, missing familiar homelands where
wild Moose, Corn fields and Salmon compose their own poems,
then wait patiently for someone to tell them to.
I sought the common root that binds us one to the other,
wet rawhide pulling us together, stretching the imagination.

Heard it said that the white man took all our poems and songs
and buried them in the drawers of their dark museums, gasping
for air, green grass and summer rain — the broken Hoop.

"See that tree over the road," old Kiowa chief Satank spoke,
"I shall not go beyond it (in slavery)." And he didn't.

Heard it said that poems live where you least expect them,
the Hoop of the People is not broken but waits in the eyes
of our children and the graying braids of our elders.
Spoke with the two Grandmothers who live alone in the woods
who light stories in the fireplace at night to keep them warm.
Spoke with teenaged writers grown wise before their time
on the streets of the city and dusty roads of the reserve.

Walked the night forest at end of day, red-purple sunset
behind black silhouette movement of Chichimeca priests,
chanting words by Firefly light and tree Frog rhythms.
Heard the Universe of our foreparents lap the River shore
with ageless voices, "We are still here. We are still here!"
Found a perfect rose Stone beneath dried stream slate Rock,
and added it to my collection of still-damp Rain Water verse.
Found our camp nestled on the green Earth near the River.
Found your warm thoughts and listened to deep sleep sounds
of our "Bear" child as I nestled in the arms of my family.
Felt the Earth move slightly as She nestled in the Universe.

So many poems to choose from.

Bear, the one year old Husky pup thinks that the newly fallen continent of white snow is meant to be plowed up by an inquisitive black snout, running free of chains and absurd rules. In the spring he raises his leg at the beautiful yellow blooming bush or digs his way to Tiananmen Square, leaving holes in the greening lawn. It is all quite tentative to him. He understands only the here and now. He flings the wet snow into the air above him with wild abandon, pretending to hunt a careless groundhog or rabbit.

Bear, the wonder dog, has heard the rumors that circulate among the white men. Tales of brave Ulysses on the lands of Mu in the Pacific Ocean and Atlantis in the Atlantic Ocean, filled with the Anglo people who have fathered our many Native nations. Bear loves to feel the hard, smooth rock floor beneath his feet and listen to the gurgle of the creek water while Mu and Atlantis erode their legends at the bottom of the deepest of waters. Creek Water Spirits tell Bear how the Navajo People emerged at the Grand Canyon at a time when the land was submerged beneath a thin mantel of sea water. They speak nothing of Mu or Atlantis except on colorful pages of comic books or between the lines of *Mein Kampf*.

Bear the full-blood refugee from Siberia laughs at the notion that space invaders from a distant solar system carved the images of Earth Spirits on the Nazca Plain, or built the great temples at Teotihuacan. He scoffs at the handful of Roman and Greek coins found on Indian land that are used to prove that our great civilizations are a product of platonic logic and Roman forums. Bear prefers to live in the world of his ancestors as he sniffs the cool air for scent of automobile exhaust and gray smokestack sacrifice to the gods of progress, straining the leash to chase the rapidly moving culprits down the highway, annoyed by the noise and anonymity. He feels he rules through the natural power of the Earth when he wanders the woods and streams, racing toward natural movements and sounds in the shadows.

Who are these strange people who think they can buy and sell the Earth, posting NO TRESPASSING signs to keep Bear from running the woods? If we Native People had posted no trespassing signs on the land would Columbus and Cortez have landed?

Of course they would have landed, so Bear ignores the funny writing and roars past the sign after the rascal squirrel who had taunted him.

Robert Gish

Coastal Mountain Train

Bishop's Peak.
        To the West. Stalwart. Stationary.

Shadowy in the night.
Shrouded in morning fog.
At noon looming large —
        Boulders warming to sunrise.
King snake wriggles into warmth.
Turkey vultures soar on thermal highs.

Through the window on Westness.
Beyond rows of patterned, pineapple palms,
        mounding branches to match
        the mountain's angled rise,
Always Bishop's Peak. Present. Permanent. west.

Come time. Come 3:05 P.M. Come silver-sided
        red and blue striped lines.
Sounding, blowing motion before them. After them.
Amtrak approaches. Slowing for the city.
SLO, San Luis Obispo. Mission town. Historic. Old/New
        up-scale shopping mecca of North County yearnings.
Headed south for L.A. For *Los Angeles*.

Angelic bound California coastal mountain train
Down from Seattle. San Francisco. Atascadero!
Down the line. Fronting the hard rock peak. The Bishop.

Permanence meet change. Motion see stillness.
Time merge with timelessness.

On the Central Coast way to Santa Barbara.
On the way to lala land.
On the way to
         the temporary tinsel town of HOLLYWOOD.

Diane Glancy

Genealogy

I was not raised in the traditional way, and you can ask what right have I got to speak? But the Native American voice is the one I hear when I write.

My father's people were Cherokee. I remember him telling me we were Indian. I remember asking, what kind?

My great-grandfather, Woods Lewis, was born in 1843 near Sallisaw, Oklahoma. He got in trouble around the Civil War and fled Oklahoma Territory. After serving in the 4th Company, Tennessee Cavalry, he tried to return to Oklahoma, which was still Indian Territory at the time, but word got out, and he had to settle in northern Arkansas where he farmed until his death in 1904.

My father went north to Kansas City to work in the stockyards just before the Depression. He buried his heritage as my great-grandfather, and my grandmother, had done. He married a German/English woman and I was raised in the white culture knowing little of my father's heritage. But even in the white schools and churches I attended, I was always asked the inevitable question by teachers. What nationality was I?

They knew I was something other, but they weren't sure what.

In some of us, the heritage has been rendered nearly invisible. At least unrecognizable. The voice can't be seen anyway. But I felt it moving in me for years, and it finally found visibility in the written word.

I think I speak for a lot of Native Americans who have mixed blood and who know little of their culture and language. But the heritage shows up now and then like the Indian ancestors, who I know sometimes, when I wake in the morning, have been there in the night.

Hides

I can't say I'm of the bear clan or the elk people.
Just a man who came north for work
and left all that.

I have been questioned as a white.
I have been questioned as Indian.
I am neither of both worlds.
But one of my own making.
Mainly by words.

I speak with a mixed voice.
An acculturated voice.
Because my Indian heritage was picked off.
I remember the smallpox-vaccination-scab on my arm.
Picking it off.
And it dropping to the ground.
I remember picking it up.
Trying to stick it back on.

Anyway.

I guess you want to hear about the land. And how the
Indian ancestors followed the buffalo. And how the sky
spoke to them in the smoke signals of its clouds. And
how the rocks were known to turn and speak the way you're
walking with someone somewhere and they say something you
know right then you'll remember all your life. But you
know it isn't that way. Though I know a rock. The
weight of it in my hand like a heart. Sometimes I hold it
to my ear and say, hey rock — How you? And I know

the open prairie where you drive for days and still don't
see the end. You go on forever and know nothing except
a few lonely cafes and a motel room for the night. You
know my father asked me if I wanted some animal hides.
He worked for the stockyards and could get them. But I didn't
know what to do. Whad he expect? Moccasins and
dresses? A reconstruction of the drum? Where would I
get the heartbeat? After the earth was paved and covered
with the rattle of cattle trucks. But you know. I guess
you can hear anything again. You can still scrape hides.
If only through the imagination in your own head.

Mary Goose

Clay Man

Years ago I met a blind sculptor

CLAY MAN

> He asked me what I looked like when I met him
> I didn't know how to describe myself
> because I had never told anyone how
> I thought I looked
>
> So he asked if he could touch my face
> and when I felt the fingers barely skim the
> surface of my skin
>
> I knew the extremely small circular ridges
> on his fingertips were more sensitive to the touch
> than mine and he didn't need light to see anything
> and that they could remember the structure of my heart
> like the memory of how soft and warm
> gray clay feels squeezed between the fingers
>
> A hand that could open palms up
> and catch any individual water droplet from
> a thunderstorm even while standing under the
> shelter of a dense and tall evergreen forest
>
> When the fingers moved around the
> curve of the bone of my eyes
> the nose of the sculptor flared as though
> he had seen the rim of the world

as he caught a glimpse of the tanned moose hide bag
that hung on that wall of that faraway room
behind a closed door, and beyond
to recall which stone was from Iowa, from California,
from Canada . . .
small stones that you can hold between two fingers
yet get heavier the longer you hold them
together

As the fingers gently lifted off my face
the sculptor took a deep breath,
and as the sea smoke gray eyes blinked
his head nodded up and down, slowly — Yes.

Yes?

The Common Color of Red

The film's narrator said that you could still see
claw marks on the brick walls of the shower rooms
as those human fingers had tried to escape their barbed wire lined coffin

Limp bodies existed in the film and those photos that looked
like a pile of broken twigs and fallen leaves being
swept into a human garbage dump by a bulldozer   or
being thrown into a mass grave by gloved hands and covered by
a mound of dirt

> People said these two tribes did not fit the blue-eyed blond
> image that Hitler, Custer and others had of what humans should
> look like

Could I be bold enough
to say that is why they died with
memories tattooed and indelibly etched on the bodies and minds of
   these people

forever reminders to each his own of:
      attendants with black swastikas that walked down the
      arms of these people in numbers   or
      of wool blankets designed with smallpox embellishments
      and those red tear-shaped footprints in snow

Could I be bold enough
to say that the bricks and the earth
both now dried to a rust and brown color were once blood red.

Roxy Gordon

I Used to Know an Assiniboine Girl

I used to know an Indian girl up north
on the northern plains.
I'm sorry that I don't know her anymore.

She'd just come home from boarding school,
just turned nineteen,
so all she wanted then most was more.

So the men that she stayed with were not
the gentlest kind.
I saw her walk the roads with swollen eyes.
She'd come to my door in the darker hours of night,
asking drunk for help while she cried.

Sometimes when she spoke to me, she'd ask without words;
she would offer herself for my caress
and her hair it was black shiny, her skin
was brown and soft.
I ached for the fullness of her breasts.

But I had another woman and I never said a word.
I kept all I wanted to myself.
So she came to spit at me, came to call
my name with fire, offered actually to fight me with her fists.

And, my God, I loved her then: I looked
behind her brown eyes,
I saw a nation that's gone, born again.

I saw lean and screaming riders race for buffalo.
I saw a hundred-thousand free and haughty men.

Now that I don't live on the plains anymore,
I haven't seen her, but I heard that she tried
to kill herself one morning in the house where she stays
with a drinker from some southwestern tribe.

And, God I loved her then, I looked behind her brown eyes,
I saw a nation that's gone, born again.
And I saw a woman, who always wanted more.
And I wish to god she'd found that kind of man.

Indians

Hank Williams was an Indian,
John Kennedy was not.

Chuck Berry is an Indian,
Michael Jackson ain't.

Street people are Indians,
presidents ain't.

Pancho Villa was an Indian,
Che Guevara was not.

Los Angeles is an Indian,
New York City ain't.

Africa is an Indian,
Europe ain't.

Baseball is an Indian,
football ain't.

Crazy Horse was an Indian,
Custer was not.

Sitting Bull was an Indian,
so were the Indian policemen who killed him.

Poetry is an Indian,
journalism ain't and
proper punctuation ain't.

Circles are Indians,
and random lines are Indians.
Straight lines ain't.

Red meat is an Indian,
corn is an Indian,
potatoes are Indians,
fry bread is Indian.
Health food stores try
hard to be Indian.

Living is Indian,
expecting to live forever ain't.

Murder

I saw him walk off the ship. He
    was a strong man and young, younger
    than me. His hair was deep dark red and
    long, braided down his back. I
    knew him of all the travelers. This
    was in the colony of Virginia in
    1724.

I said to him, "I am your descendent from
    two centuries
    in the future."
    The Scotsman looked at me uncomprehending,
    and I said,
    "I've come to kill you."

And then the Scotsman knew me,
    saw his blood after all
    in my veins.

"My God," he said, "you
cannot kill me." He said, "I
am your ancestor." He said,
"Without me,
you cannot be."

I said, "I must." I said, "I
must stop the thing that
you'll become." I said,
"I must stop the thing that
I myself
might become."

The Scotsman said, "My God, I'm a good man."
He said, "I'll marry a good woman." He said,
"We'll found a dynasty
of good Presbyterian Scots-Americans."
He said, "We'll love and help our brothers." He said,
"We will bring God to
this dark and godless place." He said,
"We'll bring good Scot sense to build a rich and
bountiful place
in this wilderness."
But then the Scotsman
saw the bow, the wood and horn bound bow, he saw
the stone-tipped arrow, the black obsidian
tipped-arrow. I said,
"I will
kill
you
now."

"My God," the Scotsman said, knowing his death was
near. "My God," he said, "my God. You cannot
be that cruel. I am your past." The Scotsman said,
"How can you kill the part of you that I
myself began?"
So then
I shot him.

The arrow penetrated the upper half
     of the Scotsman's heart. The black
     obsidian point driven by wood and
     horn went
     all the way
     through the Scotsman's body.
     He looked at me in pain and in confusion.
     And blood slowly started,
     dripping from
     the corners
     of his mouth and then
     dripping from his nose.
     And the Scotsman let go;
     the Scotsman died.

I had his long, deep dark red hair in one
     hand and my knife in the other.

Janice Gould

Snow

Snow had fallen during the night,
snow on snow. The streets were white and muffled,
and hard banks had piled up along the sidewalks,
on the boulevard where city buses chuffed to a stop.
It seemed we disembarked into caves of ice,
into dirty igloos broken through by passersby
heading for home after the five-fifteen
rush from downtown.

I liked the snow, the way the city slowed
to accommodate Nature, who slid her hand
over the northwest, from Puget Sound
to the Willamette Valley,
from Tillamook to Hood River,
until fields, forests,
the rounded hills and orchards
all lay in a deep frosty dream:
ponds frozen over,
cattails split like cornhusks.
Horses stood in pastures,
breath steaming, icicles
hanging from their shaggy coats.

The morning after the snow it was just growing light.
And probably for the first time
I saw two adults in love.
He had walked out from their basement apartment,

laughing as he pushed through that trench of cold powder,
a stocky black man in a bus driver's uniform.
She was at the door, laughing with him,
her blond hair disheveled, her face puffy.
She smoked a cigarette, he held
a cup of coffee.
Before quite reaching the street
he had come back to kiss her.

That is what I saw, I don't remember how.
Perhaps I watched from an upstairs window:
him waving to her from the corner
he strode through the snow,
the fresh swirl blown down like feathers
or cottony seeds.
                    I only know
it was a time of transition. Yet everything
seemed to fit together: how you and I read Vallejo,
ate chocolate,
and listened to the blind man
play the accordion.
How the soft sounds of Portuguese
fit in my mouth
as we studied from your book.
We loved the romantic languages!
How every day we passed the family of women
who stood in a storefront window
at the foot of Ankeny Bridge,
women young and old,
their faces bitter,
black hair pulled back tight
against their thin heads.
I imagined them gypsies
who could see into my soul.

I was in love with you,
a girl who was a little crazy,
who had hung her heart
in the icy branches of a tree that winter,
just beyond the reach of any of us,

father, mother, or lover. How stupidly
I behaved with you. But I was young,
frightened, and also crazy. I didn't know then
the dimensions of abuse and violence,
I was still unnerved by the word lesbian,
how it began with a shameful lateral,
how the sibilance of its interior
fit against the body with its wetness,
its caverns,
its long dream of winter.
When we made love I never
took my clothes off, I sometimes
slept in my shoes.

Perhaps that's why I like to think of the busman
and his woman, the warmth that flooded out their door
as if they'd stepped from their hot sheets
to the shower, to the breakfast table with its
cups of coffee, how their flesh was still flushed
with blood and kisses.
                        I know this now, the depth
of roses, the laughter that resounds in frozen air,
the first shove through January snowfall.
After years I grew up,
married a woman who isn't crazy.
I like to imagine how I've come back to kiss her,
time after time on snowy mornings,
her lips warm, the room steaming,
the smell of sex still in our bed
delicious as hot rolls
and tangerines.

Richard Green

Resurrection

Silly Rubyann. She pressed her nose against the jewelry store's window glass for a better view of the object inside. This made her nose look like a pig's. Done by a 27-year-old Mohawk woman, this city-child's antic was unlikely. A turtle shell rattle bore the heat of her stare.

Anthony, her live-with man, didn't notice her attention until she tugged at his hand and fetched him. In the window's display, the rattle lay partially hidden under strings of sweet grass amongst flawless pottery with Mimbres designs and woven Chemehuevi baskets. Anthony guessed at what her favored Indian thing would be; perhaps it was the silver Zuni squash blossom necklace, turquoise watchbands or rings. These are what he saw.

"I'm going inside," Rubyann said.

She released Anthony's hand, pulled at an oversized brass door handle and made an entry bell jingle. Anthony, realizing the shop was actually a jewelry store, joyfully followed. He applied authority to shut the stuck door behind him which triggered its etched window to rattle.

Rubyann went straight for the display. A brass rod held white, pleated draperies which provided a backdrop for the colorful Indian pieces. She leaned over the rail and eagerly reached for the turtle shell rattle. She uncovered its buckskin wrapped handle and in a swish held it up between them for Anthony to see.

"Are you supposed to touch that?" was his concerned message.

"This is it," Rubyann breathed. She began delicately fondling the lumpy, cantaloupe-sized shell. "I'm sure this is it." She held it to her nose and sniffed.

134

Somewhere inside Anthony, where his Italian paranoia lived, a warning light went off. This was definitely another dot in Rubyann's recent behavior pattern. Ever since some fed-up Mohawk Indians, at a faraway place called Oka, had resisted the Canadian Army, Rubyann's normal yuppy persuasions seemed distracted. Her fellow Onkwehon:we resolved to prevent an ancient forest of pine trees from being destroyed by golf course construction. They had dutifully defended their sacred forest with guns and put their lives on the line for trees.

"Smell this." Rubyann held up the belly side of the rattle. "Nothing smells like a turtle," she goaded. "You'll never forget it."

Anthony sniffed. "Just what is it that I'm supposed to smell?"

Rubyann pushed the rattle against his nose. "Now take a good smell," she demanded. "This shell's pretty old — you have to really get into it."

Anthony, now 40, wondered about his suddenly aggressive soulmate. In the decade they shared, he'd never seen her like this except when he had introduced her to alcohol at what he guessed to be her first cocktail party. She had foregone the aftereffects of sipping too much white wine and became violent. That night he got slapped. Though he had always suspected she was provoking something bigger he never knew what.

"I don't smell anything," Anthony said. Believing he had made some sort of slip, he grasped the rattle, sniffed again, recoiled from an imagined sour odor and wrinkled his nose. "It is different," he uttered in monotone. He released the rattle to Rubyann before realizing a third presence loomed.

"We have a policy here," came a frigid tone from an elderly man. "You break it and you have just purchased it." This thought seemed to actuate pleasure, for a sweeping smile drove his steel-framed glasses up and his bald head rippled. "That particular item is valued at $350." He reached for the rattle, palm outward.

Rubyann admired the lumpy shell at close range. It contrasted with the smooth veneer her brown skin gave to her high cheekbones. "Buy it for me, Anthony," she said. "I left my purse in the car so I'll have to write you a check when we get back to the parking lot."

"Why do you want an old, smelly thing like that . . . ?"

Rubyann pulled him aside. "Because I helped my uncle, Oron:ia ka-ron, make this rattle when I was a kid," she whispered. "It would mean lots to me if I could have it . . . sort of like a family memento."

Inside Anthony's head, blurry pictures spun like slot machine wheels.

Family. So this has to do with family. Suddenly, three turtles stuttered to a stop in his register window. Of course. That was it. Rubyann wanted the rattle because she is turtle clan. Didn't she reveal that piece of identity during one of their courtship discussions about North America being a turtle's back? He remembered something about Bears, Turtles, and Wolves, yet he couldn't be sure.

"I first saw it when I was four, during a visit with Oron:ia karon at his log house on the Rez. I watched it hanging from a clothesline with wire around its neck. I remember how the blood dripped from its tail and formed a little pool; how its delicate skeleton was attached to the shell."

"What's that? Looks like some sort of hole near where the tail should be."

"Oron:ia karon blamed it on somebody stupid . . ."

"Somebody stupid?"

"Somebody shot it with their .22 rifle. Luckily, it didn't hurt the turtle because the bullet hole's near the edge of the shell. That's how I know Oron:ia karon made this rattle."

"Wouldn't you rather have something of value? Perhaps a nice, Zuni ring you could use as a wedding ring?"

Rubyann's glare gave him his answer. It was the same scowl he had seen in a jewelry store the last time he had promoted discussion about weddings and rings. Still, Anthony schemed a plan to quench an unfulfilled desire. He'd buy an opulent, turquoise ring and see if an Indian thing would win approval for her wedding ring.

"You're an Indian, aren't you?" The old man flashed a smile at Rubyann. "You know, my great-grandmother was flavored with some Indian blood in her. Cherokee, I think it was. What kind are you?"

"Strawberry," Rubyann said. She turned to Anthony as if expecting supportive retort. Instead, Anthony pivoted and went to the window. This was an opportunity to quench his desire; he'd uncover Rubyann's preference.

"How much is that ring in the window there? The bright blue one that's shaped like a turtle."

"You have excellent taste," said the shopkeeper. He reached for the rattle, but Rubyann pulled it away. "That's Morenci turquoise." He breezed past Rubyann. "It comes from a mine out in Arizona. It's the only place where you can find genuine Morenci."

"Anthony?" Rubyann said. She hugged the rattle to her breast. "I really don't want that ring or any ring.".

"I have other rings if that one isn't suitable for madam," the shop-keeper said. "I've got an extra special ring I was saving for my daughter, but I could let you have it . . ."

Rubyann asked: "How do you know that it'll fit?"

"Nooo problem. Any ring can easily be sized to fit any of madam's delicate fingers." He held up the ring between his thumb and forefinger so as to form a silver O. "You have beautiful hands, my dear." He presented the O to her so she could place her ring finger in it. "Do you play piano?"

"Was your craftsman an Indian?"

"Why yes. Zuni, I think."

"Try it on honey . . . go ahead."

"Notice the exact, miniature detail of the turtle . . ."

"I can put it on myself, thank-you," Rubyann said. She tucked the rattle under her arm, took the ring and slipped it upon her finger.

"It's gorgeous," Anthony said.

"A gorgeous ring for a gorgeous lady," the shopkeeper said.

Rubyann pushed her arm out and assessed the delicate turquoise ring. Its miniature turtle shell inlay and highly polished silver revealed superior quality. Normally Rubyann would have accepted this booty; she was fond of pretty things.

"How's the fit?" asked the shopkeeper.

"What's the price?" asked Anthony.

"It's nice, but I don't want it." Rubyann took off the ring and held it out toward the shopkeeper.

"But madam. This is an authentic piece fashioned by one of the country's foremost Zuni craftsmen. Lucero, I think his name was . . ."

Rubyann flipped the ring in the air. It was Anthony who caught it. "What's the asking price," he said.

"I could easily sell this ring for $1,200 . . . it's valued at much more than that."

Rubyann walked back toward the window. She began to rattle the shell in a slow, rhythmic beat. "Can your ring cure cancer? This can."

"Bottom line," Anthony said. "What's your bottom line?"

"I suppose I could let you have it for, say, $1,000. It's so perfect for madam. I'd like to see her have it."

Rubyann put the turtle shell rattle back in the window display. She held a sweet grass braid to her nose and inhaled deeply. She placed it atop the shell and arranged all of the braids into a camouflage clump. "Don't sell that rattle to anyone else," she said. "I'll be right back."

Anthony shrugged. "I guess she really wants that silly rattle," he said.

"Perhaps a diamond ring with a large stone would dissuade madam," the shopkeeper said.

Anthony sensed some sort of pending doom. He looked at the ring, gauged its value and handed it back to the shopkeeper. "I guess she doesn't want it," he said.

"Let me get the other ring; the one I had specially made for my daughter. It's gold anodized silver and has coral, wampum, and turquoise settings. I'm sure madam will find it quite attractive."

". . . and expensive, I'll bet. . . ."

"One gets what one pays for. . . ."

During his wait, Anthony browsed. Door bell tinkle followed by window rattle announced Rubyann's return. Anthony stood, with his hands in his pockets awaiting indication of Rubyann's mood. She marched straight for the window, uncovered the turtle shell rattle and as she approached him, her eyes bristled with determination.

"He wants $350 but this one's only worth $100 to $125 tops." She held up the rattle with authority. "The rule is: the smaller the costlier — because little turtles are harder to catch."

"Plus, this one's damaged," Anthony joined in.

"What's damaged?" A smiling shopkeeper held up a black velvet ring box. "As I said, this was custom-made to my personal specifications by a skilled, local craftsman. You'll note the wolf's head is in coral and set in wampum inside a turquoise-circle border."

Before Anthony could see, Rubyann thrust the rattle into his hands, took the ring and attempted to slide it on her middle finger. "How much do you want for this?" She struggled with a finger joint, slipped it off and pushed it on her index finger. "I can't get it on," she said. "It's too small . . . do you have any soap?"

The shopkeeper pushed back his glasses. "Well," he sighed, "as I said, it can easily be re-sized. . . ."

"Try it on your wedding finger," Anthony said. "If it fits, I'll buy it for you."

Instead, Rubyann slid it onto her baby finger. She quickly raised her hand to accommodate her audience and it slipped off and was propelled into the shopkeeper's chest. Trapping it against his shirt, his head reflex sent his glasses askew.

"If madam pleases." He held the ring in an "O" formation of his fingers and straightened his glasses with the back of his hand. "I believe madam has one last wedding finger left." He slid the ring to her knuckle. "It fits," he said.

"It fits," Anthony said.

"It fits," Rubyann said.

They didn't agree as easily when it came time for price negotiations. The shopkeeper expected $1,000 for the rattle and ring but Rubyann would have none of it. Anthony challenged the jeweler to a gambling game he called Moola but to no avail. Finally, since the rattle's shell was slightly damaged and his daughter didn't want the custom ring anymore because her dog had died and because he was part Cherokee after all, the shopkeeper agreed to affordable terms.

When they left the shop neither spoke. Rubyann carried the turtle rattle next to her purse loops and every time a passerby gawked she'd hold it up and rattle the rattle. Anthony's mind computed several financial adjustment figures.

They crossed the parking lot and headed, diagonally, for Anthony's sports coupe. Before unlocking the car door he stood meekly and looked at Rubyann. Curiosity overcame him and pestered him until: "I know why you wanted the turtle shell rattle but why did you want the wolf's head ring?"

Rubyann seemed more radiant than usual. "Because it's my clan," she said. "I'm wolf clan."

Anthony almost snorted with surprise. *He* thought she was turtle family and that blunder has cost him. So is this about a woman thing . . . or an Indian thing? "Then the only reason you wanted the turtle shell rattle was for sentiment?"

"Sentiment and because we need it."

"What would we possibly need a rattle for?" Before *for* vibrated from his vocal chords, a possibility struck like a thunderbolt. Maybe *they* wouldn't need the rattle, but perhaps somebody else would. Like a baby. He fumbled with his door key and jabbed at the slot. "Are you . . . are *we* going to have a baby?" He twisted the key and pulled the door open. A nervous smile fought with a smile and he stared at Rubyann's face with anticipation.

"Of course not, silly," she giggled. "How could you be so silly? Besides being a keepsake, we need this rattle because it's a calendar."

They climbed in the car and Rubyann told how the thirteen squares on a turtle's back are the moons of the year. She said that the outer ring usually has twenty-eight separations for the days of each moon. This is what Oron:ia karon taught her while sanctifying the rattle.

Anthony twisted the ignition key and the engine rumbled to life. As Rubyann continued her story, pointed to each square, and recited the name of its moon in the Mohawk language, Anthony admired the ring on her wedding finger.

Raven Hail

Return of the Goddess

The Very Important Woman is alive and well
and living on Turtle Island

For five hundred years the followers of Columbus have been stomping the Cherokee Goddess religion into the ground. From the very first, the Spaniards maintained the notion that they came only for the purpose of saving the souls of the heathen savages of the New World. At the same time, it was perfectly obvious to all but the most simple-minded that they came in search of gold and pearls and slaves to carry back to the Old Country. And, of course, new worlds to conquer and enslave. In the islands of the Caribbean where Columbus set up his domain, the gentle peoples were decimated in just a few short years.

Around 1540 De Soto made a pass through the Cherokee country. To his mind, he explained to them that there is one God, who created heaven and earth. This was accomplished through signs, for there was a language barrier. That was how he saw it. To the Cherokee, there was a different slant to the story. They were quick to interpret the speaking of forked tongues — that's why so many of them survived the onslaught of the whites. The message they got was that this white man with his warriors and his big thunder guns would wipe them off the face of the earth if they did not profess belief in his new God. Since only those Cherokees who accepted conversion were allowed to live, the old Goddess beliefs quickly went underground with the poor souls who refused to make the changeover.

The next wave of immigrants said that they came to the New World to escape religious persecution in the Old World. How odd that the very first thing they did upon settling in was to enact laws against all the American Indian religious beliefs; now that these new residents were no longer oppressed, they would allow no religious freedom but their own.

The last hope of gathering up the remnants of the old Cherokee Religion should have been in the early 1700s when James Adair lived among the Cherokees and their neighboring tribes. His "History of the American Indian" was published in London in 1775 and is such a classic on the subject that it has been reprinted as recently as 1971. Unfortunately, Adair was a perfect example of the saying, "I've already made up my mind, don't bother me with the facts!" For he was firmly convinced from the very beginning that the American Indians were descended from one of the Lost Tribes of Israel. He was absolutely certain they were worshipping Jehovah.

Now, to anyone who has danced in the "stomp dances," it is obvious that the dance songs are liberally sprinkled with the syllables ye, hey, yah, ho, wo, wa, weh, heh, ha, and such. So it is easy to see where even a rank outsider might feel he was hearing "Ye ho wah" if that was what he was listening for (even though the nearest Adair claimed to hear was Yo he wah). To point out the foolishness of such claims, I would mention that he could just as easily have thought he heard "Ho Ho Ho" and thereby proved that those early Cherokees were worshipping Santa Claus.

He seemed to find very little significance whatsoever in the fact that the Cherokees always had a fire in the center when dancing or sitting in council. And that they addressed the Divine Fire, threw offerings of sacred tobacco on it, and puffed tobacco smoke toward The Sun. In my younger years I was a cigarette smoker. When hecklers asked me why I smoked so much, I explained that tobacco smoke carried petitions to The Great Spirit — and I needed all the help I could get. Perhaps only another Cherokee would see the humor here.

When William Bartram traveled among the Cherokees around the same time as Adair, he observed that they had no graven images or idols, nor any religious rites that he could see. Whether this be true, or whether he just did not recognize their ceremonies as such, excavations of the southern Mound Builders later uncovered religious artifacts of the prehistoric inhabitants of that same area.

By the time James Mooney came to study the Cherokees of North Carolina in 1887, the overzealous missionaries had conditioned the Cherokees to Christianity and had trained them to avoid mentioning any other beliefs. But by some trick of fate, long before then, Sequoyah had created his Cherokee Syllabary and by 1850 most of The People could read and write in their own language. And here is where the miracle occurred. In the secret formulas which the Medicine Men and Women had written down, there still appeared the sacred names for The Sun Goddess.

When these sacred words slipped through, in the formulas, Mooney questioned each informant in turn to find the significance of such words.

Now, James Mooney was very popular with the Cherokee people. He treated them with proper respect, which was of major importance; and in addition, he was paying them for their information. In their reduced financial circumstances, since all their land had been taken from them by force — not once, but twice — this payment was most welcome. So they were as cooperative as they knew how to be. But Mooney was, after all, a non-Cherokee man, and a Roman Catholic; they had learned from bitter experience not to tell outsiders what they obviously wouldn't want to hear.

They were most reluctant to admit that The Spirit Moon was called Sudaltihi (Sixkiller) and referred to Him only as "Grandfather." And even more reluctant to admit the names for The Spirit Sun: Unehlanunhi (The Provider) and Agehyagugun (The Very Important Woman). Also Ancient White, Ancient Red and Ancient One (The Fire — The Sun on Earth, or alter ego of The Sun).

They were all eager to point out that the physical moon and the physical sun were both "nunda" — the nunda that lives in the night is the moon, and the nunda that lives in the daytime is the sun. As for the sacred names for these two luminaries, they all took refuge in the usual Indian escape route since the coming of the insurgents, by insisting that they "didn't know."

Even after Mooney accepted The Cherokee Spirit Sun as feminine, he still referred to Unehlanunhi as "he." It's hard for a white male Christian to get used to referring to The Great Spirit as "She."

Another bit of information that came with translating the formulas was the Cherokee concept of heaven. There are Seven Heavens, or six different levels of upward progression aspired to before reaching the seventh, which is perfection: the abode of The Sun Goddess.

Five hundred years is only the blink of an eye in the mind of The Goddess. No more enough to destroy Her than to destroy the sun or to stamp out fire. Or to stop the gentle rain and the rising of the new moon.

In the words of The Goddess:

I AM THE SONG, AND THE SONG LIVES ON!

Joy Harjo

Wolf Warrior

For all the warriors

A white butterfly speckled with pollen joined me in my prayers
yesterday morning as I thought of you in Washington. I didn't want
the pain of repeated history to break your back. In my blanket of
hope I walked with you, wolf warrior, and the council of tribes to
what used to be the Department of War to discuss justice. When a
people institute a bureaucratic department to serve justice, then be
suspicious. False justice is not justified by massive structure, just
as the sacred is not confinable to buildings constructed for the
purpose of worship.

I pray these words don't obstruct the meaning I am searching to give
you, a gift like love so you can approach that strange mind without
going insane. So we can all walk with you, sober, our children
empowered with the clothes of memory in which they are never
hungry for love, or justice.

An old Cherokee who prizes wisdom above the decisions rendered by
departments of justice in this world told me this story. It isn't
Cherokee but a gift given to him from the people in the North. I know
I carried this story for a reason, and now I understand I am to give it
to you. A young man, about your age or mine, went camping with his
dogs. It was just a few years ago, not long after the eruption of
Mount St. Helens, when white ash covered the northern cities, an
event predicting a turning of the worlds. I imagine October and
bears fat with berries of the brilliant harvest, before the freezing

144

breath of the north settles in and the moon is easier to reach by flight without planes. His journey was a journey toward the unknowable, and that night as he built a fire out of twigs and broken boughs he remembered the thousand white butterflies climbing toward the sun when he had camped there last summer.

Dogs were his beloved companions in the land that had chosen him through the door of his mother. His mother continued to teach him well, and it was she who had reminded him that the sound of pumping oil wells might kill him, turn him toward money. So he and his dogs traveled out into the land that remembered everything, including butterflies, and the stories that were told when light flickered from grease.

That night as he boiled water for coffee and peeled potatoes he saw a wolf walking toward camp on her hind legs. It had been generations since wolves had visited his people. The dogs were awed to see their ancient relatives and moved over to make room for them at the fire. The lead wolf motioned for her companions to come with her and they approached humbly, welcomed by the young man who had heard of such goings-on but the people had not been so blessed since the church had fought for their souls. He did not quite know the protocol, but knew the wolves as relatives and offered them coffee, store meat, and fried potatoes which they relished in silence. He stoked the fire and sat quiet with them as the moon in the form of a knife for scaling fish came up and a light wind ruffled the flame.

The soundlessness in which they communed is what I imagined when I talked with the sun yesterday. It is the current in the river of your spinal cord that carries memory from sacred places, the sound of a thousand butterflies taking flight in windlessness.

He knew this meeting was unusual and she concurred, then told the story of how the world as they knew it had changed and could no longer support the sacred purpose of life. Food was scarce, pups were being born deformed, and their migrations, which were in essence a ceremony for renewal, were restricted by fences. The world as all life on earth knew it would end, and there was still time in the circle of hope to turn back the destruction.

That's why they had waited for him, called him here from the town a day away over the rolling hills, from his job constructing offices for the immigrants. They shared a smoke and he took the story into his blood, his bones, while the stars nodded their heads, while the dogs murmured their agreement. "We can't stay long," the wolf said. "We have others with whom to speak and we haven't much time." He packed the wolf people some food to take with them, some tobacco, and they prayed together for safety on this journey. As they left the first flakes of winter began falling and covered their tracks. It was as if they had never been there.

But the story burned in the heart of this human from the north and he told it to everyone who would listen, including my elder friend who told it to me one day while we ate biscuits and eggs in Arizona. The story now belongs to you, too, and much as pollen on the legs of a butterfly is nourishment carried by the butterfly from one flowering to another, this is an ongoing prayer for strength for us all.

Gordon Henry

Song for Oshawanung Manitoequay

This wing feather
I give you

not for love
not for memory
not for the hidden bone
beneath the smooth blue feather
not for the shadow it
brushes away in your hand
not in exchange for the
gold wolf at your ear
not for the mist that rolls
through your lips to cross
the garden in gray air
not for the man I want
you to destroy
not for a moment
not for moving smoke
or hot days
not for the lies I gave
for the stories I told
not for the dreamtime artist
who keeps you awake at night
not for the power to hold off
collection agents
not to remove layers of dust
from the possession of the dead

or distant
not to blow out the candle
you've lit for prayer
not to gather your amazement
and release it as my own
not for you to excite my skin
not for fletching
for any particular arrow
not for floating free for a few
moments above ground in
an August whirlwind
not to represent the stone
I found it on
not that you may fly
or walk differently
not that the wing will
come back as a whole
bird for me when I am
starving or alone
No, this wing feather
I give you
you who know
I can't fly
you who know
I will.

_____

At once you recall
the thunder song.

a village leaves every door open
and no one returns.

Old Stone Woman smudges
blue dishes under blue-scarred moon
at the guild hall.

Bingo night eats up
the aspirin girl
on the blue television.

Messages are never received
for one reason.

For another, a wild
dog upsets garbage.

Auntie uses an air rifle
to silence the screaming
of passionate cats.

None of the singers
will go into the mission.

Under the influence
of gasoline fumes
a boy runs, naked, into
a barbed wire fence.

The tribal custodian
dances with a BIA mop.

The chairman's deep in a dream
of information
about using information
more effectively.

From steep bluffs
you look deep into
the river
held back by pointless dreams
and simple songs of home.
Be with me
in starlight, in sunlight,
with the people.

As old man Tobacco Song
buries the intellectual shadow
beyond stations of memory.

My home is far away,
farther than
a hundred sleeping places
beside winter fires.

Out where youth sing
in sunlight bands
one crow calls
from the offering cloth.

Chant on Being Photographed

The picture will
come out dark
and the soul
will not leave.
The picture will
not take the soul.
Eyes rely
on the aperture
The soul will not leave
without the proper lens.
The picture will
come out dark
and the eyes
will take nothing
without the proper lens.
The soul will not leave.

Wolf Dancer

I am seeking the
dancer who killed
the golden retriever,
the same clown
with somebody in love

written all over him.

When I find him
I will change his name
and chain him
to a fence
to see if he can
escape his own
barking shadow.

If I find him
I will find him
a home among strangers
who feed him ·
and send him out in the dark
to relieve himself.

In time he will be
the first to hear everything.
He will distrust strangers
and take pleasure
in deep smells.
He will fear dancers
and the chaos
of human activity.

Old man,
I will guide your silver canoe
to the center of the water,
where the Loon father
carries children on his back.
If I'm quiet
I will arrive as a call
from another shore,
close enough to see
the fantastic eyes
seeing me
drifting alone.

Lance Henson

two fragments

a murmur of geese
follow the angling river north
clothed in a dream
their wings sore with dusk

north country rain
a birds hushed song caught in a droplet on a tree branch
no thunder
i sit in lamplight
an occasional car whines by outside
this is the time lorca named duende
an hour made of essential things
flowers in lightless water
a horse wandering aimlessly toward a village with no name

guilderland, ny
march 1992

midland poem #3

tomorrow night the moon will be full
tonight small skeletons of moths
are blowing across the parking lot

by the dim lamp i trace the age that has
scarred my hands

i have grown up among men who love
their loneliness

dark flowers on the dresser reflect in
the mirror
and waiting in the locket of a prayer

a child is watching us
in his dreams

6/5/90–3/2/92

translation on a sleepless night

it is near dawn
and the storm off the mediterranean has
awakened me to this hour
and what outside the window lace and glass
watches us sleep

the moon thin as a dream hangs on in the midst
of a rainstorm

a shadow moves across the room
wringing its hands
the earth moaning now among damp flowers

a small sound presses its face against the night
this night that is lost

a tin can outside fills
with a weary rain

3/2/89–2/18/92
riva trigoso italy

a great darkness

it is an old loneliness
voices weeping softly against the earth

a gray wing hovers above us
in the midst of the rain

i have arrived here sleepless and empty

tying my names to the cloth of night

4/4/91–3/20/92
rensselaerville ny

Linda Hogan

Bush's Mourning Feast

"The house is crying," I said to her as steam ran down the walls. The cooking stove heated the house. Windows were frozen over with white feathers and ferns. It was a long week of cooking, and there was no music.

"The house can withstand it," Bush said. She stepped outside and brought in an armload of wood. I caught the sweet odor of it and a wind of cold air as she brushed by me. She placed a log in the stove. It was still damp, and when the red hands of flame grabbed it, the wood spat and hissed.

I didn't for a minute believe the house could withstand it. I knew already it was going to collapse. It was a wooden house, dark inside, and spare. The floors creaked as she swept about, still wearing the cold. The branches of trees scraped against the windows, trying to get in. Perhaps they protested the fire and what it lived on.

Bush unjointed the oxtails and browned them in suet. She worked so slowly, you would have thought it was swamp balm, not fat and backbone, that she touched. I thought of the old days when oxen with their heavy hooves arrived in black train cars from the dark, flat fields of Kansas, diseased beasts that had been yoked together in burden. All the land, even our lost land, was shaped by them and by the hated thing that held them together as rain and sunlight and snow fell on their toiling backs.

The shadows of fish were afloat in the sink. Bush did her own hunting then, and she had a bag of poor, thin winter rabbits. She removed their fur the way you would take off a stocking. She dredged them in flour. In the kitchen, their lives rose up in steam.

Day and night she worked. In her night clothes, she boiled roots that still held the taste of mud. She stirred a black kettle and two pots. In her dark skirt, she cut onions. I didn't understand, until it was over, what it was she had to do. I didn't know what had taken hold of her and to what lengths she must go in order to escape its grip.

She had black hair then, beautiful and soft. She folded blankets and clothing and placed them on the floor in the center of that one dark room. She took down the curtains, shook out the dust, washed them in the sink and hung them on lines from wall to wall. All the while, bones floated up in broth the way a dream rises to the top of sleep.

Your mother entered my dreaming once, not floating **upward** that way, but crashing through, the way deer break through ice, or a stone falls into water, tumbling down to the bottom. In the dream, I was fishing in Lake Grand when the water froze suddenly, like when the two winds meet against each other and stop everything in their path, the way they do in waking life, the way they left a man frozen that time, standing in place at the bank of Spirit River. In the dream, your mother was beneath ice in the center of the lake. I was afraid of her. We all were. What was wrong with her we couldn't name and we distrusted such things that had no name. She was a deep and magnetic force like the iron underground that pulls the needle of a compass to false north and sets it spinning. My heart beat fast. The part of me that was awake feared I was having a heart attack, but I could not shake myself out of the dream.

Whatever your mother was in that dream, it wasn't human. It wasn't animal or fish. It was nothing I could recognize by sight or feel. The water became solid and the thing she was, or that had turned into her, pulled me toward it, out across the ice. I was standing, still and upright, drawn out that way to the terrible and magnetic center of what I feared. I reached an arm, as if to grab for anything that might stop me, but nothing was there, and I slid across the glaring surface of ice. Standing like a statue, being pulled that way, helpless and pale in the ice light, old stories I'd heard from some of the Cree began to play across my mind, stories about the frozen heart of evil that was hunger, envy, and greed, and how it tricked people into death or illness. The only thing, finally, that could save them was to find a way to thaw it, to warm it back into water.

But where your mother, Hannah Wing, stood was at the bottomless passage to an underworld. And there was no thawing to it.

Bush had struggled with your mother's ice cold world. There was the time she heard you crying in the house when you were not there. I heard it, too, your voice, crying for help, or I would not have believed her. It was a chilling sound. Bush turned desperate as a caged animal, wanting to get you out of the clutch of the nameless thing that held you.

In her battle with that underworld, whatever it was, Bush didn't win, but she didn't lose either. It was a tie, a fragile balance that at any time could go either way. That was why she cooked the mourning feast. That was why she baked the bread and soaked corn in lye and ashes until it became the sweetest hominy, and who would have believed such a caustic thing could sweeten and fatten the corn. That was why she cooked the wild rice we harvested two years earlier with Frenchie poling in the canoe. The rice was the most important thing; you had gone with us that fall day, wrapped in cotton and with netting over your face so that the little bugs and dust wouldn't bother you as we drifted through the plants, clicking the sticks that knocked rice into the boat.

And when Bush opened the jar of swamp tea, it smelled like medicine to me. It smelled like healing. It was what we needed. It reminded me of the days when the old women put eagle down inside wounds and they would heal.

Bush is a quiet woman, little given to words, and she never takes kindly to being told what to do. So while she prepared the feast, I let her be, even when she did a poor job on the rice soup. I knitted and sat in the chair by the window and looked outside, straight at the face of winter. There was a silence so deep it seemed that all things prepared for what would follow, then and for years to come, years when the rest of us would be gone, when the land itself would tremble in fear of drowning.

The windows had frozen over so it was through ice that I saw them coming, the people, arriving that cold Sunday of the feast. Across ice, they were like shadows against a darkening winter evening, and the ice shifted as they approached. Wind had blown snow from the surface of the lake. In places the ice was shining like something old and polished by hands. Maybe it was the hands of wind, but the ice shone beneath their feet. I scraped the window with my fingernails and peered out. Jarrell Illinois, gone now, wore a miner's headlamp even though it wasn't quite dark, and the others walked close to him, as if convinced that night had fallen. As they grew closer, I saw that their shadows and reflections walked alongside them like ghosts or their own deaths that would rise up and meet them one day. So it looked like they were more. My breath steamed the window, I remember. I wiped it again for a better look.

Some of the people were wrapped in the hides we used to wear; others wore large wool coats, or had blankets wrapped around them. They walked together like spirits from the thick forest behind winter. They were straight and tall. None of them talked.

"Here they come," I said. Bush, for a change, was nervous. She stirred the iron pot one last time, then she untied her hair. It was long and thick. Hair is a woman's glory, they say. Her glory fell down her back. The teakettle began to sing as if it remembered old songs some of us had long since forgotten. Its breath rose up in the air as she poured boiling water over the small oval leaves of swamp tea. The house smelled of it and of cedar.

"Look at that," I said. "They look beautiful."

Bush bent over the table and looked out the window as the people came through a path in snow. The air was shimmering in the light of the miner's lamp and a lantern one woman carried. Bush wiped her hands on her apron. And then they came through the door and filled up the crying house. Some of them stamped their feet from the habit of deep snow, their cheeks red with cold. They took off their boots and left them by the fire. They greeted us. Some of them admired the food or warmed their hands near the stove, and all of them looked at the pictures of you that sat on the table, but after greeting us, they said very little. After all the years she had lived here, they were still uncomfortable around Bush. They had never understood her. To get them to her banquet, she had told them this was her tradition, and it was the only thing that could help her. There wasn't one among us who didn't suspect that she had made this ceremony up, at least in part, but mourning was our common ground and that's why they came, out of loyalty for the act of grief.

Bush put a piece of each kind of food in her blue bowl for the spirits, wiped her hands on her apron, and took the bowl outside. When she left the doorway and went out, heat rose from the bowl, going up like a story carried to the sky, begging any and all gods in the low clouds to listen. The aching joints of my hands told me it was a bone-chilling, hurting cold, the worst of winters, and the temperature was below zero. Bush held up the bowl for sky to see, for the spirit of ice, for what lived inside clouds, for the night-wind people who would soon be present because they lived on Fur Island and returned there each night. I could barely make out her shape in the newly swirling snow, but when she came back in, she smiled. I remember that. She smiled at the people. As if a burden was already lifted.

158

One by one the people took their places, settling into chairs or on the couch that was covered with a throw I had made, or they sat at the long table. They hadn't been there before and so they looked around the little, now-stripped house with curiosity. It was stained wood and wallpaper. There were places where rain had seeped through. It was lighter without curtains than it had been a few days before.

When Bush served up the food, it came to me that I didn't want to eat. I was a large woman then, I loved my food, but I must have known that eating this meal would change me. I only picked at it.

At first, we hardly spoke except for a few exchanges of small talk, then there was just the sound of forks on plates, spoons in bowls. We were such quiet eaters that when the wind died down for a moment you could hear the snow hitting against the wood of the house, dying against the windows, tapping as if it, too, was hungry and wanted in. I could only think of the island where she lived, the frozen waters, the other lands with their sloping distances, even the light and dust of solar storms that love our cold, eerie poles.

There was moose meat, rice, and fish. The room was hot. There were white-haired people, black-haired, and the mixed-bloods in colorful clothes. Frenchie was there, dressed in a blue dress. It was low-cut and she wore rhinestones at her neck, and large rubber boots. We were used to her way of dress, so we didn't think it was strange attire. We just believed she was one kind of woman on top and another below the waist.

It was so damp and warm inside, the wallpaper, full of leaves, began to loosen from the moist walls. It troubled my mother, Dora-Rouge, who sat with her back against the wall. She was always an orderly woman and accustomed to taking care of things. When Bush wasn't looking she tried to stick it back up, holding edges and corners with her hands until it became too much for her so she sat back down and took the fine bones out of her fish and placed them together on the side of her plate in a neat arrangement.

Jarrell Illinois took some tobacco out of a tin and pinched it into his cheek and smiled all around the room.

The house grew smaller. It settled. The floors sloped as if they knew the place would soon be abandoned, the island quiet and alone with just its memory of what had happened there, even the shipwreck of long ago.

I don't know how to measure love. Not by cup or bowl, not in distance either, but that's what rose from the iron pot as steam, that was the food taken into our bodies. It was the holy sacrament of you we ate that day. We ate from evening through to near light, or as light as it gets in winter. The fire cast shadows on the walls as almost all cleaned their plates. The old men picked the bones, then piled them up like ancient tellers of fortune. They ate the bowls empty, clear to the bottom. By then, people were talking and some even laughing, and there was just something in the air, and that night, in front of everyone, Bush cut her long hair. It held a memory of you and she had to free it.

And when the dishes were all piled up, she went to the middle of the room where she had placed her earthly goods, then gave each diner present some part of her world. It was only your things she parted with unwillingly, holding them as if she dreaded their absence, and now and then a tear would try to gather in her eye, but she was fierce and determined. She gave away your hand-made blanket, T-shirt, shoes, socks — gave one here, one there. Some of the people cried. Not only for her, or for you, but for all the children lost to us.

That was how I came to have the cradleboard Bush beaded for you in the dim light of the house that cried. It is made of soft buckskin with red and blue beads. I leave the small doll laced inside it. It has been this way all these years. Inside the smaller bag are your hair and nail clippings. Your mother, Hannah Wing, did not save your stem, so it was all Bush, who loved you so, could think to close inside, to call you home again to us, and it worked.

Then she gave her quilts away, and the hawk feathers that had survived both flood and fire. She gave the carved fish decoys my son Harold made. They were weighted just right to drop through ice and lure many a slow and hungry winter fish. No one else had weights as good as those. She gave her fishing poles and line, and her rifle. She gave the silverware. At the end she stood there in her white sleeping gown for she had even given what she wore that day, the black skirt, the sweater.

With all the moisture of cooking and breath, the door froze shut, and when the people were ready to leave, John Husk struggled to open it until finally it gave. And when they went through it each person carried away a part of her. She said it was her tradition. No one questioned her out loud or showed a hint of a doubting face, though they knew she had created this ceremony for the ending of her grief.

They came to love her that night. She had gone to the old ways, the way we used to live. From the map inside ourselves. Maybe it reminded us that we had made our own ways here and were ourselves something like outcasts and runaways from other lands and tribes to start with.

When they left through the unstuck, pried-open door, night had turned over. The vast white silence of winter was broken only by the moaning sound of the lake.

I was glad to remain in the hot kitchen with Bush, but I watched the others walk away with their arms full. Going back that morning, in the blue northern light, their stomachs were filled, their arms laden with blankets, food, and some of the beaver pelts Bush had stolen and been ar-rested for — from the trappers who had trespassed the island. Anything that could be carried away, they took. Frenchie pushed a chair before her across the ice, leaving the track of wooden legs in shining lines. Beneath her coat, she wore Bush's black sweater over the dress and rhinestones. But the largest thing they carried was Bush's sorrow. We all had it, after that. It became our own. Some of us have since wanted to give it back to her, but once we felt it we knew it was too large for a single person.

They walked through the drifts that had formed when the wind blew, then seemed to merge with the outlines of trees. I was worried, thinking as they neared the mainland that Frenchie might fall into the warm spot where the lake never freezes. Others had fallen before her.

When the people were no longer in sight, Bush went outside to get the bowl. It was empty and there were no tracks. Or maybe the wind had covered them. But a bowl without its soup is such a hopeful thing, and like the bowl, Bush was left with emptiness, a place waiting and ready to be filled, one she could move inside and shape about her. And finally, she was able to sleep. She had made her grief small and child-sized, one that would slide its hand inside one of ours and walk away with us, across the frozen water.

After that, she didn't talk about you anymore, or wear black. But we did. We were the ones who began to wear black, not to defy ghosts as in other days, but out of pain. And after that, we were never together with-out you in our hearts. Your absence sat at every table, occupied every room, walked through the doors of every house.

The next evening, Bush said it was time for me to leave. "Go on," she said, handing me my coat and hat. I hesitated. She had little more than a few pieces of firewood and some cooking pots. She had given away even the food. She saw me look about the house at what wasn't there. I sipped hot tea. We had slept near each other for warmth the night before, my bear coat over us. Once Bush sat up and said, "This coat is singing." I told her it was just the sound of ice outside the door.

I must have looked worried. "I'll be fine," she said, holding up the coat to help me into it.

At least, I remember thinking, if she'd kept her long hair she would be warmer. But I said, "What about me? It's getting close to dark." She wasn't fooled. She knew I walked late at night just to hear the sounds of winter and see the sky and snow. She handed me my gloves and hat. I left unwillingly. It was all I could do to go out the door. I felt terrible leaving her in all that emptiness. I guess it was her sadness already come over me. I wanted to cry, but I knew the wind, on its way to the island where it lived, would freeze my tears.

I took my time getting home. Above me there were the shimmering hints of light. The sky itself was a bowl of milk.

Four days later, food and blankets appeared at Bush's door. She never knew who left them and there were no tracks on the ice. But I was beside myself with worry, and one night that worry got the best of me. I laced up my boots and went back over the frozen water. She was thinner, but she looked happy, and she didn't argue when I opened this bear coat I've always worn and wrapped it around the both of us. We walked together back to the mainland. The only sound was our feet on ice, the snap and groan of the lake. We were two people inside the fur of this bear. She said she could see the cubs that had lived inside and been born from this skin, and I said, "Yes."

Andrew Hope

On Kaagwaantaan Street

He's here
He's back
Walking
Sitka Indian Village streets
Again
He left us in 1968
The village was
Empty and dark for a time
Black and white photos
Of broken houses
Rain faded wood
Dreaming of his spirit
Was he always there?
Or was he reborn in my dream?

On Kaagwaantaan II

When I was a teenager
I remember standing on Katlian street
Looking up at the face
Of my grandparents' house
When they were out of town
Waiting for them to return

From the fishing grounds
From the cannery
From the Indian conventions
From the Presbyterian missions
Thinking they would never leave
Somehow, I know they are back
The Spirit of the house
On Kaagwaantaan Street
Lives on forever

LeAnne Howe

A Story for Shatanni Ohoyo

Nahotina, the second daughter of Opa Hatanchi, pulled the flap of her shelter back and walked into the night. She yawned and watched a fragile star blister, then burst and fall silently through the air.

The night smelled sweet with burning cedar's breath. The sky shone full-moon white.

By midnight, every fire in the temporary encampment had burned an offering for protection from what the Choctaws call *kon-wi anun-kasha*, That Which Moves at Night.

As Nahotina started toward the center of the encampment to join the others for the Starting Dance Song, she took two steps, another, then stopped. A faint movement in the air, something from the West, startled her. The trees murmured, not enough to stir up the breeze, but enough to chill the sweat on the back of her neck. She looked behind her. Nothing.

A nesting bird sensed her approach. The wings took shape in the air, then escaped into the surrounding woods. Nahotilla thought she had heard heavy feet moving along with her. She held tight her mother's porcupine sash as she began walking down a narrow, twisting path to find her relatives who were preparing for the all-night sing-along.

The soil was wet. The prairie grass along the path struggled against heavy dew to keep its ends up. She stopped and put out her hand to catch a firefly. The feet which had been running behind her suddenly stopped too. The tiny hairs on her head stood on end. Again she looked around her. No one. How many times would this happen, she wondered?

"Intek aliha. Sisterhood!" called Nahotina in a low voice as she bent over to pull a small moist shell out of the ground that gleamed like a silver lure in the moonlight. "I am growing stronger now," she warned as she looked back toward the woods with compassion.

Leaving the shell behind, she set out once more and immediately heard the muffled tread of feet over the moist earth a few paces behind her. Little by little the feet gained courage and drew closer to Nahotina.

Soon it sounded as if the feet would catch her. As she continued down the path, she whispered, "Intek aliha, I am calling on you. Intek aliha. Sisterhood. Help, before it pounces on me."

Just then Nahotina reached the center of camp. She saw Atokotubbee standing at the big fire next to Haya, Anoleta, Talilusa and Nitakechi. Her nostrils sniffed the air. She watched the smoke twist and ascend around her uncle's head. Her sisters began shouting, "Ae, Ae, Ae!" "See, she is always the last one," said Haya.

Surprised, the old man turned. When he saw his niece, he smiled and banged his striking sticks together.

"*A-chuk-ma,* are you ready, *alla ek?*"

Nahotina's world grew calm again. She glanced back toward the footsteps. There was nothing. The sound of the feet had vanished. She laughed revealing her small white teeth and said, "I am ready, Imoshe."

* * * *

A group of Nahotina's relatives had been singing continuously. When they stopped to eat, another *iksa* took their place and continued singing at the big fire in the center of the Choctaw encampment.

Nahotina was glad she arrived in time to see her favorite uncle assemble everyone at the *ahila,* a plot of ground about a hundred yards away from the big fire prepared for the purpose of dancing. Dancing was at the center of Choctaw life. Nahotina loved the sounds of Atokotubbee's striking sticks, too. Despite his age, there remained something youthful about his playing and dancing. His eyes always held a kind of sweet mocking, full of so deep a knowledge that all the children of the iksa obeyed him without question.

Even though she never remembered exactly what happened, she knew it had been Atokotubbee who resurrected her after the attack in the southeastern borderlands which belonged to her people.

It had happened during the month of the Sun of Blackberries. She had been gathering fruit with her mother and two sisters when she got lost in the dense woods. After frantically searching Yan'abe, Shakbatina called her entire iksa together to hunt for her small daughter. On the second day of the disappearance, Shakbatina sent word to her husband, Koi Chitto, who was staying at his sister's cabin, to come back to Yan'abe because their daughter was missing. When the men found Nahotilla's unconscious body several miles from the village, no one expected her to live. She was an awkward tangle of matted hair and blood. Her knees had been badly gashed and she had a two-inch wound scratched across her right cheek.

When Atokotubbee saw Nahotina, he said, *"Alla tek, a-chuk-ma taha che. This girl will be well."*

The oldest member of the iksa danced all through the night, singing his family's most ancient songs. The next day, he burned a special plant and blew the smoke up the child's nose. Without speaking, as if that was the end of it, Nahotilla sat up. After a few minutes, during which the women worked over the girl's body, Nahotina drank some water and ate a small portion of dried deer meat.

Haya, Anoleta, Nitakechi, and the tenderhearted Koi Chitto stood in the doorway of the cabin waiting to see if the girl would remember anything. Shakbatina placed her hand on her daughter's head and caressed her lightly, so that she would not frighten Nahotina further.

"Try to remember what happened on that green morning," she urged. "This is sometimes the way we are given things. Fight hard to remember, so you will know the meaning of this."

Shakbatina stepped aside with respect and motioned for Atokotubbee to come next to the girl. He took Nahotilla's hand and patted it, but did not speak. At that moment, a fat buck ran in front of the door of their cabin and headed toward the woods. The animal had shown himself and several Choctaw hunters went chasing after him.

Nahotina, too, saw the deer, and something else riding on top of the animal. However, when she tried tell her mother what she saw, her voice left her and she could no longer speak, or even mouth the words. And it was then, the young girl realized she had lost her ability to speak.

Frantic at first, Nahotina cried and would not be comforted. After several months, her legs healed, but she was still mute. Her uncle began to take her hunting with him. He taught her about the woodland animals and how to depend on her other senses to communicate with animals and people. Like a baby learning how to squeeze a lazy tongue behind new teeth, she struggled to make words. After a time she began to be able to speak a few phrases. And the following year she was talking again with her two sisters.

The wound on her cheek also left a scar. Some said, Shatanni Ohoyo, the Tick Woman, had kidnapped Nahotina, marked her for a purpose, and made her mute until she learned the intended lesson. Tick Woman was known to play tricks on the Choctaw: sometimes bringing a fever-sickness to them, sometimes to their enemies. Tick Woman could also be a helper. Many times Shatanni Ohoyo had been seen running her herd out of the burning forests into the arrows of hungry Choctaw hunters. For this reason, the Choctaw named their dance, Shatanni Hila, for the one who teaches the wild deer to dance in the people's fires.

As for Nahotilla, she was never very sure of what had happened to her, except that over the years, she had become an excellent tracker of wild game. She developed her gifts, eventually learning to tell whether people were sick or well by their different smells. So when Atokotubbee asked his niece to choose the first Naholla for a dance, she first walked up to this first white stranger to arrive in the Choctaw camp and breathed in his scent.

"Teach that one to dance, alla tek," he said again, pointing her toward the white man seated close to the Choctaw fire.

Motioning for the Spanish trader to get up and join her in a Jump Dance, Nahotina memoried the white man's scent. He was not sick or well. It was unlike any Choctaw smell she knew. Slowly, she understood why her uncle sent her to this man. "To track the animal you must first learn the scent." This is what someone had said to her.

When the dance was finished she took this Naholla across the path toward *kon-wi anun-kasha,* That Which Moves at Night. And she taught him how to dance in the Choctaw fire. And that was the lesson of Shatanni Ohoyo.

Sun and Wind

Part I
Each morning, Hashi, the stark red creator rises,
swelling,
she passes over the ground, spilling a drop or two of her blood
which grows the corn, and the people: Choctaw that is we.
Naked, she goes down on us,

her flaming hair burns us brown.
Finally, in the month of Tek Inhashi, the Sun of Women,
when we are navel deep in red sumac, we cut the leaves and
smoke to her success. Sing her praises.
Hashiq, Creator Sun, won't forget.

Part II

When Ohoyo Ikbi pulled
freshly-made Choctaw
out of her red thighs,
we were very wet, so
one-by-one,
she stacked us
on the mound,
and Hashi kissed our
bodies with her morning lips
and painted our faces with afternoon fire,
and, in the month of Hashi Hoponi, the Sun of Cooking,
we were made.

Part III

It is said that
once-a-month warriors can kill a thing with spit.
So when the soldiers came,
our mothers stood on the tops of the
ramparts and made the *tashka* call
urging their men on.
Whirling their tongues and hatchets in rhythm,
they pulled red water and fire from their bodies
and covered their chests with bullet-proof blood.
And when it was over,
they made a fire bed on the prairie that
blew across the people like a storm;
melded our souls with iron.
And in the month of Hashi Mali, the Sun of Wind,
we listen for the voices
that still urge us on
at sunrise.

Alex Jacobs

Indian Machismo or Skin to Skin

this is the Blue Jean Nation speakin', bro
and these are the Red Man's Blues, sista
hey ya hey ya hey, what can I say
you could say, cuz, we missed the boat
yeah, the Mayflower, or was it the Nonie, Pinto & Santo Domingo,
i dunno, i wasn't in school that day
but, yo! we ain't no alcatraz, no aim, no wounded knee
we don't vote, but who votes anyway
you kick out the blood-sucking scum
they just come back wiser, richer, hard-core thieves
you can't kick out what you come to depend on?!
they need us weak and weak we get
so what? so what?! so what!
you do your part, you get diddly squat
how many meetings, how many cops, how many knocks
in the dark, leave me alone, just do your thang!

hey, hey, hey, we missed:
Floyd Westerman, Buffy Ste. Marie, Russell Means
Dennis Banks, we even missed Iron Eyes Cody and
this tear's for you, we missed national indian day
we missed the Trail of Broken Treaties, Plymouth Rock,
the Longest Walk, the fish-ins, the sit-ins, the marches
NO, we dont know tom petty, the allmans, the grateful dead,
we dont know jackson browne, bruce cockburn, neil young,

NO, we dont know fritz scholder or jamake highwater
& MAN, WE DON'T WANT TO
we missed: FORT LAWTON, PIT RIVER, FRANKS LANDING,
we missed: SCOTTSDALE, CUSTER, PINE RIDGE, ROSEBUD
we missed: CROW DOG'S PARADISE, THE FBI RAIDS,
we missed: GANIENKEH & AKWESASNE & MORE FBI RAIDS
THE MOHAWKS DREW A LINE IN THE DIRT & SAID TO THE NY
STATE TROOPERS: "CROSS THIS LINE AND WE WILL ATTICA YOU!"
TROOPERS BEATING BATONS ON THEIR RIOT SHIELDS
THEY WOULD NOT TAKE THAT LAST STEP
TO COLLECT THAT LAST EARTHLY PAYCHECK . . .
we missed them outlawing the Native American Church
we missed them tearing up 4 Corners, fencing Big Mountain
we missed the Vatican wanting to put up a telescope
called Columbus on an Apache Sacred Mountain . . .
we missed: RED & BARRIER & LUBICON LAKES, PARLIAMENT HILL,
we missed: JAMES BAY & OKA & THE TV NEWS
we missed all the new Redman movies
NO, we dont know, brando, dylan, fonda, costner
but, bro, i say, not proud, not wise, just reality
& human-size, from the beat of the street & not a drum

We are the Skins that drink in the ditch
We are the Skins that fill the tanks, cells, jails, wards
We are the Skins that need that spare change, bottle, baggie
We are the Lou Reed Skins, the Funky Skins, the Cowboy Skins
We are the ghosts of Seattle, homeless walking urban spirits
We are the frozen dead of Bigfoot's Band
WE ARE BURNING CORNFIELDS!
We are burned down boarding schools, trashed BIA toilets
government trailer trash, broken glass, broken treaties!
You mean you still believe in treaties?
you be bad, bad judges of character, like the faith of clowns
you trust too much, you believe in people's smiles,
you mean you never seen 'em smile when they stab you in the
back, jack, Billy Jack, what show you been watchin'?
this ain't no rerun! it's reality! it's goin' on right now!

IT'S HAPPENED EVERY DAY FOR 500 YEARS!
but i bet you be there in your buckskins when the politicos
celebrate Cristofo Mofo Colombo in 1992 & make him an
honorary Cherosiouxapapanavajibhawk too! aaaaiiiieeee-yahhhh!

But don't forget to invite us to your par-tee, boyz
we are the skins that fill the bingos, the bootleggers,
the afterhours clubs, we are the skins that speak the language
of currency: toyota, cadillac, colombian, sinsemillian, jim beam,
jack daniels, cuervo, honda, sushi, gilley's hard rock cafe,
santa mantra fe, coors, bud, it's miller time, zenith, motorola,
sony, phony feathers, patent leather, kragers, headers, spoilers
VCR, VHS, CD, DAT, BFA, MFA, PHD, BIA, BMW, LSMFT
machined decks and state of the art funky crapola,
it's all payola, make you feel like the Marlboro-man, aaay! S.A.!

Where we put this stuff, i don't know, but it makes the rounds
thas fer shur, we can't help what we ain't got,
what we ain't got, izzit what we lookin' for?
I think we lookin' for help, that a flash or what?
U can call me bad, bro, but you did it, too, pretty slick of you
to forget to add it to you res-u-may, compadre
we can pass the buck all night long, asking
"How much did you get for your soul?"
but this soul's been punctured, splintered, folded & mutilated
sewn back together into a crazy quilt that catches the wind
it's the only way this soul knows how to pray. I'm sending
signals, bro!, using my genuine, authentic, rubber slicker, neon
patch, imitation yellow tanned bodybag, the same bodybag that
will carry me home when the last round-up happens in some
bloody border bar. Say, bro, say, sista, can you help me read the
signs, i musta missed survival school that day . . .

BUT, WHEN THEY KILL, YOU, ACTIVE
DO WE, PASSIVE, BECOME VICTIMS OR GHOSTS . . . OR SURVIVALISTS
DO WE EVEN KNOW HOW TO SURVIVE OUTSIDE OF A CITY
& WHY DOES IT ALWAYS COME DOWN TO
SURVIVAL & SURVIVORS . . . EXTINCTION OR SUBMISSION

but i tell you what, Indians makin' babies will take over
this country, this continent, from the inside out . . .
& i'm not gonna be another sad indian story
passed around the table after midnight

Lenore Keeshig-Tobias

my grandmother's house

hardwood floors and walls
slats all waxed and shiny
everything
basks in sunlight and order

it is a good place
it is a clean place
it is a bright place
like my grandmother's house

but it does not feel right
something is wrong
something has been changed

i turn quick to exit
and as my feet touch
the grass outside, gray wings
unfold and i fly
high into the trees,
i circle to swoop
down past the house again
and again wings brushing
the windows as people peer
out to see the great owl

i circle once more
before perching in an old maple
its bark in decay

wings spread and
i reel back into the sky
swooping past the house

this is not my grandmother's house
i cry this is not
my grandmother's house

January 28, 1992

in my grandmother's house

waking
i am in bed,
my youngest daughter beside me
we are in my grandmother's house
and it is empty

paint peels in patches
from the walls and ceiling
in the room where
gramma and papa would sit

i tell my daughter
this is my grandmother's house
come see

i hurry through the
empty room to the garden door
i want to look out and see
the great owl, see if it's
still perched outside

i open the door and
look out, stretching to catch

a glimpse of it
tall and quiet over the eaves

there is a sudden rustling
at my feet
something, keeping close to
the wall and the floor,
scuttles past me, laughing and joking

ha ha ha
i've got you now,
i'm Harry
i've tricked you now

i stop
step back carefully
and scoop
the fledgling owl
up in my hands and take
it quickly
outside where i fling it about,
shaking it in my fury,
my indignation,
rending it shapeless

how dare you
how dare you trick me,
try to fool with me this way,
try to sneak into this house

and then i think
this is preposterous,
this is crazy
this is not nice
i should do such a thing,
rend this creature so,
shake it about like this

poor little owl

i set it down in the grass
and smooth back its feathers,

telling it never
never to fool me this way again

i return to the house,
the livingroom where my little girl
has crawled back into the bed

i chase out the stray cats,
the black and white one,
the orange and white one and
push them out the door
as I sprinkle tobacco
over the threshold

but the orange and white
cat struggles to get back in
and i thrust
my tobacco pouch into its face
it sneezes and runs away

i sprinkle tobacco over
the threshold of the garden
door and then the kitchen door

perhaps from the kitchen
window i will see the bear
when he comes, if he come

February 2, 1992

Maurice Kenny

Sky Woman

In the night
I see her fall
sometimes
clutching vines
of ripe strawberries,
sometimes sweetgrass,
other times
seeds
which will sprout.
Always
loon or crane
fly with her.

I

I imagine her standing
by the cauldron stirring,
her naked flesh spattered
by bubbling corn mush.
Dogs come from the dark,
wolves, to lick her flesh.
Blood runs from wounds
the dogs have made
with their sharp tongues.

She will mother me
for generations.
Her endurance assures mine.

2

He pulled a great tree by its roots
from the sky earth
and left a gaping hole showing
the dark. Waters rumbled.
She was enticed to look deep
into the hole. She clutched
her abdomen, the child she carried,
and falls . . .
Water birds attend her . . . loon,
crane, mallard. Turtle stretched,
quakes, rises to surface dark waters
and awaits her passage.

She filled woods with trilliums, baneberry;
she gave hawk flight, thrush song,
and seeded cedar and sumac.
She flecked her hand in cold waters
and fish came to nibble fingertips.
All about her was wonder.
She brought grains to the fields
and deer to sweet meadows;
she touched maples
and juices ran down the trunks:
she looked back — up and rains
fell . . . she brought surprise.

All this her grandsons made,
and the face in the mountain rock,
river currents, deadly nightshade,
forests of elm, tamarack, birch, white pine;
the little spirits and the red people;
wolf and wolverine and bear.
She brought delight . . .
the greenness of things.

This her grandsons knew,
the birthed twins . . . Sapling and Flint:
she brought beauty under nourishing sun
and illumination of the moon
and stars over winds blowing
from all directions.

I'll look
tonight
for her to fall
again
from among stars
with strawberries
or sweetgrass
held tightly in her hands.

"Now it seems there were brothers . . ."

Black-caps scent July
under milkweed's sweet and heavy fumes.
Mountains rise with morning sun.
Rain sits on the mountain shoulders,
heavy brows of clouds frown on the hour
as winds still and a stark tamarack
shades the last wild raspberries of the season.

Tanzy cannot light the moment.
A naked youth emerges from the river,
shakes his black hair of diamonds,
and climbs into his clothes. A younger boy
pulls in a trout and jumps in glee
as the first tatters of rain fall.
Thunder rocks the skies; black clouds
erase summer, even the blue hare-bells
seem to pale while the boys' brown flesh
shivers as they gather up things for home
and set off downstream in a long canoe.

Only the aged mountains remain constant.
Lightning cracks around the peaks
and the thunderers beat stone against stone
frightening whatever creature caught on the trail.

Suddenly as it came, suddenly it ends.
The river is swollen and flushed,
carries broken branches in its breath.
Milkweed scent grows heavier,
afternoon wades across the day;
silence in the black-cap brambles;
the swimmer allows a loud hoot;
bees buzz and a single finch flies.

This was a day of long ago.
A boy fishing, a youth swimming clean
waters as berries ripened all around
as they pushed feet into moccasins
to tread quietly home to the longhouse
but paused to leave a pinch of tobacco.
Adowe.
Now it seems these grand-fathers were brothers.

Harold Littlebird

In a child's memory
kerosene lanterns faintly glow
clean water & alfalfa offerings
in freshly swept corrals
welcome their arrival

Summer's flowered shawl fades, retreats
wrinkled in Autumn's icy howl
first snow dusts Mt. Taylor's distant peaks
seemingly edible layer of purple popcorn clouds
swim the frigid, evening sky
as October gloomily departs
but, I remember, it is always much like this
Somehow
just before they come
bringing our loving relations, long departed

Grandfathers & Grandmothers, Mothers & Fathers
Aunts, Uncles, Brothers & Sisters
all our loved-ones, returning
reunited
feasting with the living

Hear now, the wagon wheels groan
and their tired horses' hooves plod
familiar dirt roads

On the earthen floor, prayerfully
prepared food is placed
steaming pottery bowls of red & green chile
with chunks of soft, mushy potatoes in savory broth
racks of greasy, roasted mutton ribs
piles of fresh tortillas, & sliced loaves of oven-baked bread
cups of dark, creamed coffee
sweetened, in remembrance
with heaping spoons of white crystal sugar
fresh, golden corn-on-the-cob, salt & peppered
and glasses of cool, refreshing water

All their favorite foods
peeled, squishy bananas
for Granpa, because he had no teeth
or baked apples, soft, shriveled & cut
slippery, oily sardines with thin, pungent slices of onion
stewed prune pies with flaky, Crisco crusts
tangy fruit sections nestled in porcelain bowls

And for you, Mom, a special soft salmon salad
mashed & boned, mixed with creamy mayonnaise
crisp celery chunks, chopped onion & strong, crushed garlic
just the way you liked it
and the way Marsha and I remember

vapors sweet, spiced & scented
fill our waiting home

We open the doors, and quietly, pray

> "Come in, sit down, eat
> We've been waiting . . .
> Welcome, all of you
> Eat lots
> You make us happy that you have come!"

Grandfather!
Like before and after, followers of the Stone-people lodge
I am an Indian-Giver

Learning to give
Swim in breath stroke
Earthly tides of joy & sorrow
Sail hidden swells that ebb & flow
Praying primordial heat & blessing
For Giveness & healing
Breathing singing stone

I am an Indian-Giver
On bended knee, Grandfather!
Giving all that is given
Breath returned
Jubilantly in song
Childlike & playful
Rolling among Autumnal leaves
Descending into memory mists of recovery

Oh Grandfather!
In Love, for Giving
I give lovingly
For I am an Indian-Giver, returning . . .

Mary Lockwood

A Tribal Situation

A vision comes to me. My sight comes from far above, like an arctic tern gliding in long August light. I see a slow spread of people dotting a low valley before a huge, shallow bay.

Faintly, I recall the efforts and talk of planning one last tribal foraging at Kweguk. An abundant crop of berries caused a flurry of discussion about harvest. So plentiful were the berries that four families agreed to spend two days picking berries up the coast at Kweguk. Each segment of the Nashalook clan had their own fish camp scattered throughout the Unalakleet basin.

Auntie Lillian Ivanoff and Uncle Henry Nashalook and Mom had large families, which kept the men busy throughout the seasons to harvest the natural abundance for food. Traditional life is hard work, and timing is essential to reap the sudden flushes of plants and animals. There was always danger waiting to destroy the unwary, taking away an important person to greet. With the advent of Alaskan statehood, more cash-paying jobs lured my aunt and uncles away from the harvests of the land.

Yes, it was during these infant days of statehood when the great synchronized efforts were made with the various families of the Nashalook clan to gather berries. My uncles got ready to do their part by repairing backboards of canvas and rope to carry the ten-gallon barrels up Kweguk Valley. They cleaned and repaired hunting equipment, fixed the tears in the gill nets, and chose their camping gear amidst preparations of our women.

Mom baked biscuits and packed berry buckets. Hers was a special bucket made of steamed curved wood, sewn at the seam with tough walrus thongs, which secured a fitted bowl at the bottom. It had an old yellow ivory handle. Different sizes of coffee and Crisco cans were made into buckets by fitting a wire handle through two opposite holes at the top and twisting several strands of wires to create a thickness that did not cut one's hand.

All the children were fitted with rubber boots, hats or scarves, and pants and jackets for two days of living outside. We needed mosquito repellent and bedding, ways to deal with the baby, collect and pack cooking and eating utensils. The process became progress in four different households as we finally put everything in wooden boats and made our way up the northern coast to Kweguk.

There, the hodge-podge cargo was unloaded on the rocky shore, and the lightened boats went out to set nets perpendicular to the shoreline for late salmon or maybe seal. Canvas tents were set up along flat dry spots near the tundra, while children gathered firewood amidst the strewn logs at the tideline.

After setting the nets, the men hoisted the barrels upon their board packs, took up their rifles, and made out for the tundra. The rounded oak barrels swayed with their gait as they went up a gentle incline. One man dropped a barrel in an open space and quietly moved ahead of the others toward a ridge to be on the lookout for moose or bear. Another deposited a barrel further up a hill and headed toward the opposite ridge. One kept up the valley and dropped a barrel by willows growing near a stream and looked for signs of beaver or rabbits. The last went through a thicket and placed a barrel on the far hillside.

Back at the beach, the women had all the children fed and ready to harvest blueberries, salmon berries, blackberries, and cranberries. Off we went to the lush tough growth of the tundra to harvest what was offered in creation. Slowly buckets would fill, and the larger children were sent to the scattered barrels to pour the delicious contents in — with instructions not to trip on the clumpy muskeg. Fears of wandering into the jeopardy of wild carnivores were eased as a woman pointed to a man watching over the group from his vantage place on top of a ridge.

Reassured, we spread out more, reaching for the dusky blueberries or the shiny heads of the salmon, blackberries, and cranberries. Random wanderings broke apart mechanical movements, until the swagger and reach and sway of the wild trail of harvest led one into earth's sweet embrace.

The day grew long and we children eventually became hungry for other food than berries. A woman would wave for us to come over, signaling lunch with an upraised dried fish, and off we would rush to surround her with blue-stained hands and faces, reaching for biscuits or smoked salmon strips to gnaw on. She laughed at her joy of feeding a pack of kids — so tall and brown skinned, flashing white teeth — her cloth par-kikuspuk waving in the breeze.

Mom would arrive with her deliberate pace and pour out her full bucket in the storage barrels, pursing her lips and whistling for the wind to blow and carry away the tundra leaves from her harvest . . . and to keep away the mosquitoes. She gave the empty bucket to my oldest brother, Chuck, to rinse it, then fill it from the creek for heating water after lunch. She asked the other children to collect dry wood while she found a sandy place to make a fire.

Soon, my aunts and Grandmother came along, happy to be in this gathering of the full, rich autumn. A bittersweet sense came over those who knew this would be over in a few days. Yet, it was humorous or awesome stories that were told around the low mealtime fire. As the special outdoor wood smoke wafted around the little gathering and we listened to the connecting web of life, the very soil melded into our beings.

I remember getting so tired, then. Back at the beach, we gathered more wood and logs for a bonfire. Nets were checked for fish which were then cleaned at the creek. Children splashed in the water, going to one side of the creek, then back again. The older ones pole-vaulted across, and some kids just threw rocks in for a big splash, or skipped stones in the shallow sea.

Another late firetime meal by the flickering pastel colors of a wide, wide ocean with a curved horizon that hid the continent of Russia. The bonfire licked flames to shy new stars emerging after a summer's absence from the land and season of continual daylight. The setting sun glowed strongly between purple Besboro Island and the stern and handsome Indian Head cliff.

Attracted to the orange light, some villagers came over to our camp to visit. Dad brought out his guitar from our cabin and strummed lovely Hawaiian songs.

Evelina Zuni Lucero

Deer Dance

Trini had been told not to come because nothing good ever happened at the bar.

Now here she was dancing with Reynard with his cool, distant air, and the half-moon curve of his smile. She remembered the Deer Man. Trini smiled when she caught herself looking at Reynard's feet. His shiny leather boots were as fancy as the rest of him. Reynard's shirt, a crisp, black-and-white checkered print, had thunderbirds cross-stitched on the front yokes and was neatly tucked into his bluejeans. A large silver buckle sat atop his firm belly, threading a leather tooled belt which blazed REYNARD on the back. He was like a buck, sleek and full, well muscled, surefooted; his neck was smooth and graceful, his skin an even bronze tone. He possessed an easy smile that flashed like a lightning bolt, illuminating his face and sparking movement behind his photogreys.

Yes, he was good-looking enough to fit the story that Auntie Rosalee liked to spook them with as children:

The tall, handsome stranger strode into a wedding dance, commanding attention with his silent entrance, looking neither to the left or right. No one knew who he was though he looked vaguely familiar, like someone's cousin's cousin. The bride's family thought he must be the guest of the groom's family, and the groom's family assumed he was known by the bride's side. He carried himself with grace and sureness, head erect, meeting all questioning eyes and answering them with careful indifference. Large turquoise stones, conspicuously old and heavy, dangled from his earlobes. His long hair was pulled back in an old-time style. He leaned against the wall, smoking a cigarette, a glint of amusement in his dark, slanted eyes.

All the young, single women and even the restless married ones watched, ready to catch his eye, hoping to be the one he'd ask to dance. After a long time — the dance was almost over — he asked the prettiest, most popular girl to dance. The other women sighed and pretended they didn't care, but they watched enviously out of the corner of their eyes. They saw how he tenderly gazed into the depths of her eyes, and how he spun her across the room in movements as smooth as silk against silk.

The girl forgot who she came with, forgot that her sweetheart might have meant something to her, that he stood in the corner sulking. A woman letting her hair down, she danced on with the stranger. The songs became soft sighs, each dance a yearning. As the last song was ending, screams and shouts filled the air. The band stopped. The crowd parted. The young girl who was dancing with the handsome stranger lay lifeless on the floor.

In the confusion of the moment, the stranger almost slipped away, but he was stopped at the door by belligerent, red-eyed young men. Once again, terrified screams paralyzed the crowd. In the sudden hush that came upon the room, someone cried out, "Look! Look at his feet! He has the feet of a deer!" The stranger smiled, brazen and fearless. He pushed his way to the door unchallenged and walked out.

Later, his deer tracks were found beneath all the windows of the hall.

Rosalee heard the story while she was at the Indian School from the matrons who insisted that it was true. During the deer-hunting season, Rosalee and other women would joke, saying, "Now that the men are gone, let's go on a hunt of our own for a two-legged *dear*." It took a while before Trini caught the pun. She used to wonder why they would want to look for the Deer Man and risk being danced to death.

Only in a place like this could that happen.

Reynard smiled at her.

She looked away.

Going Across

In memory of my brother, Ken, who crossed to the other side

Across the river muddy brown, going am I
    Silent, powerful, steady moves it
    Holding all memories in murky depths
    Flowing past fields of corn and alfalfa
        now lying cold, yet waiting and listening in winter beds.

        Chasing clouds swift as painted ponies across the darkening
        sky

From the mother village going am I
    Holds she the people close to her breast
    Keeping them warm in the comfort of nearness she does.
    Singing a song at my back, the wind it is
    Toward the fields go I
    The fields so cold and quiet,
        waiting to receive the seed they do;
    Bursting through the earth, warm and moist,
    Rising up to greet the sun in spring,
    The seed it will

Going across am I
    From the other side turn I to look
    And seeing the sun slip down
        in a blaze of red deep as blood splashes it upon the pony
        sky.
    Ke-beh-mohe-wue-wui. I will see you again, say I
    Singing a song at my back, the wind it does
    Sending my hair flying like the mane of a pony

Going Across have I
    Turn I south down the valley
        Darkness it holds me, no fear have I
            Going Across have I.

Mazii / Rex Lee Jim

Sight

The heart
of the earth explodes
from the depth
of the crater.
A single voice
    a plea
    is heard.
The eagle
encircles
the vision pit.
The eagle sees
    the man
      is
still blind.

Black Tears

Sometimes when I stutter
utterances of intimacies
choke in my throat.
There are times too when
words flow from my mouth
like diamonds trickling upon
a murmuring creek,

hopping from pebble to pebble,
down mountain gorges
betwixt columns of pine.

My feelings and my thoughts
rush out into the world
where they tiptoe along the blue
that curves around the earth,
where the arches of the feet
become the bend of the she-rain
as she dances across the land,
a touch on the mesa,
a caress along the contours of mountains,
through dripping canyons,
toenails undressing into planting sticks,
planting seeds of growth.

Choked words, sobbed expressions,
sung words, laughed expressions
become tears of creation slowly seeping into earth.
Greens shoot out of the ground,
defying gravity, turning into flowers,
yellow, red, blue, pink, white.
The crows sing, the yellow warbler croaks,
the winds whine, the thunders laugh.
Dancing at the edge of dawn,
as I recall that day when we walked
at dawn in the swaying drizzle,
we crossed the bridge going west.
I laughed and talked,
you listened and walked.
Words have their function and time.

Now I sit silently,
remembering that time,
that place as pain piercing my heart;
tantalizing memories shun my feelings.
I can no longer cry,
but my feelings return,
my healing begins

as black tears slowly, hesitantly,
a drop at a time,
begin to flow from the tips
of my fingers.

Dipping

As my pen struggles against
the smooth surface of a tree that was once alive,
I wonder how my pen could ever possibly
take a grip on this slithery highway of death,
and cling onto a life that once was, or
one that hardly flickers in the heat
of my burning memory.
Still I recall that day,
lying on my back, staring into the faint blue.
I see the pupil of God, a mere speck in the sky.
It isn't something in my eye or in my mind.
The eye blinks and a shattering brilliance
cuts the air, the razor-edged wings of the silver
crow. Strings of clouds roll toward the west,
gather in huge thunderclouds just above Black Mesa,
and soon the smell of rain comes upon the breeze.
A dust devil kicks up dirt as
the crow surfs upon the current above.
How could I have known that an ordinary
creature could embellish the heavens in daylight
when the stars can do no better with the night.
I follow the contour of the crow's flight and
come to realize that "as the crow flies" not
only gets you there shortly, but that you have
always been there, here and now.
A fluttering of wings, a curving dive, and a
gentle rise on carved clouds, and even
an occasional dangling of claws
uncover in the sky those seen sculptures

not yet seen by earthly eyes.
I recall that day,
the silver spark flips over,
and disappears into sacred time.
I recall this day,
that distant spot reappears on this blue paper,
as the first drop of ink at the top,
the risk of that flip into nothingness,
disappearing from the sight of God,
reemerging at the tip of my pen.
I blink and dip the pen into the ink,
and think, "Just the way life should be."

Planting seeds,
or that's what I thought
I was doing when I sent
those words of love
folded up in an 8 by 11
ruled white writing tablet,
purchased at the local supermarket,
my heart pranced
upon anticipated thrills of
happiness.
Dancing to the music of
unseen whirlwinds,
observing the long
dark hair of the gentle
she-rain in the distance,
I think of her in those
Montana hills,
or on those Hopi mesas,
or even in one of those obscure
canyons in my backyard.
Two doves dance on tips of
leaves entwined in golden
quivering rays of heat.

The rubber pellet from
the play gun doesn't miss its aim.
Jealousy goes straight to the target,
and the remaining dove disappears into
the concrete jungle of East Chicago.

Acceptance

The sun shone today

Indeed
there was light at the end of the tunnel
for those born today

Oh the taste of dew
Child Born of Water
Oh the sense of light
Slayer of Monsters

        suspense

in the shimmering pollen of sun rays
in the dancing silk of heat waves

that of the father
and
that of the mother

the sun shone today
The tasks yet to be overcome
The father has yet to proclaim
his heir

the son has yet to smile

I am of the Redhouse clan.
I am from Rock Point.
I am from the household of Hastiin Ohodiiteel.

Daniel David Moses

Blues Around a Barn

Hurry past the weathered
boards — for there are no words
in white wash there. There are
no names or questions now
against that ingrained red.
Whoever wanted you

to answer *Where will you
be in eternity?*
is gone already, lost
as the farm. There's only
the wind here, wandering
in the fallow fields

beyond, too despondent
to do more than sigh. *Why
is it we never know
who they were, farmers and
their sons?* The wind settles
down, a wreathe for the barn.

Lament Under the Moon

Where am I? Here
beside the wide
river of night,
watching the moon's
reflection float.

And you? There, out
in the current
ahead — though you
are the younger
somewhere between

me and the light,
that waning light.
Soon you will dive
underwater,
try with one breath

to reach the far
shore and not leave
that moon crazy
in your wake. You
won't wait for me.

Too late for that.
Soon you will rest
beyond the moon,
another great
bear made of stars.

Julie Moss

The Forgotten

An award of achievement is announced
self-inflicted prestige to a red-skinned sellout
success is so very fine
incidentally, he helped the Indians too
he wears his concern and his tie from 9 to 5
he smiles and takes his bows

Far in the distant woods
an obscure shaman lives in a shack
he is humble in his obscurity
he practices his calling
his doors never close

Crowds of card-carrying Indians
stare with admiring eyes
at the outstanding Indian politician
who capitalizes on his blood
on the campaign road
promises of power and what it will do
he tours the poverty of his kinsmen
                    in his cadillac

Blood tribespeople are left to themselves
as it should be
seekers of their own destiny
within the Great Mysteries

While charms of fortune rise and fall
they carry on
they carry on . . . .

Joe Dale Tate Nevaquaya

Bruised inside
the soft touch of samovars
fear is boiling through the circumference
of eyes, broken
as bitter cups in their season
of scuffed shoes and empty table

watching the slate blue dusk
of winter, stagger through wayward
slush of home
chilling the bones arthritic
(the bellied stove of far memory)
knotty as scrub oak,
and Arctic thunder smashing the old bread,
their legs shiver and fall as spiders
in porcelain,
chipped as teeth
and blood hissing a crimson steam
long frozen before hitting the ground.

Duane Niatum

North American Native Writers Journey to a Place Where the Air Is a Gift of Promise

> "A people without history is like the wind on the buffalo grass."
> LAKOTA PROVERB

Their journey will be remembered as a sacred place where the voices of many tribes gathered to be one body and one spirit on this earth. The trek back to this center started with the collective knowledge that we are slowly drifting away from the origins of our songs, stories, and dreams, the words that have their nests in trees, flowers, buffalo grass, stone, and river. We have come to Oklahoma country in the belief that the mound builders of this land will give our blood a new dream path if we thank our elders in a way that links all things to our recovery of the ritual dance of words. We have decided to sit in a circle and wait until the spirit helpers of the language and the land enter our chant like morning sunlight. We will watch for the tiny miracle of rain to show us the path to the clarity of the five senses. Then we will have a good reason to move like the wind swirls until the changes are a delight to every nerve.

We have traveled great distances to reach this lifeline of memory, family, and faith, to hold the thread that will lead us to our animal bodies, the field where the words will form from the mountain river that will rush before us like the wolves showing us the multi-faceted shield of survival in their songs. We carriers of the people's torch through the darkness know in our hearts that this circle we are weaving with the sinews of our lives for our children's children has a special purpose, meaning, and direction. We are waking up to the reality that the majority of the people around the world are almost completely indifferent to the destruction of the earth, sea, and air, and continue to deny the consequences of this destruction. It is becoming more plain to us now that they don't want to understand or appreciate the extent of our grief that circles the earth like the sea. We know that if we stand by and do nothing while this great mother dies, then we will die with her. Our ancestors never imagined such an end could come to pass. Unfortunately, we recognize only too well that it could be our end. Thus we are here to ask the young not to mime the self-destruction they see each day. We, therefore, are here for our youth; we want to show them how important it is for us to find the path to those original songs, the ones embedded in rock and shell and bone, and that our reason for gathering the tribes this summer is to embrace our fear and ignorance and loss, thus prevent ourselves from being swept away by the plunder of the New World that wants to destroy not only our bodies but our songlines that have their heartbeats in the inner nature of Mother Earth.

So we came together to this Returning the Gift festival carrying proudly the doubled-edged arrow of our vision. We have returned home to touch the deepest layer of our soul, and to tell our young that we don't want our bones or spirits to be found in the mass graves mushrooming across this land and beyond. Today we have watched the four corners of the earth become man's killing field. In fact, who any longer can remain blind to the way the world is becoming one giant grave, since the living creatures that inhabit each corner of the earth are not alive to any song of a green awakening or a greener repose? Thus we link hearts in our pilgrimage to the origins of our people.

We have learned in our long battles with loss and denial and defeat that what is most difficult to face is not ourselves, but the pain of the ancestors in our dreams. It is the agony we see in their eyes and hear in their keens that led us to the mound builders' sanctuary, the healing rainbow of ancestors. We are attempting again to live fully in the geology of our bones, in the stories of our cells. We have united in spirit to celebrate the myths and legends of our great grandparents round dancing in our genes. We ask in our most humble way that tomorrow's life be only as honorable and as beautiful as the shawls and quilts of our sacred, but very real, guardians. We merged at this point on the medicine-wheel to fly like the erotic monarch butterflies migrating far south on the golden airstreams of ecstasy. We have one last chance and we are taking it.

Seattle
Moon of Harvest, 1992

202

Muskogee Carrier of the Stories

In memory, Louis Little Raccoon Oliver, 1904–1991

Louis will always be there at Koweta Town,
sitting before the fire of those
who come from the stars to tell
the ancient stories. He learned
from the Old Ones that Yahola, first
teacher of the Creeks, came to offer
the story of the ball of fire and the red seed
arrow the people can follow day and night.
Yahola said to walk in the direction
of the arrow and chase the sun,
the gift of the seven clans.

So Louis built from memory's cave the Bighouse,
Chukomako, out of rock and cedar
and sage and pitch, out of love
for his grandmother and aunts who told him
of the ball of fire, the birthplace
of his clan, the way to burn the sacred
wood: sycamore, cane, and elm.

His grandmother spoke of how their home
began at Chatahoche, rock of the elders.
Tekapay'cha circled the fire until
the birthplace of her grandson's yearning
flew back to its badger's burrow,
turtle tracks under red willow
on the banks of the Okmulgee River.

He played his flute and his aunts stomp
danced around him; asked their musician
please bring the night and morning sun,
down to their hearts; chew and swallow
history and defeat like the roots
they made into tea. His grandmother heard
from the mountain spirits that he
brought his aunts the kindling
for the dawn song. They offered him

an herb potion, the gift that would build
new life from the chipped-flint
of the people's sorrow; they sprinkled
sage into the fire and sang
of the star people leading to the Chukomako,
the Bighouse where in the shadow of Raccoon,
the sacred fire returns the people
to the deepest river in the earth.

They told him this was the path
of blood, the four steady points
of the heart, the gift of ancestors
that fills the night with light.
They reminded him of the story
when he was a child that the enemy
wears so many masks and words
as hollow as bamboo that he must
learn the language of herbs and trees,
catfish and trout, wolf and deer,
squirrel and bear, bee and butterfly,
so not to be betrayed
by their diseased language.

He painted on animal skins and visited
the sweatlodge the days no sun
rose from its yellow basket.
Sometimes his voice abandoned him,
the ancestors sang little more than stars.
Silence was an empty grave;
ancestors would not tell where
to trade bones and directions,
scars and confusions. He then danced
for green corn and sanity
and another fire ceremony.

His grandmother leaned back into shadow
in the opposite direction to fool
the Little People who might trick his dreams.
She said stand like thunder being
even if a wing catches fire in a wind

rage over the deaths of so many guardians
of the path, the animals carrying in
their backbones the seasoned drums
of stone and story.

Little Raccoon stokes the fire again;
we hear the blanket stories
build a path to the lodge beyond pain,
the sacked villages and towns,
the words trapped in treeless darkness,
the body tearing itself
from the dream-wheel's home.

O listen inwardly, listen to your own
voice forming a rainbow over our lives.
O watch the night people
change the round dance of light.

Find your path, the lightning snake's!

Seattle
Moon of Ripe Berries, 1992

Jim Northrup

Veterans' Dance

Don't sweat the small shit, Lug thought; it's all small shit unless they're shooting at you.

The tall, skinny Shinnob finished changing the tire on his car. It took longer than usual because he had to improvise with the jack. Summer in Minnesota and Lug was on his way to a powwow.

The powwow was on its second day. The dancers were getting ready for their third grand entry. Singers around the various drums had found their rhythm. Old bones were loosening up. The emcee was entertaining the crowd with jokes. Some of the jokes brought laughs and others brought groans. Kids were weaving through the people that circled the dance arena. The drum-sound knitted the people together.

Lug brushed his long hair away from his face as he looked in the sky for eagles. He had been away from home a long time and was looking forward to seeing his friends and relatives again.

He really enjoyed powwows, although he didn't dance. Lug was content to be with his people again. Ever since the war he had felt disconnected from the things that made people happy.

The first time he walked around the arena he just concentrated on faces. He was looking for family. While walking along he grazed at the food stands. He smelled then sampled the fry bread, moose meat, and wild rice soup.

The Shinnobs walking around the dance arena looked like a river that was going in two directions. Groups of people would stop and talk. Lug smiled at the laughing circles of Shinnobs. He looked at faces and eyes.

That little one there, she looked like his sister Judy did when she was that age. Lug wondered if he would see her here. Judy was a jingle-dress dancer and should be at this powwow. After all, she only lived a mile away from the powwow grounds.

The guy walking in front of him looked like his cousin that went to Vietnam. Nope, couldn't be him. Lug had heard that he died in a single-car accident last fall.

Sitting in a red and white striped powwow chair was an old lady that looked like his grandma. She wore heavy brown stockings that were held up with a big round knot at the knees. She chewed Copenhagen and spit the juice in a coffee can just like his gram. Of course, Lug's grandma had been dead for ten years, but it was still a good feeling to see someone who looked like her.

Lug recognized the woman walking toward him. She was his old used-to-be girlfriend. He hoped she didn't want to talk about what went wrong with them. She didn't, just snapped her eyes and looked away. Lug knew it was his fault he couldn't feel close to anyone. His face was a wooden mask as they passed each other. He could feel her looking up at him out of the corner of her eyes. Maybe, he thought, just maybe.

He stopped at a food stand called Stand Here. Lug had black coffee and a bag of mini-donuts. The sugar and cinnamon coating stuck to his fingers when he finished. He brushed off his hands and lit a smoke. Lug watched the snaggers 8 to 68 cruising through the river of Shinnobs.

That jingle-dress dancer walking toward him looked like his sister Judy. Yup it was her. The maroon dress made a tinkling, jingling sound as she came closer. She looks healthy, Lug thought. A few more gray hairs, but she moves like she was twenty years younger. They both smiled just hard as their eyes met. Warm brown eyes reached for wary ones.

She noticed the lines on his face were deeper. The lines fanned out from the edges of his eyes. He looked like he had lost some weight since the last time she saw him. His bluejean jacket just hung on him, she thought.

Lug and Judy shook hands and hugged each other. Her black-beaded bag hit him on the back as they embraced. They were together again after a long time apart. Both leaned back to get a better look at each other.

"C'mon over to the house when they break for supper," she said.

"Got any cornbread?" he asked.

"I can whip some up for you," she promised.

"Sounds good," he said.

Eating cornbread was a reminder of when they were young together. Sometimes it was the only thing to eat in the house. Cornbread was the first thing she made him when he came back from Vietnam.

"I have to get in line for the grand entry so I'll see you later. I want to talk to you about something," she said.

"Okay, dance a round for me," Lug said.

"I will, just like I always do."

Lug watched the grand entry. He saw several relatives in their dance outfits. He nodded to friends that were standing around the dance arena. Lug sipped hot coffee as the grand entry song was sung. He saw Judy come dancing by. Lug turned and looked at his car.

He walked to it as the flag song started. He almost moved in time to the beat as he walked. Lug decided to get his tire fixed at the truck stop. He got in and closed the car door as the veteran's song came over the public address system.

Lug left the powwow grounds and slipped a tape in his cassette player. The Animals singing "Sky Pilot" filled the car. Lug sang along with the vintage music.

He drove to the truck stop and read the newspaper while the mechanic fixed his tire. Lug put the tire in his trunk, paid the guy and drove to his sister's house. He listened to the Righteous Brothers do "Soul and Inspiration" on the way.

Judy's car was in the driveway, so he knew she was home. He parked and walked up to the front door. He rang the doorbell and walked in. He smelled cornbread.

She was in the kitchen making coffee. He sat at the kitchen table as she took the cornbread out of the oven. The steaming yellow bread made his mouth moist. Judy poured him a cup of coffee and sat down at the table.

"How have you been?" she asked.

"Okay, my health is okay."

"Where have you been? I haven't heard from you in quite a while."

"Oh you know, just traveling here and there. I'd work a little bit and then move on. For a while there I was looking for guys I knew in the war."

"Where was that you called from last March?" she asked.

"D.C., I was in Washington D.C. I went to the Wall and after being there I felt like I had to talk to someone I knew."

"You did sound troubled about something."

"I found a friend's name on the Wall. He died after I left Vietnam. I felt like killing myself."

"I'm glad you didn't."

"Me too, we wouldn't be having this conversation if I had gone through with it."

She got up, cut the cornbread and brought it to the table. He buttered a piece and began taking bites from the hot bread. She refilled his cup.

"Remember when we used to have to haul water when we were kids? I was thinking about it the other day, that one time it was thirty below and the cream cans fell off the sled? You somehow convinced me it was my fault. I had to pump the water to fill the cans again. You told me it was so I could stay warm. I guess in your own way you were looking out for me," she said.

"Nahh, I just wanted to see if I could get you to do all the work." Lug smiled at his sister.

"I thought it was good of you to send the folks money from your first military paycheck so we could get our own pump. We didn't have to bum water from the neighbor after that."

"I had to, I didn't want you to break your back lugging those cream cans around."

"Yah, I really hated wash days. Ma had me hauling water all day when she washed clothes."

She got up and got a glass of water from the kitchen faucet. As she came back to the table she said, "I've been talking to a spiritual leader about you. He wants you to come and see him. Don't forget to take him tobacco."

"That sounds like a good idea. I've been wanting to talk to someone," he said.

"What was it like in the war? You never talked much about it."

Lug stared deep into his black medicine water as if expecting an answer to scroll across. He trusted his sister, but it was still difficult talking about the terrible memories.

His eyes retreated into his head as he told her what happened to him, what he did in the war. She later learned that this was called the thousand yard stare. His eyes looked like he was trying to see something that was that far away. The laugh lines were erased from his face.

"Sometimes I'd get so scared I couldn't get scared anymore," he said, hunched over his coffee cup.

Judy touched his arm. Her face said she was ready to listen to her brother.

"One night they were shooting at us. No one was getting hurt. It got to be a drag ducking every time they fired. The gunfire wasn't very heavy, just a rifle round every couple of minutes. We didn't know if it was the prelude to a big attack or just one guy out there with a case of ammo and a hard on. We laid in our holes, counted the rounds going by and tried to shrink up inside our helmets. The bullets went by for at least a half hour. I counted seventeen of them. The ones that went high made a buzzing noise as they went by. The close ones made a crack sound. First you'd hear the bullet go by then the sound of where it came from."

"I got tired of that shit. I crawled up out of my hole and just stood there. I wanted to see where the bad guy was shooting from. The guys in the next hole told me to get down, but I was in a fuck-it mood. I didn't care what happened, didn't care if I lived or died."

Lug stood up to show his sister what it was like standing in the dark. He was leaning forward trying to see through the night. His hands clutched an imaginary rifle. Lug's head was swiveling back and forth as he looked for the hidden rifleman. He jerked as a rifle bullet came close to him. He turned his head toward the sound.

Judy watched Lug. She could feel her eyes burning and the tears building up. Using only willpower she held the tears back. Judy somehow knew the tears would stop the flood of memories coming out of her brother. She waited.

"I finally saw the muzzle flash. I knew where the bastard was firing from. After he fired the next time we all returned fire. We must have shot 500 rounds at him. The bad guy didn't shoot anymore. We either killed him or scared the shit out of him. After the noise died down I started getting scared. I realized I could have been killed standing up like that."

He paused before speaking again.

"That shows you how dangerous a fuck-it attitude is. I guess I have been living my life with a fuck-it attitude."

Lug sat back down and reached for another piece of cornbread. He ate it silently. When he finished the cornbread he lit a cigarette.

She touched his shoulder as she poured more coffee. Lug accepted this as permission to continue fighting the war. Judy sat down and lit her own cigarette.

"It was really crazy at times. One time we were caught out in this big rice paddy. They started shooting at us. I was close to the front of the formation so I got inside the treeline quick. The bad guys couldn't see me. When I leaned over to catch my breath I heard the snick, snick, bang sound of someone firing a bolt-action rifle. The enemy soldier was firing at the guys still out in the rice paddy. I figured out where the bad guy was from the sound — snick, snick, bang. I fired a three-round burst at the noise. That asshole turned and fired at me. I remember the muzzle flash and the bullet going-by noise happened together. I fired again as I moved closer. Through a little opening in the brush I could see what looked like a pile of rags, bloody rags. I fired another round into his head. We used to do that all the time — one in the head to make sure. The 7.62 bullet knocked his hat off. When the hat came off all this hair came spilling out. It was a woman."

Lug slumped at the kitchen table unable to continue his story. He held his coffee cup as if warming his hands. Judy sat there looking at him. Tears were running down her cheeks and puddling up on the table.

Lug coughed and lit a cigarette. Judy reached for one of her own and Lug lit it for her. Their eyes met. She got up to blow her nose and wipe her eyes. Judy was trembling as she came back and sat at the table. She wanted to cradle her brother but couldn't.

"Her hair looked like grandma's hair used to look. Remember her long, black shiny hair? This woman had hair like that. I knew killing people was wrong somehow but this made it worse when it turned out to be a woman."

Lug was slowly rocking his head back and forth.

When it looked like Lug was not going to talk anymore Judy got up and opened the back door. She poured more coffee and sat there looking at him. He couldn't meet her eyes.

"Tell me how you got wounded. You never did talk about it. All we knew was that you had won a Purple Heart," she probed.

After a long silence, Lug answered. "Ha, won a Purple Heart? We used to call them Idiot Awards. It meant that you fucked up somehow. Standing in the wrong place at the wrong time, something like that."

Lug's shoulders tightened up as he began telling her about his wounds. He reached down for his leg. "I don't know what happened to my leg. It was a long firefight, lots of explosions. After it was over, after the medivac choppers left, we were sitting around talking about what happened.

"I looked down and noticed blood on my leg. I thought it was from the guys we carried in from the listening post. The pain started about then. I rolled up my pants and saw a piece of shrapnel sticking out. Doc came over and pulled it out. He bandaged it up and must have written me up for a Heart. I remember that it took a long time to heal because we were always in the water of the rice paddies."

Lug was absently rubbing his leg as he told his sister about his wound.

He suddenly stood up and changed the subject. He didn't talk about his other wounds. He drained his cup.

"I gotta go, I think I talked too much already. I don't want you to think I am crazy because of what I did in the war. I'll see you at the pow-wow," said Lug, walking to the door.

As she looked at his back she wished there was something she could do to ease his memories of the war. "Wait a minute," Judy told her brother.

She lit some sage and smudged him with an eagle feather. He stood there with his eyes closed, palms facing out.

He thanked her and walked out the door.

While cleaning up after her brother left, Judy remembered hearing the ads on TV for the Vet's Center. She looked the number up in the book and called. Judy spoke to a counselor who listened. The counselor suggested an Inpatient Post-Traumatic Stress Disorder program.

The closest one was located in southern Minnesota. Judy got the address for her brother.

She went back to the powwow and found Lug standing on the edge of the crowd. "They have a program for treating PTSD," she told Lug.

"Yah, I saw something on TV about PTSD."

"What did you think of it? What do you think of entering a treatment program?"

"It might do some good. I was talking to a guy who went through it. He said it helped him. It might be worth a shot," Lug said.

"I talked to a counselor after you left. She said you can come in anytime."

"How about right now? Do you think they are open right now?"

"Sure, they must keep regular hours."

When she saw him walking to his car she thought it didn't take much to get him started.

Lug left the powwow and drove to the Vet's Center. On the way he listened to Dylan singing "Blowing in the Wind."

At the Vet's Center Lug found out he could enter the program in a couple of days. His stay would be about a month.

Lug talked to the spiritual man before he went in for the program.

He remembered to bring him a package of Prince Albert tobacco and a pair of warm socks.

In talking with the man, Lug learned that veterans were respected because of the sacrifices they had made in the war. He told Lug he would pray for him. The spiritual man told Lug to come back and see him when he got out of the Veterans Hospital.

Lug went to see the counselor and she helped him fill out the paperwork. He thanked her and drove to his sister's house. He parked his car and went inside. She showed him where he could leave his car parked while he was gone.

Judy drove Lug to the brick hospital. He took his bag of clothes and walked up the steps. Judy waved from her car. As he turned and looked, he noticed she was parked under an American flag.

He walked into the building. The smell of disinfectant reminded him of other official buildings he had been through.

He was ready for whatever was to come. Don't sweat the small shit, he thought.

Lug quickly learned that he was not the only one having trouble coping with memories of the war. He felt comfortable talking with other vets who had similar experiences.

Living in the Vets Hospital felt like being in the military again. He slept in a warm bed and ate warm food. He spent most of his time with guys his age who had been to Vietnam. His time was structured for him.

In the group therapy sessions they told war stories at first. After being together a while they began to talk about feelings. Lug became aware that he had been acting normal in what was an abnormal situation. He felt like he was leaving some of his memories at the hospital.

In spite of the camaraderie he felt, Lug was anxious to rejoin his community. He wanted to go home. He knew he would complete the program but didn't expect to spend one extra minute at the hospital.

While he was gone Judy was busy. She was making Lug a pair of moccasins. The toes had the traditional beaded floral design. Around the cuffs she stitched the colors of the Vietnam campaign ribbon. She had called the counselor at the Vets Center to make sure the colors were right. It was green, then yellow with three red stripes, yellow than green again. The smoke-tanned hide smell came to her as she sewed.

The hardest part was going down in the basement for the trunk her husband had left when he went to Vietnam. The trunk contained the traditional dance outfit he used to wear. It had been packed away because he didn't come back from the war.

Judy drove to the hospital and picked Lug up when he had completed the PTSD program. Looked like he put on some weight she thought when she first saw him.

She drove to the spiritual man's house, and listened to a powwow tape while driving. Lug tapped his hand on his knee in time to the drum. On the way Lug told hospital stories. She could see his laugh lines as he talked about the month with the other vets.

At the house Judy waited outside while the two men talked and smoked. She listened to both sides of the tape twice before Lug came out. He had a smile and walked light on his feet. Lug got in the car.

Judy drove to her house. They listened to the powwow on the way. She could see that Lug was enjoying the music.

"I've got that extra bedroom downstairs. You can stay there until you get your own place," she told him.

"Sounds like a winner. Cornbread every day?"

"Nope, special occasions only."

"I might be eligible for a disability pension, but I'd rather get a job," Lug said.

"Do what you want to do," she said.

"Where are we going now?" Lug asked.

"We're going to a powwow. I got my tent set up already and I want to dance in the first grand entry."

"Okay, it'll feel good to see familiar faces again."

"Did the hospital do anything for you?" she asked.

"I think so, but it felt better talking to the spiritual man," he answered.

When they got to the powwow grounds Judy drove to her tent. Lug perched on the fender when she went inside to change into her jingle dress.

Sure the hospital was nice but it felt better being here with his relatives, Lug thought. He breathed deep in the cool air. He could hear his sister's jingle dress begin to make sounds as she got dressed. He was trying to decide which food stand to start with when his sister came out.

"Tie this up for me, will you?" she asked.

Judy handed him the eagle fluff and medicine wheel. He used rawhide to tie it to her small braid. After she checked to make sure it was the way she wanted it, Judy said, "Go in the tent and get your present."

"Okay," he said, jumping off the fender and unzipping the tent.

Inside the tent he saw a pair of moccasins on top of a traditional dance outfit. The colors of the campaign ribbon on the moccasins caught his eye. He took off his sneakers and put on the moccasins.

"Hey, thanks a lot, I needed some moccasins," said Lug.

"The rest of the outfit belongs to you too," she said.

"Really?" he recognized the dance outfit. He knew who used to own it. He thought of his brother-in-law and the Vietnam war.

"Hurry up and put it on. It is almost time for grand entry," Judy told him.

Lug put on the dance outfit and walked out for the inspection he knew she would give. He did a couple of steps to show her how it fit. She smiled her approval.

They walked to where the people were lining up. He was laughing as he joined the traditional dancers. He saw his cousin Fuzzy who was a Vietnam vet.

"Didja hear? They got a new flavor for Vietnam vets," Lug said.

"Yah, what is it?" asked the guy who had been in Khe San in '68.

"Agent Grape," said Lug.

They both laughed at themselves for laughing.

Lug danced the grand entry song with slow dignity; he felt proud. He moved with the drum during the flag song.

When the veteran's song began Lug moved back to join his sister. Both of them had tears showing as they danced the veteran's honor song together.

nila northSun

red flags yellow flags

i don't get it
i'm in my 40's and i still don't get it
why do good women fall for outlaws?
course i'm flattering myself
and giving them the benefit of the doubt
i know there's no perfection
that would be boring anyway
and perhaps that's the key
i don't feel like being bored
so i court disaster
enjoy the roller coaster of tumultuous
relationships
that's probably why my vocation is crisis
resolution
i'm good at it with other people's lives
i can balance 6 figure budgets and develop
program goals but my own checks keep bouncing
and i don't know what i'm doing a year from now
and these men
these men
keep coming into my life
i must be inviting them in
but like an unwanted salesman
or seventh day adventist
i get strong and shoo them away

and then wonder why nobody knocks at my door
until the next onslaught
what worries me more is that some of these men
seem to be boys
and some of these men are grandpas
soon to be great-grandpas
i wonder if i should seek solace in women
but already i know
would be more of the same
and like marlene dietrich
sometimes i just vunt to be alone.

stupid questions

after a lifetime of stupid questions
you'd think i'd have grown
more tolerant
more patient
or at least come up with
snappy comebacks
to
are you really indian?
(no, i just say that so you can ask me
stupid questions)
you don't look indian
(you mean i don't look like the guy on
the nickel)
well, you sure are a beautiful shoshone
woman
(as if beautiful shoshone were an oxymoron)
you know, my great-grandmother was a cherokee
princess
(you know, she must have been one helluva whore
cause everybody has that same great-grandmother)
do you have to stay on the reservation
will they let you out?

(no, i'm there because we won't let you in)
do you know, when i was a kid
i used to pretend i was indian
(and for halloween i dressed as a yuppie
and nobody thought i was in costume)
i'm really sympathetic about the way indians
were treated, lands taken, treaties broken
(oh good, does that mean you donate generously
to the reservation nearest you, that you sponsor
a scholarship fund? that you donate turkeys for
the elders' thanksgiving baskets so they have something
to eat? that you give canned goods to the social
service program so they can help others? that you
sponsor a child or family at christmas so they can
get a warm coat or toy?)
fuck it
don't waste my breath
put your money where your mouth is
send books, donations, your time and involvement
to the reservation nearest you
call it
'in memory of my cherokee princess grandma'

Simon Ortiz

February and Violet

Two days after Valentine's Day,
the intermittent rain still falls.
Or is it snow? Days, weeks, months
of bone and muscle tightness, tension
of holding little warmth to body.
This morning though, I look outside
and right out there beyond the ledge
are tulips. Maybe those are not them,
but they're something beginning, violet
petals. Or are they the color purple?
What their name is, this precious now,
is my discovery, the significant act
I need — rain or snow, tulips or not,
yesterday or tomorrow — and for this,
I am alive. Intermittent desires, gain
and loss, warmth and fleeting wishes
will still be here, more than momentary,
even eternal, but the moment of seeing,
looking outside and right there, always
will be the discovery offered to us.

Making Quiltwork

Like the coat of many colors, the letters, quilts,
all those odds and bits we live by, we have come
to know. Folks here live by the pretty quilts
they make, more than make actually, more than pretty.
They are histories, their lives and their quilts.
Indian people who have been scattered, sundered
into odds and bits, determined to remake wholecloth.
Nothing quits. It changes many times, sometimes
to something we don't want, but we again gather
the pieces, study them, decide, make decisions
yes and fit them to color, necessity, conditions,
beauty, and start again. Our lives are quilts,
letters odds and bits, but always the loving
thread through them, the compassionate knowledge
that what we make is worth it and will outlast
anything that was before and will be worthy
of any people's art, endeavor, and final triumph.

Here, look at my clothes, quilts, coats of many colors!

"And the Land Is Just as Dry"

Line from a song by Peter LaFarge

The horizons are still mine.
The ragged peaks,
the cactus, the brush, the hard brittle plants,
these are mine and yours.
We must be humble with them.

The green fields,
a few, a very few,
Interstate Highway 10 to Tucson,
Sacaton, Bapchule,
my home is right there
off the road to Tucson,

before the junction.
On the map, it is yellow
and dry, very dry.
Breathe tough, swallow,
look for rain and rain.

Used to know Ira, he said,
his tongue slow, spit on his lips,
in Mesa used to chop cotton.
Coming into Phoenix from the north,
you pass by John Jacobs' Farm.
Many of the people there,
they live in one-room shacks,
they're provided for by John Jacobs.
Who pays them $5 per day in sun,
enough for a quart of wine on Friday.
Ira got his water all right.
Used to know him in Mesa in the sun.
My home is brown adobe
and tin roof and lots of children,
broken down cars, that pink Ford
up on those railroad ties.
Still paying for it
and it's been two years since
it ran, motor burned out,
had to pull it back from Phoenix.

Gila River, the Interstate sign says
at the cement bridge over bed
full of brush and sand and rusty cans.
Where's the water, the water
which you think about sometimes
in empty desperation?
It's in those green, very green fields
which are not mine.

You call me a drunk Indian, go ahead.

Juanita Pahdopony

The Old Dead Unconscious Me

Like a balloon
I flew around the room
wildly darting
about
in a loud display
of jettisoned hot air
finally
when all the air escaped
and
nothing was left,
my flattened rubber brown
skin
lay silent and unmoving
like a discarded
used
rubber
a crowd gathered
and
everyone had an opinion
about what happened
to the old
dead unconscious
me.

Elise Paschen

Two Standards

At "Returning the Gift" in Norman, Oklahoma

Joan's one-eighth. I'm a quarter.
When we walk into Billy's
I want to look like her,
full Osage. She tells me,
"You wouldn't find any Indians
here if not for the conference."

Like the cigar-in-hand
van driver on the highway
from the Will Rogers Airport,
leaning towards me, confided:
"I never seen so many
Indians all in one spot."

The bar's packed like a bar
should be. Joan shows me off,
introducing her friends
to this light-haired, East Coast–
educated outsider
whose mother, Betty Tallchief,

is Oklahoma's pride.
"At that table are some
Osages you should meet."
An only child, I'm glad
my family has grown.
They know my relatives

in Fairfax, though they come
from Pawhuska, Pawnee.
Angela says the Tallchiefs,
the keepers of the drum,
will host the Osage dances
next June. "Will you join us?

You'll be given your Osage
name." I would pretend, when young,
my name was Tallchief Paschen
(like my mother). In school
I proved my heritage
by demonstrating how

Indians danced in our play,
"Peter Pan," until I was silenced
by my teacher and asked
to sit down. My grandmother
Tallchief once shared with me
a photo of my mother

and aunt when they were twelve,
eleven wearing Osage
dress, dancing at a powwow.
My mother said her father's
mother had taught her the dances.
"Tall, dark and quiet," my Osage

grandfather died before
I turned one. My grandmother,
Scots Irish, Dutch, lived out
the next twenty-two years
in their house on the hill
overlooking the church

where she'd go Wednesday nights
for Bingo, Sundays to mass,
and where we held her funeral.
I haven't been back to Fairfax
since her death. They've restored
the house to honor her

daughters, sister ballet
stars. I always answer,
when asked, I never wanted
to dance, but in this bar
with the jukebox repeating
the Beatles' "Twist and Shout"

all I want is to dance
and to adopt my mother's
Osage name "Wa-Xthe-thon-ba"
which also means "Two Standards."
More than the quarter in me
wants to tell Angela,

yes, but New York is half
a continent away.
I try to see my grandfather
as he lifts me in air,
months before I will learn
to say my given name.

Robert L. Perea

Eagle Bull's Song

Lowanpi. . . . They are singing. . . . Lowanpi. . . .

They are singing.

"Hey, Blue, get over here and sing one," a voice in the room said. A man's voice.

"What do you want me to sing? A bit of Willie or Waylon?" Cliff Blue Dog was the one all of us really wanted to hear. The young kid was all right. He could play the guitar pretty good. He had a decent voice. But Cliff Blue Dog was the one we all really wanted to hear.

"After he finishes this song," a soft pretty voice said, "start recording." A pretty, but sad voice. A young voice. A young woman's voice had spoken.

Cliff Blue Dog picked up the other guitar. "Where do you get your A at?" he asked the young kid. "You don't use a straight A, the Hillbilly A."

"Lot of people use it like that," was the answer from the young kid.

"They wanna tape your warrior song. 'The Warrior Song.' "* The words came from Ronnie. A deep voice. A slow, deep, instantly recognizable voice. Ronnie's voice. Ronnie Eagle Bull's voice. Ronnie Eagle's voice. Roland Eagle Bull's voice. Roland Eagle's voice. Ro's voice. One voice. One single voice.

But they weren't listening to Ronnie, Roland, Ro'. Blue Dog and the young kid went right into "Johnny B. Goode." Two guitars, two voices, and a roomful of Indians clapping. "Go, go Johnny go, go, go. . . ." I could hear the voices straining.

Lowanpi. . . . They are singing.

The singing stopped, the dogs started. Outside the mobile home. First

226

one dog on top of the hill. Then another dog close by. Then one of the dogs in the yard. Then all the dogs in the yard. Howling loudly. Howling together.

"The dogs are singing, too," I laughed. No one else thought it was funny.

"It's somebody going to the other trailer," Ro' said.

"Pine Ridge dogs," Cliff Blue Dog said. "They let you know when somebody's coming 'round."

"In Arizona it's too hot for the dogs to bark," I said. Nobody thought that was funny either.

"Blue, they wanna tape your warrior song," the deep, slow voice said. Ro's voice. Eagle Bull's voice. But there was too much noise again in the mobile home. Too many voices. Laughing voices. Joking voices. Ro's voice was drowned out. Eagle Bull's voice was drowned out.

"I hope you like this one, eh," joked the young kid. This time it was one guitar. "Yesterday" by the Beatles. "All my troubles seemed so far away. . . ." Nice enough, but we wanted to hear Blue. Cliff Blue Dog. Singing Willie or Waylon or anything else. Looking like Waylon or Willie with his cowboy hat, jeans, and boots. Black cowboy shirt. The young kid finished.

"The 'Warrior Song' . . ." Ro' said.

Blue Dog made himself comfortable on the chair. Adjusted his guitar. The young kid put his guitar down and got ready to listen.

"Would you do me a favor and turn this way an' play it," Ro' said. "They're gonna tape you on the tape."

My sister turned on the tape. I sat up on the couch. She had already taped Roland's introduction.

"Testing, testing," she said. The voice of a teacher. With authority. "Testing, testing," she repeated, then laughed.

Wanna wicasa ki lowan. . . . Now, the man is singing.

Lowan. . . . He is singing.

The scaffolds have all fallen, the bones have turned to dust,

Lowan. . . . He sings.

My buffalo shield has fallen, my knife has turned to rust,

Lowan. . . . He sings.

The lodges have all fallen, the scaffolds are all gone, the Great Spirit's callin', I must go home.

Lowan. . . . He sings.

But someday I will rise again and grab my trusty horse. Gather up my fallen warriors, and ride the plains again. Where have all the warriors gone, the eagle flies alone, in the dreams of every man, in the dreams of every child.

Lowan. . . . He sings.

"Hey-yo, hey-ya, hey-ya, hey-yo . . ." many voices joined in. Lowanpi . . . . We are singing.

Lowanpi. . . . They are singing.

"Hey-yo, hey-ya, hey-ya, hey-yo," many voices. Lowanpi. . . . They sing.

"He wrote that," the pretty, young voice spoke.

"He did?" asked my sister.

"He did," was the answer. The pretty voice. The sad voice. Dressed in tight jeans, cowboy boots. A baggy T-shirt. "A good song, en it?"

More songs were sung. But the words of that one song stayed with me. Fallen warriors. . . . In the dreams of every man. . . .

The next night there were no songs. There were stories. Stories of Eagle Bull. Roland Eagle Bull. Roland. Ro'.

Ro' and a buddy had decided to burn down a house. Just down the alley. The reason. Ro' gave one reason. Later, I heard different reasons. Ro' was a member of A.I.M. The people in the house were shooting at A.I.M. people. I'd heard that. The people in the house weren't Indians. They didn't belong on the reservation. I'd heard that,too. The reason wasn't certain, the result was. Ro' and his buddy poured gasoline on the side of the house. They poured a trail of gasoline leading from the house to the alley. But Ro's buddy lit the match too soon. Before Ro' could get out of the way. Eagle Bull caught on fire, the house didn't. Eagle Bull burned, the house didn't. They flew him to Denver. To save his life. To a hospital specializing in serious burns. He'd been burned over his entire body, except his face and parts of his arms. They saved his life. Later the F.B.I. questioned him. He said nothing. No one pressed charges. That was that.

That night there were no songs. There were more stories. The words of one song stayed. Fallen warriors. . . . Hey-ya, hey-ya, hey-ya, hey-yo. . . .

A recent story. Just last week. Ro' had been in Hot Springs. Off the reservation. Living with his wife. Their two young boys. What was once a good marriage was no more. They argued. They fought. She called the police. The police came and they were still fighting. He made a run for it. Into the night. Into the hills. The police running behind. In hot pursuit.

228

Eagle Bull had to do something. Something quick. An old Indian trick, he told us laughing. He dove into a clump of bushes and covered himself up. The police were everywhere, roaming the hills. Police cars followed. Headlights probed the side of the hill. White police determined to corner one Indian. But the old Indian trick worked. The white police finally got tired of looking. They left. But Eagle Bull had been tricked, too. The bushes that had hid him, that had saved him were poison ivy. Poison ivy. Eagle Bull barely made it to the Indian hospital. Eyes almost completely swollen shut. Every inch of skin on his body broken out and red. And the itching. One giant itch over his entire body. It would have taken twenty hands and a hundred fingers to relieve the itching. Eagle Bull didn't know where to start scratching. An old Indian trick.

Lakota kin tatanka ktepi. . . . The Sioux Indians killed the buffalo. Lakota kin tatanka ktepi. . . . The Sioux killed the buffalo. An older story. Ro' would hunt near Tasunka Witko, near Crazy Horse Mountain. The mountain where they were carving the giant statue of the great Lakota warrior. Tasunka Witko. The bravest of the brave. Fought the whites to the end. The Strange Man. Our Strange Man. Curly. The Light-haired one. Medium blonde hair. The great Lakota warrior. Crazy Horse. Ro' didn't hunt near Mount Rushmore. He hunted near Tasunka Witko — the great Lakota. Bringing down many deer. The great Oglala. Deer to feed the family. Like the great Oglala Lakota warriors of the past. Eagle Bull. Roland Eagle Bull.

The Eagle flies alone. . . . The words of that song. . . .

Lowanpi. . . . They are singing.

Talk turned to Ro's older brother. Half-brother Robert Janis. Vietnam soldier. Vietnam warrior. His name on the Pine Ridge Wall.

"I wish I coulda' been there," Ro' said. "I missed out on a chance to kill," he added. I looked at Ro'. I'd been there. To Vietnam. Ro' had never been there, but he knew what he was talking about. I never killed directly. I was ready a few times. I am glad I didn't have to kill directly. Eagle Bull knew what he was talking about.

Ro' and his brother Hobert started arguing. At Wounded Knee one had been with A.I.M., the other against. They'd fought each other. Now it was over. But there were still strong feelings.

"Today, Russell Means wouldn't know you from a buffalo turd," Hobert said. Ro' didn't answer.

Tatanka. . . . The buffalo.

Lakota kin tatanka ktepi. . . . The Lakota killed the buffalo.

"Ro'," it was my voice again.

"Whadda ya want?" the instantly recognizable voice answered.

"How do you say 'I love you' in Lakota?" I asked.

Eagle Bull laughed. He saw I was watching a winyan waste, a wicincala walking by. She had nice bouncing big tits.

"I just say 'Spread the legs,'" Eagle Bull laughed.

"Wastecilake," said Jay. Returns-from-Scout. "That's 'I love you' in Lakota."

"I just say 'Spread the legs,'" Ro' repeated, laughing again. "Ce mazaska," Ro' said.

"What's that?" I asked.

"Iron dick," Ro' answered matter-of-factly. All the men in the trailer laughed.

The singing had ended. The storytelling had ended. The people had all left. Except Eagle Bull. Eagle Bull was alone. The horse was outside. The one that liked to eat the corn that grew by the trailer. Eagle Bull wanted to ride the horse. Like he'd done many times before. But he couldn't. Blood came from his mouth. There was no one there to help him. Nothing could help him now. Not even the sacrifice of the Sun Dance.

Wiwangwacipi. . . . The Sun, they dance.

It was too late. I had wanted to help. It was too late now. Eagle Bull saw the horse. He knew he could not reach the horse. He'd accepted that before. But still, the struggle. The white man was too strong. He beat you down, then beat you some more. An Indian could never be what he wanted to be.

Later, the mobile home went up in flames. Indian anger. . . . Indian hatred. . . .

The Eagle flies alone. . . . Fallen warriors. . . .

That song. I can't get it out of my mind.

Eagle Bull. He had given me a feather. An eagle feather. He knew the time was near. Eagle Bull knew. It is difficult. I don't know the words. I am learning. I try to sing. I try to be a Lakota. It is difficult. My voice, it cracks. There is hatred. The white man beats you, beats you. Offers you a hand, then beats you more. Tries to beat the Indian out of you.

I hold the eagle feather.

Eagle Bull gave it to me.

I try.

A few words.
It is so hard to sing.
A word.
I sing.
Walowan. . . . I am singing.

* "The Warrior Song" is an original song written and sung by Cliff Blue Dog of the Pine Ridge Sioux Indian Reservation, South Dakota. The song remains unrecorded and also unpublished except for this short story. The author was allowed to tape the song for use in this story with permission of the song writer.

Suzanne Rancourt

Thunderbeings

My grandmother was struck and killed by lightning
gazing through a window for a split-atomic second,
her left finger touching one of the four brass posters
as gently as one touches the cheeks of newborns
as though she had pressed a doorbell,
a button on an elevator — ascend please —
then the lightning arched and she crossed over
leaving a fingerprint
and a strong smell of uric acid.

Her name was Dorothy, an artist
taught by the Nuns. She painted in oils
the light and dark of all things —
ships full sail on calm oceans —
I could not reach them, hanging on the wall,
so I'd pull a chair under these two paintings
one new-moon dark, the other full-moon light —
I would press my finger on each brush stroke, each sail
wondering where these ships were sailing
in my Memere's head.

Her name was Dorothy, a Parisienne farm woman
who on bad days when the horse and carriage
couldn't make the twenty miles of hardscrabble to Mass
would open up the parlor and hold her own, chanting Hail Marys.

The next year the lightning
came back, took the barn, took the horses.
The bed, where my cooling Memere had lain the year before
was removed from the house, stored in the shed
until forty years later when I polished for days
the spokes and posters. A brass lamp of sorts
illuminated images of a woman
I never knew. I rubbed
until the chalky, thunderhead blue dissolved
and the metal shone lightning yellow.
For years I slept in this bed,
and often heard her
still humming in the brass.

Haunting Full Blood

I

Oh. Indian woman that sold butter,
Rispah,
my unsettled blood
speak to me through the generations
of crossed out names and altered paperwork.

Rispah. Grandmother to grandmothers
whose grave cannot be found
perhaps you never died
but simply traveled
to another place and time —
perhaps you returned to your people, your ways,
that no one spoke of.
In a pasteboard box, at someone's wake, buried among
your framed in-laws and children's children
my hand found you — you found me.

Were you anything more than a photograph?
Oh, yes, Rispah, Grandmother, my subtle bridge
over flooding time — shhh —
I am breathing proof.

II

there is something hard in my cheek bones.
sharp like Eagle beaks.

when i release my breath
to the gray and motionless sky
something behind my facial planes
melts
into meandering notes of a soprano sax,
washes
into droplets,
trickles down the keyboard, flat ivory,
gentle rain on river,
where my grandmothers bathed
and the rocks are that smooth.

Carter Revard / Nompewathe

Cities

are a way of keeping grass
from growing under feet

of spreading oil upon
the troubled earth

of squaring heaven, setting
pillars of fire, pillars of smoke

around a hi-fi voicebox that
speaks but cannot answer —

have crumbs for winged beings
who decorate its leaders' heads,

are inside-out cathedrals
brightest at night, staining

their darkness visible
with green gold and scarlet

— they make sure pale faces pass,
signing them onto exit-ramps,

put space-probes into Venus,
fingers of doubting aThomists —

know how we must be saved:
BE NUMBER, OR YOU PERISH!

nothing we plant in one
is food or medicine; feeds

the eye or banks into
a sharp-eyed pocket:

where flowers know their place
illuminating margins,

where wild things paw the trash
around white reservations

that darken spread and flake
like ringworm in green hair.

Q: Name several American Holocausts, the nations involved, and the places where these were accomplished.

A: Missouri, Illinois, Miami, New England, Virginia, and most place names in the United States. For more advanced students, the answer can extend to North and South America.

Q: What kind of un-American creep would give that answer?

A: A Native American. Of course, a truly patriotic American might have known better than to ask the question. In such cases, silence is the only effective way to avoid acknowledging guilt. There have been no American Holocausts, and we all should realize this truth. It is self-evident, since we believe all men are created equal, that we would not do what those nasty Europeans did. They are racist bigots, We are the people who got rid of the old prejudices and refused to do terrible things. We have pure hearts, pure motives, and pure history.

Q: What advantages are there to the true Americans if they deny that there has been any American Holocaust?

A: It allows them to be outraged at other monsters. Also, it lets them focus on the terrible things done overseas so that no one will notice what is still going on here. Since there was only the one Holocaust, we can be wonderfully virtuous in supporting its victims, and we know that we do not have to worry about being on the right side. So this justifies our putting up a monument in Washington, D.C. to that one Holocaust, and not putting anything there which hints that there was anything like it in this country.

Q: Is this matter relevant to the origins, makeup, and functions of the United Nations?

A: Yes. I do not dare, however, answer in more detail. No true American can afford to consider the question of whether Native American nations are truly sovereign. *De facto, de Deo,* must be their only refuge. When Franklin Roosevelt, about 1942, discussed the postwar realignments with Winston Churchill, he reminded Churchill of what the English were doing in their African colonies. Churchill then reminded Roosevelt of two cases: blacks in Mississippi, and Navajos in Arizona. Roosevelt shut up. It is the only safe answer.

Q: So your conclusion is that American history should not be taught?

A: Of course not: it never has been, and this is no time to begin doing so.

When Earth Brings

For Joy and Daisy, grandmothers; for Simon, grandfather; for Rainy Dawn and Chris, parents; for Krista Rae, child; and for all our relatives.

When earth brings the sun
into deep translucent
morning around us, when stars go quietly into
blue air behind him, we know
they are telling us:
Grandchildren, here is one of us,
we have arranged for you to see
the world you have been given on this day
by the clear brilliance of
our brother only, at this time,
but we are here, we have not gone away,
the earth will bring us back to you,
return us to each other and you will see
with our little sister's light, and all of ours,
how you move always among our many worlds,
the light and darkness we are given that
we give to you.
Dawn
is a good word to tell you
how children come into a world
again and again and how grandparents see ahead
in the blue dazzle where
a rainy light descends upon the earth,
where light comes back into the children's eyes with word
of how the earth meets heaven and how, one special time,
each child will look into the rain that lives
again on earth in a small pool and say:
I see myself, I see the stars,
now light and water give me back again

the world and heaven in which I live
and move and have my being,
here where the earth has brought
us everything, this day.

Wendy Rose

Dry Lightning

I could no more close my ears to your sound
than bring home the useless bright skin
of murdered serpents, moist ribbons
of transparent beads that stretch
and twist in the wind. But I have done that
a thousand times.

> Did everyone agree
> I would come to no good?
> That men must be tricked
> into fatherhood?
> And women destined
> to whirl away
> wincing in the storm,
> daughters crumbling
> with small hands desperate
> to cover the scars
> left moaning on their bones?

Two hundred acres of madrone burst into flame.
Under helicopters that dip & hover like dragonflies,
manzanita explodes from sudden heat.
Rusted gray bombers push pink semen from their bodies
& trucks rumble past, rounding up the men
who live on the mountain.
From the westernmost point of the dissolving sky,

the Sierras abandon themselves
turning to red smoke
as the valley lays into fog.

Coarsegold
1990

Forty, Trembling

She bore no children
but ghosts emerged
from between her legs.

Dare to believe
that roots can be built
like a pot
in ascending circles
and that skin
will just naturally form
copper sheets on the bones.
Promise that a name will appear
blazing from the cliff,
that this harvest is large enough
for her life and her life
is not half empty
but has much farther to go.
Step softly.

She is not of this world
and no one rides
to the rescue.

Coarsegold
1992

Armand Garnet Ruffo

No Questions Asked

Gradually you lose your tongue
and hardly notice.
How can you? It doesn't fall from your mouth
and you don't bite it off
and swallow it (if you did you probably wouldn't be here).
The process is subtle. For the longest time
you even keep thinking it's still attached
and continue to use it
to chew or gargle. Tho all the while
you are saying less: Conversations
become a burden,
a portage of words;

in your blunted mouth they become gnarled
and convoluted, so you accede, resign yourself
to this mute fate. Soon
you learn to live without a tongue.
Who needs one anyway, why speak?
You even begin to enjoy your new position
and use it to your advantage.
Your work and play become a silent and private deal,
while everywhere, in the sky, on the ground,
there are raw signs demanding your voice
and you are empty.
Nothing to say.
No excuses required.
No questions asked.

Christoforo Colombo Claims America, 1492

Upon the occasion of the Pope's visit to the NWT, 1987

I

Those who made the journey believed
in God and His goodness. Provider
of hope. Back home many starved — but
not all. A King, someone claiming a divine right
to wealth and power, ruled alongside the Church,
which in turn claimed God (and hope.
Let us just say between them they had all
the angles covered.)

II

High noon and drummers chant
under spruce bows. Fancy Dancers whorl
round, as I admire blanket patterns in sunlight.
The South American Indian guests
at the microphone translate an ancient Chief:
We're all in this together. Recognize
and renew your strengths.
In shade looking out, I think of understanding
and energy.

III

Both King and Church had much
in common. Both believed Explorers were opportunists.
Necessary. Loyal only if controlled, if rewarded.
Explorers lived a deep fear, endured sky, sea,
the unknown. Lived for gold and plunder
and were Heroes when they did. After the fast
came the plenty. And plenty of it.
Titles and Women. Song and Dance
in the streets of Seville.

IV

Once I stared at the sea from high in a castle
and thought distance and time.

Enough to bring a smile to Carl Gustav Jung's lips
as he clasps his hands and says in a deliberate
hushed tone: about your dreams . . .
Worlds collide. Satellites blast-off
in a flash to send back photographs
while the dancers smile
for the clicking cameras.

V

Up at Moose Factory a conference
will bring together Elders and Youth
announces the Grand-Speaker.
The Pope will visit.
The Prime Minister and
Governor General will greet him.
Drums will beat time to Mother Earth.
Explorers will have come
and gone. America will have been claimed.

Let the Oppressed Sing

1988

Let the oppressed sing of Chile,
the Ojibway who last night
told me he'd just got out of prison
after being inside for eight years
the warrior who lifted his tattooed arm
to the ceiling which for a moment
                              became the sky
and clenched his fist in proud defiance
while looking straight into my eyes
after being told that I too had Ojibway blood.

Let the oppressed sing of Chile,
that Anishnawbe who excused himself for drinking,
but said he only wanted to have some fun,
that man with the woman nobody else wanted,

that big man who'd just been released from concrete and steel
to a world that for him is
                    concrete and steel,
that Mississauga Indian who told me there were only
13 hundred of his people left,
and who like so many others of his kind
had fallen between the fiscal cracks
of a corporate society gone money mad.

Let the oppressed sing of Chile,
where mother earth has become infected by nuclear waste,
where father sky has become infected by industrial waste,
where traditional homelands have been flooded,
clear-cut or mined in the name of progress,
where one-half of the world's population starves
while the other half grows fat in both body and mind,
where law means wealth and power and a strong arm
                    carrying a big stick
and where justice is just another word.

Let the oppressed sing of Chile,
Minnie Sutherland, an Indian woman struck
by a car New Year's morning in Hull, Quebec,
and dragged to the side of the road
                    by police officers
just doing their duty (To Serve & Protect?)
while witnesses to the accident pleaded
that an ambulance be called.
Yes. Let Minnie sing of Chile
along with all those other mothers and children
who have died needlessly, senselessly,
unjustly — Let all of them sing of Chile.
For Chile is more than a country, it is a people
dispossessed   the world over.

Ralph Salisbury

"Among the Savages . . ."

Hill, frosted, white
cathedral dome in France,
and Indian corn's cruciform,
communion-wine dawn resurrect
Père Priber, who lost,
in an English Colonial prison,
he'd earlier saved from flames,
his life and his Cherokee dictionary,
five years of devoted work "among the savages."

A century later, Sikwaya did it again, and —
bark book burned, by his wife — again, and died,
revered and old, while trying
to find our people who'd fled their persecutors.

My Cherokee dawn-prayers said
for two great men, breath rising, as white as smoke,
my wife in our home, below this field, writing poems —
with Germanic words, which invaded ancient England —
I think of the Anglican Church and Rome
fighting like dogs over bones,
which dance, in Earth,
around Sun, thanks
for this gift of corn.

Some of the Life and Times of Wise-Wolf Salt-Town

January 24, 1926, eight-and-a-half pounds of Indian, Irish, and English centuries of mating happenstance, was yanked, butt first, into an under-heated Iowa farmhouse, first whack from the world delivered by a doctor, whose ribs had been broken when his horse-drawn sled hit a blizzard-obscured milepost intended to inform motorists of how far they had come, how far they had yet to go.

Ralph, my first name, was that of a man who had saved my father's life. Ralph was derived from an old, European tribal name Radwulf, meaning, I record, without intending to vaunt my poor powers, "Wise Wolf." The name reminds me of what European Americans usually forget, that Native Americans are not the only Americans with a tribal past, to be remembered and to be honored while we fulfill our destinies as part of the human race. My last name, Salisbury, is a coupling of Roman and English and it means Salt Town.

Wisewolf Saltown was born, in a Northeast Iowa farmhouse during a blizzard, to a skeptically Protestant Irish-American mother and a Cherokee-English father. Half of the underheated, two-story farmhouse had been moved, a generation before, many horses and many incredibly knowledgeable humans having moved the immense burden half a mile, intact, and joined it, not quite perfectly, to an already existing house.

I think I was born in the migrant half. I think my mother said that I, my three brothers and one sister were all born in what was then called "the north bedroom," my parents' nuptial chamber at that time. My birth-space has now been opened, like so much of my life bared for fiction and poems, to be part of what my childhood knew as "the front room," the living-room of the, remodeled, house in which my sister, now vice-president of a bank, and her university-educated, now a farmer, husband live. I remember standing, four years and one month old, on an iron rung at the foot of my parents' bed, seeing my newly born brother. I think I remember that the room was cold, I think I feel the cold, in flesh 62 years from the lived-moment, but perhaps I only know the room was always cold in February, the month of my brother's birth. I think I have kept an impression of what I saw, my mother, her image strikingly young in my mind as I write, she then in her mid-forties, her loving face, still haggard from a hard birth, raised, her auburn hair, a lock of which survives, dark against a white pillow, her body beneath heavy quilts, maybe even under the heavy sled robe, two pictures of horses woven into it, the robe which had maybe protected the doctor's fractured ribs as my father righted the sled, giddapped the black Percheron horses and drove over barbed-wire fences buried under weeks of frozen snow, to help me enter the same cold room where I'd stand shivering, a cast-iron bed rung gouging through the soles of my shoes, seeing a small, red face, from whose shadowy, tiny nostrils my sniffles and coughs were distanced. I was witnessing the moment I had lived four years before.

Was I, with monstrous, natural egocentricity, jealous of my younger brother? Today, as I write, he lies in bed again, 62, now, having survived, as I did six years ago, and as our father and our older brother did not, a heart attack.

I taught him to walk, my baby brother. That is an early memory. I put all of the dining room chairs on their sides, as we children often did in playing house or in making fences for the little calves we sometimes liked to be, although not to the point where, bellowing pitifully, they disappeared into a truck, their child-bestowed pet names, White Star, Red Fire, Black Diamond, Little Lily, changed to "veal." I started my toddler brother around the ring of chairs, teaching him to hold on to the chairs and to make his little legs move in the motions of walking. That was, probably, my first effort at teaching.

This June, just weeks from now, I will have completed my fortieth year as a university teacher. Like most of my life and like all of my books, this teaching career was unplanned. Eighteen, my trigger finger and eye were practiced from over six years of hunting, and, tests convicting me of a high intelligence, I was offered the job of aerial gunnery instructor instead of combat. I chose combat.

My brother eight years older than I, my half brother, had fought in Algeria and was, by then, an escaped and a returned prisoner of war. I wanted to kill his captors, the Germans, who'd been so evil, in the official history books of twelve years of state schools, in three wars. The fact that my half brother's father had been a German American, who'd died in the American army in World War One, didn't mean much compared to all the newsreel film propaganda, accompanied by stirring background music, which made me feel I was part of something Big, even though I was only five foot seven, and made me feel I was an important part of something Important. In school after school, I learned more and more complicated ways of killing fellow human beings and ended the war in Albuquerque, New Mexico, still training to electronically machine-gun and cannon any kamikaze pilots who might try to prevent my Harvard-educated bombardier from electronically toggling tons of fire bombs onto Tokyo civilians.

Yesterday, the high school daughter of a neighbor asked me if she can interview me about World War Two in a day or so. What should I tell her? That all of the approximately two hundred Americans I saw exploded, crushed, or burned — all were killed by Americans, hastily undertrained, like myself, by slipshod American "know-how" but not "why" technology or, simply, by uncontrollable weather. Should I tell her that East Coast inheritors of wealth possibly doomed the U.S. by forcing us, yet again, into alliance with our old imperialist master, England, though quite possibly we should have stayed neutral and devoted our energies to our numerous and even now worsening social problems and that, possibly, we should have allied ourselves with the European prototype of our present-day Hispanic American, Muslim, and Asian Allies, Hitlerian Germany, taking an inhumane, narrowly military view.

Here, the page making everything safely, blessedly unreal, can tell a girl younger than my daughter that World War Two was part of my youth, sex surging into divine confusions with love, cosmic harmony and other impossible-to-define dimensions of existence, idealism, however misdirected by propaganda, impelling me to risk my life. Perhaps I should merely say that, in the Vietnam defeat, my brother I taught to walk lived to be the man thought to become in World War Two, a pilot, an heroic medal winner for courage in combat. "I love the gutsy little fucker," I wrote in a poem I either published or lost, and, here, I say the same, as he lies in peril of his life. And I love the gutsy little eighteen-year-old World War Two volunteer, as much a mystery to me, still, as the four-year-old shivering, with the iron rung at the foot of his parents' bed gouging into his instep, witnessing the miracle of birth, as he would witness fourteen years later, the miracle of death.

Tomorrow I will return to the farm where I was born. Tomorrow, God willing, I will sleep on a couch in the corner of the house where I was born, the northwest corner. In a few days I will stand by the grave of my father, my mother, my aunt, my brother who'd be two years older than me and the brother dead in infancy before I was born.

Today, the first of the several bullets which have been aimed my way frightens me awake in the dark, shattered glass clattering down against my baby-blanket-swaddled body, blizzard chilling little nostrils, chilling toothless mouth yelling up at God, yelling for Ma, yelling for Pa, "yamp-ing" they would say, a family word not heard since childhood, "yamp-ing" for succor, bellowing my little lungs out, hollering fit to bust a gut, yelling my goddamned head off, pissing and moaning fit to kill, flat on my·infant back, only hope voice, only hope, yamps, yells, screams, collo-quialisms from various decades, poems from God knows where, all rever-berating against whatever daggers of glass still do battle with snowflakes, with wind, my pathetic hope that someone, someone will find me impor-tant enough to try to save.

From the living room, Mother rushes to give me again the protection of her body, while Dad blows out the kerosene lamp and slips, as he has had to do before, and as he will have to do again and again, out into our farmyard, his eyes searching darkness, searching thick blizzard flakes. A tiny horse reared onto hind legs gouges its shape into Dad's cold hand gripping a .32 automatic pistol, all that protects him and his family from whatever someone wants to do — the someone maybe a sex maniac, es-caped from the nearby state hospital; a migrant Chicago gangster casu-ally raiding a farm; or a neighbor who hates Indians. An inconsequential attack on an Iowa farmhouse in 1926 — one of several that year and for at least two decades after — rides into history on a little steel shape, en-lightening the world of potential customers that the gun is from the fac-tory of Samuel Colt, whose miracle weapons did so much to "win the west," to "subdue the savage redman," to empower Jesse James, The Sundance Kid, John Dillinger, Al Capone, and other American entrepre-neurs.

Did the man younger then than I now am, did the man who died be-fore attaining the 66 years I have now attained, did the man I first as pri-mal presence then as "Pa" then as, influenced by movies, "Dad," and, now, in my prayers as "Father," did he, that man, that brave, incredibly heroic father, who'd been abandoned by his own father, did he hunt down in the darkness and cold my attacker? Did he shoot over something moving in shadows, as I once did, not certain of target, intending to draw return fire and aim at the sound of explosion or to frighten danger away? The answer is lost, a snowflake among snowflakes, whispering together in darkness. I have lived 66 years. The enemy either died, as he sure as hell deserved to do, or was driven away to return in family stories and to return night after night for 66 years, glass shattering, shards falling onto soft blankets, glass dislodged by wind fragmenting against glass glittering in whatever light reflects off months of snow, my body, the little curled shape of flesh from which this brain-bearing form derived, my body, festooned with glass fragments, gleaming like the body of a Christmas pageant infant Christ, the enemy's bullet a bee fleeing winter into wallpaper roses, bullet hole a dimple in the bedroom wall, a belly button for me to contemplate, the center of the world, my world, and, for the enemy a compass point, a magnetic north, to return to again and again.

Why crime, why violence, why cruelty, why war?

Safety off, trigger squeezed, whatever is in the firing chamber will detonate, and whoever the barrel is aimed toward will die or live and remember.

And if the bullet from mysterious source had been lower?
He was born, he was kept alive a little while and he died.
But my story was destined to be longer, more of it doomed to be told.

My eldest brother suffered, as we all did, from malnutrition, due to corporate America's oppressive economics and to winter, and, too weak to fight off illness, my brother died before he was a year old. I nearly died, only two years older than my dead brother, fever so high the superactive chemistry of my brain holds still the image of the huge family barn, built in the time of my mother's father, balanced on one of my little fingers, balanced, the animals terrified inside, how can I bear all that weight, how can I go on sensing the center of that impossible burden and keep its invisible core of gravity joined to that centering my fingerbone? How can I keep my little pet calf, Black Diamond, or White Star, or Red Fire, or Little Lily, from plunging ass over appetite to be crushed into hamburger patty under timbers which were the forest of this place when this place was home only to Indians?

It is 500 years since 1492, the year an Italian — who must have spoken Spanish better than I do, and who must have been an awesomely more impressive commander than the twenty-year-old buck sergeant I was — discovered and invaded a land which was to provide slaves, gold, and other useful things.

It is 1992, and, an Indian, proud that he is, I consider my father, who told Indian hunting stories and taught me to hunt with Indian skill, Indian instinct and taught me, together with my probably agnostic mother, a religious view based on awareness of Creation, my father, who, at the turn of the century, preferred to be known as of the race of the father who'd abandoned him and his twelve siblings, after first robbing his children's Indian mother of land she'd inherited according to white law, another Indian treaty broken, oh well, oh well, but this was my family.

My family. And for me here everything begins and everything ends, and it begins, or fails to, again, and again.

Carol Lee Sanchez

wind song

my four wind brothers
tease me;
chase me through
nearby cities and
laugh when they
frighten me.

they say i left them
out of my song last night
and i should
remember them
every time i offer
my smoke.

sometimes
they torment me
when i forget
to sing to them.
they push me around,
dare me not to run and
hide from them.

other times they kick
sand in my face
or run cold fingers
under my clothes
across my skin

to scold me,
to remind me of
their powers.

huk-ko — now,
i am sternly reminded
again!

today, i am wind
and rain
hugging cliff edges.
first, i kiss palm trees
oil pumps and
beach sand, then i
turn superhighways
into mirrors
and sidestreets into
lakes.

today, i am wind
singing four winds songs
as my wind brothers
and i fly the 101
to ventura
together.

2/89

notes from central california

santa barbara

1. how tall our heroes were
we missed the parade that night,
where *was* the car-ni-val?

we caught a glimpse of
glitter on the street dis/solving
into pubs and eateries —
a party crowd on

mardi gras eve
shouting at each other

while the tv in the corner
snatched lulls in conversation
trying to entertain us with
the newest video rock tune

but we entertained ourselves —
roared laughter at each
other over loud voices around us
and saturday night video tunes.
was this carnival? mardi gras?
why not? i sd

(no substance here — no
careful thought
no layered meaning yet inscribed
upon this storytelling page —

we drank beer and spoke of
things and places been
noted points of variance —
discussed our backgrounds
our beginnings and
the lack of substance in
contemporary literature;

discussed
historical heroes and
fictional lake communities
and the almost fictional
chumash natives of this
central california coast.

then, i sd)
embedded substance
like buried nuggets
demands mental detectors
skillfully operated by
prospectors for meaning

elemental ores in various
combinations wait to be
unearthed, leached and separated
into different vats;
weighed, sifted, filtered
then recombined again
and again until all the
relationships are noticed,
until all the stories have been told.

some of our historical and literary
heroes *were* tall
and far bolder,
more innovative than we
are today (or so it seems.
perhaps future generations
will find treasure buried
in our mundane writings;
perhaps this central coast
will one day yield more than
the bones of those unknown
unnamed native chumash heroes
that preceded us.

2. some of our heroes are unknown to us
the fathers/los padres surround us;
hold free life and no trespass
behind the same fence
while los osos/the bears stand watch
between the fathers and
el mar pacifico/the peaceful water.

somewhere
in this region, ancient rocks
carry picture stories about
a happening that seemed
important to make note of.

the exact meanings
are lost to me

the translators were
re/educated and baptized
into new beginnings.

'running bear' became 'jose'
'little deer' turned into 'ignacio'
'bird with no song' was called 'esperanza'
and 'quiet water' married a 'lopez'
who left *his* name as the
origin of that laguna/lake
outside arroyo grande/the big dry wash.
my pen cracks ink
into the blanks;
ignores recent historical
coatings of asphalt conquests
and old victorians oozing with
substance and legend.

ignores yet older missions
(those pearls of civilization
whipped from blood caked mud
by fra junipero serra —
testaments to the victory of
bartolomé de las casas:
champion of the heathen souls.

renamed, replaced
civilized into encomiendas
re/invented on the spot.
san — santa
san — santa
san — santa

"ruega por nosotros
nuestro padre, nuestro señor."
(pray for us
our father, our lord)

santa barbara, san ardo
san juan bautista, santa maria
santa rosa, san miguel

san ysidro, santa ynéz
renamed, replaced
re-invented on the spot.

in 1548
great scholars, great thinkers
journeyed to valladolid —
royal capital of carlos cinco
el rey of 16th century spain
to debate the true nature
of those native inhabitants
of nueva españa.

juan ginés sepúlveda,
world-renowned scholar and jurist
called them slaves!
natural slaves as described in
aristotelian doctrine (that great
ancestor of american thought)
and argued for a papal bull —
a declaration to the world
of the soulless nature of los índios
inhabiting the new world.

but — the dominican padre
insisted the indian contained
a soul!
could be civilized
should be baptized
and saved!

for three years they battled
at the court of carlos cinco
and in 1550
holy mother church and
bartolomé de las casas
won the day,
the soul of the indian,
and moral sanction
to proceed with conquest

in the name of dios
and carlos rey of spain.

san — santa
san — santa
san — santa
san luis obispo
san juan capistrano
santa margarita
san ramón.

somewhere around here,
ancient rocks carry
picture stories about
pre/balboan times
of heroic moments
and ordinary days
that missionized 'juanita'
might interpret for me

or maybe old man 'pedro's'
grandfather, chumash 'diego,'
remembers the stories
his grandfather
told about coyote
the tides
the whales
the mollusks
the swallows
grasses and grains
sun — moon — and earth
and the nine thousand year history
of the chumash people.

mardi gras 1986 recounted,
documented,
retold.
mr lincoln
was a tall man we sd.
a hero and a paradox
we sd.

bartolomé de las casas
was a hero
and a paradox
and — some of our heroes
are still unknown
to us

renamed, replaced
re-invented on the spot.

Cheryl Savageau

Survival

On Cape Cod
the colonists bring their
animals tied to the yoke
and plow the mother's breast
planting in long rows,
separating one crop
from the other

the corn's feet grow cold
the harvest small, and eaten
by raccoons who raid nightly
with no squash bristles
to threaten their delicate feet

In winter, angry winds
carry the earth
someplace else
til there is nothing left
but this sand
where white pine,
shrunk from grandfather forests
to these survivors,
hold hands across the dunes

I know that inside the white pine
there is food to survive a winter
that the wide plantain leaves

pushing up through the old driveway
could make a salad, that the furry berries
of the staghorn sumac will make
a winter tea for me, and be first food
to returning birds come spring

how much is forgotten?

the earth is cold now
but when the dogwood blossoms
it will be warm enough
to hold the seed corn
and coax it into growth

see how the hill catches the sun
for the young roots of corn
see how the corn stays the winter
holding the earth safe
through furious winds

Michael Simpson

Sweating It Out

I tend to the fire the stone people dream in.
They come to the sweat lodge knowing our problems.
We bathe in their ancient solutions,
after giving greetings to the six directions,
respects to the bear deer elk snake eagle coyote raven and salmon,
the green growing things water wind sun moon planets stars
all our relations forever reborn in our grandfather's flames.

My brothers and sisters all stand together
in mists they gather and wait with ashes in their hair.
Wrapped only in wind perhaps seeking visions
or health that comes always upon returning
to the womb of our great mother
we must always go back into sometimes.

Our leader brings us the sacred pipe
as a Sun Dancer
he burns tobacco and sage
cedar and songs into our minds
we seekers who walk once around
the circle behind he who speaks to the spirits
who sanctifies air with the old prayers
who takes us into our journey
where we join creation going in just one direction.

I heat the stones in the roaring pit.
They breathe flame they carry within

then give us our sweat when we pour
the Grandfather water upon them.
This is the old way of healing
this is the way of the first people.
Into darkness and warmth we all go as we came
into the hearth drum and spirit chant
into the place where we are all naked and faceless
O let us be wiser than fate and learn of its messages
so soon there may be a great healing of everyone passing
into the world on the world above the world
beyond the world of the world.
Here we join to send prayers on the smoke
into the heavens and through all our ancestors
as their blood turns its tides in us
as the seasons return as we live and die here
often returning.

Four rounds of seven stones each I am giving
four times the drum song and prayer leader takes us
into every direction we sweat out the harm that is in us
we learn to sit in our earth and love it.

Virginia Driving Hawk Sneve

The First Christmas

From a work in progress

Violet didn't know what to think, but that evening when she stood in line with the other girls, she was uneasy with the expectant air gripping the boarding school. All of this talk of Christmas tomorrow — it must be more special than any other day. But why was Christmas to start tonight with a service in the agency chapel?

Violet quietly joined the march from the school to the chapel. Snow crunched under her hard-soled shoes which she still hated even though the blisters had healed. It was odd to be going to church in the dark, and Violet's gaze sought the darker depths of the river breaks. Could she slip out of line without being seen and run? but she heard teacher's stern, "Keep moving!" and the girl knew she couldn't get away.

Amber streams of light flowed from the windows of the small frame building and the march quickened toward the beckoning warmth. The first student stepped onto the porch, the door opened and Mr. Burt, in his white robe, cried, "Merry Christmas!"

The girls filled the left side of the aisle. The boys sat on the other side with the biggest boys in the rear near the potbellied stove. It was their duty to keep the fire going during the service.

Violet stared at the transformation of the plain chapel. Swags of green cedar boughs were draped over each window, above the altar, and on the organ where Mrs. Burt, smiling a welcome at the little ones, began a carol they had practiced.

Violet stood with the others as she had been trained and sang, then knelt as Mr. Burt prayed. She gratefully listened to the Dakota words which she seldom heard above a whisper, but as she sat, she was disappointed to hear English.

"A child was born," Mr. Burt began, and Violet strained to comprehend the story. She knew about birth; it was a natural event in every home, but the idea of the baby's parents being turned away was foreign to Violet, whose people who were always welcomed in any village.

Mr. Burt spoke of wise men coming to see the baby, and this she also understood. The birth of a baby was a joyous time, and the elders, wise men of the band, would welcome the birth because it meant the survival of the tribe.

The door creaked open and a draft of cold darted over Violet's ankles, but none of the well-trained children turned and only the soft shuffle of moccasins gave evidence of visitors.

Now heads turned, but excitement, if any, was not shown as young eyes followed the three Indian men moving up the aisle. Violet recognized old Drifting Goose who majestically led two elders up the aisle. All wore blankets draped over their shoulders, and behind them their blanket-wrapped women aligned themselves in back of the stove.

Mr. Burt stopped speaking and stepped forward to shake the men's hands.

The little ones' teacher fluttered up from the front pew, pulling children off the seats onto the floor, but Drifting Goose held up his hand and shook his head: he and his men sat at Mr. Burt's feet. Settled, he nodded at Mr. Burt to resume the story.

The minister spoke of shepherds watching their sheep in the cold night. "Shepherds" and "sheep?" Violet wondered what they were, and what was an angel? Was this Christmas like a vision quest?

The story ended. The children rose and sang "O Little Town of Bethlehem," which they had memorized by rote. But suddenly, as she sang, the words and the meaning came together, and Violet knew they were singing the story Mr. Burt had told.

"Mmmooo," quietly sounded from outdoors, causing the boys by the windows to stare into the dark night.

"Moooo," louder. Then the bass of men's voices rumbled over creaking leather, and again a dart of cold air swirled across ankles as the door opened. This time feet stomped and spurs jangled as two booted white men came into the church. The children stared as the strangers took off their hats, nodded to Mr. Burt and opened their mackinaws to the warmth of the stove. Violet knew of these white men who trailed cattle to the reservation — and maybe, she thought, to her home.

The men pulled out tobacco and papers and rolled a smoke. The organ wheezed as Mrs. Burt pumped and the children sang "O come all ye faithful."

Drifting Goose and his elders stood. From under his blanket the chief pulled his pipe bag and walked to the stove. He tamped knikinic into the red stone bowl and one of the white men struck a match. The old chief drew on the pipe and offered it to the sky, the earth, and each direction before he smoked and shared the pipe with the men.

The carol ended; the white men, warm and rested, left the church, raising a grateful hand to Mr. Burt. Leather creaked as they mounted their horses and followed the herd.

Drifting Goose lifted his hand in a sign of peace and farewell and led his men and women into the night.

The big boys carried sleeping little ones and led the way to back to the school. Bright stars lit their way; snow crunched underfoot, and cows mooed in the distance. A deep Dakota command urged the horses to pull the wagon. It would carry Drifting Goose to his home on the river. Violet longed to follow, but too soon the harness bells jingled away to silence.

Jean Starr

Message From the House of the Winds

A dull-normal morning: Nila was late getting ready for work, but only a little. There was time enough to catch her usual bus if she took the short-cut through the alley in back of her apartment building. As she reached the end of the alley, she saw, spray-painted in orange-red over the incomprehensible graffiti on the wall, the outline of a stylized jack-rabbit. He was holding a placard which read, "Hello, there, Nila Pigeon!"

Nila gasped, then took off, running as fast as she could in three-inch heels and a straight skirt. Panting from her dash, she pulled up at the bus stop beside the bench, which was already occupied by three hunched gray-brown figures. Nila, who was still not used to the street-people beached on park benches and bus stops and edges of sidewalks like drift-wood piled up at the high-water mark, looked straight ahead, pretending that they were really not there. Then the one closest to her said "Nila." The next one said "Nila." And the last one said "Nila PIGEON" just as a bus veered toward the curb, its doors flying open. Nila flung herself into the open door and up the steps almost in one jump, never even stopping to look at the bus number to see if it were the right one. She paid her fare and sat trembling.

A true-crime story on TV just a few days before had given Nila night-mares. A young woman, working alone in an office, as Nila often did, was kidnapped, the only clue her name, spray-painted on a wall opposite the building where she worked. Stalked, that was what they called it. Not like crime at home. "I'll never get used to this," Nila thought.

And "No, I refuse to think about home anymore." Nila had turned her back on all that home represented, the good with the bad, and had fled to the big city, to her helpful cousin Maggy, now called "Mickey" for some reason that had to do with fashion and being modern. "But Egi," Nila said, using the old Indian form of her name, "Maggy's a white girl's name, a school name, huh?"

"Old-fashioned. Worn out!" said the newly-named Mickey with a grin, "Like everything else we used to get at home. Schoolbooks without covers! Old broken-down cars! Rusty trucks! Me for plastic and chrome!" And she shook her tightly permed curls so that the frosted streaks glinted, stamped her bright red boots, and was off, dancing down the stairs, to a date, an evening class, a moonlighting job. But Mickey had the time to answer Nila's desperate letter, had given her a place to come, a place to stay, had helped her find a job. "McMahon Lumber! Typing invoices! Up in a dusty old loft, I'll bet! Well, kiddo, you'll do better than that once you get used to things," Mickey said.

And once safely at work, Nila had to laugh a little at her fears. From her desk, she looked out over the stacked boards in two-story piles sprayed with water. The air was golden with dust; the building hummed and vibrated from the action of the big saws almost a block away from her cubbyhole. As always, her work was piled up before her. No time to worry over weird stuff. No time even for lunch today; she'd have to eat a sandwich at her desk.

And on her way home, when Nila looked apprehensively into the alley, there was no drawing of a rabbit. There was no rectangle with her name in it. Everything had vanished without a trace.

"But spooky stuff like this doesn't happen in the city," Nila thought. "Not like at home, where every time something goes wrong, someone's sure to think of witchcraft, where every time somebody goes to court, even for traffic tickets, there's someone the family has paid, puffing furiously away, throwing clouds of magic smoke from remade tobacco to cloud the minds of the other side." She could remember the baffled fury and frustration when smoking was banned from the courthouse.

"Now what we s'posed to do?" muttered an elderly man. The magic-makers now dwelled furiously on the courthouse lawn, she had heard. No, Nila hadn't spoken or written to anyone from home for almost a year now. Soon it would be time to mark the anniversary of Nila's divorce from her father, and, by that act, her separation from all the rest of her relatives at home. Even now, she could not decide whether it would be a celebration or a time of regret.

Even Mickey, who almost spat at the thought of "those old-fashioned ways," who had stood by Nila's decision, resolutely telling everyone who summoned up the fortitude to dial long distance that she had no idea how to reach Nila, even Mickey couldn't understand. "But Nila," Mickey said, "What exactly was it your Dad did that was so awful? Come on, Nila, honey, you can tell me, no matter what."

"I wanted to get my driver's license," Nila bawled, breaking down completely.

"But there was more to it," she said hesitantly. She found it hard to explain why the incident had such importance for her, but it did, it did. It had all begun with driver-training, which seemed harmless enough as a thing to want, though life with Daddy always had its uncertainties. Nila needed to learn to drive officially, to have her very own license. It was freedom. It was liberation from the fear of blue bubble-lights in your rear-view mirror. It was being like the other kids.

When Nila had gone to sign up for the class, breathless with hope and anxiety, she had been given a checklist: "Must have signed Parent Consent Form" and "Must have Birth Certificate" were the last two items. The consent form was tricky, but perfectly possible. All she had to do was to wait for the right moment, when her father was not in the stage of drunkenness where making a paper airplane out of the consent form would seem amusing, for instance. She had to avoid when he was hung over, deep in guilt and despair. And she had to make sure he was not too drunk to write clearly. A couple of times she had had trouble getting shaky signatures accepted at school. But her birth certificate? She was not sure where he kept that, and she'd have to have his cooperation in order to find it.

When she asked him, her father laughed so hard he almost fell off the rickety old porch swing. When she opened up the battered brown envelope he handed her and read the contents, she knew why he thought it was so funny, and, for an instant, was filled with a fury so red-hot that, if a weapon had been within her reach, she might have killed him. There was no birth certificate. There were three items in the envelope: a permit to transport Christmas trees in Sequoia National Forest dated seventeen years before, a stock registration certificate for a Holstein heifer calf, and a Bureau of Indian Affairs Indian registration card with her name on it — spelled wrong — her date of birth — wrong — and amount of Indian blood — also wrong. The tribal identity was correct.

"Ever'body's so damn dumb, Nila-girl," he sputtered, laughing and spraying beer. "Gov'ment folks, think they SO SMART, cain't hardly talk to a man, they so much better'n me, that's what I 'rolled you in school with, girl, a stock certificate. And the tree transport paper got you your Indian enrollment. Stupid, stupid."

He looked slyly up at her expressionless face. "Bet' not go to Mexico, though, sugar, not with that damn full-blood look you got. Know why? Ain't no record you was ever IN this ole Unitee-States, nope; no, sirree! They gonna hold you back at the border for a Messican!" And he laughed until the tears rolled down his cheeks. When his eyes could focus again, Nila was gone and so was his old beat-up truck. "Musta dreamed it," he muttered to himself.

How to get a birth certificate? Nila went to her Number One Resource, the Hickory Hill Public Library. "Research paper, for government class," she lied, and in minutes, learned the ways and means. Within the hour, Nila was on the phone to her Aunt Mary, begging for help. "I gotta have three people, Aunt Mali, they all gotta be old enough so they were over eight when I was born and they gotta say they knew I was born. No, no, they don't have to be right there in the room, or even the house. They just have to know about it. What I do is, I take them to a notary and they swear to it, and I fill out this form, and pay a fee, and send it in to the state."

Nila knew that her aunt — and the neighbors — who were old-fashioned traditional Indian people, would be very reluctant to help her deal with any part of The Government. "Why, don't you know, they keep those Japanese Internment camps all painted up and ready in case the Indians start givin' 'em a hard time!" But when Aunt Mali found out Nila couldn't ever go to Mexico because she wouldn't be able to get back across the border, she was appalled. She would start that minute calling everyone until she found two more witnesses. Nila knew that since she was underage, her father would have to sign the application for the birth certificate, but this time, she planned forgery. No use taking unnecessary chances.

"Hostility, that's what it is, Egi," Nila said. "Alcoholics have this hostility, they don't like themselves, they don't like the people around them. It SAYS that in this book I read."

"But you and your Dad, you were always close."

"No, no," said Nila, trying not to cry. "That's what's so awful. I used to think the real man was who he was when he wasn't drunk. I even thought maybe it was me, if I was better somehow, he'd stay sober for me. I used to think a lot of things, but it just came to me, right then, when he was drunk, THAT was really him. It wasn't just the birth certificate. It was everything. It was my whole life. Every time, it would be the worst possible time when he got drunk and screwed up. And finally he made me just a non-person. It was too much. If that's what being in my family is, I wanted a divorce."

A week after Nila's scare with the rabbit drawing in the alley, she had an odd experience. The old bookkeeper at the lumberyard, Mr. Meyer, talked Nila into coming out to lunch. "Just a hot-dog from the stand down the street, Miss Pigeon. But it will get you out into the fresh air. All this eating at your desk, it's not good for you."

Mr. Meyer told her funny stories about his boyhood as a refugee, how he had been sent to America with a label on his coat, and his first lessons in English. They were going back to the lumberyard when they both saw something going on just ahead of them on the sidewalk. For a second, Nila thought it was two cats mating. Then she thought it was three or four cats fighting. But it was cats attacking a large bird. She ran toward the cats, yelling and swinging her handbag. They fled, yowling, leaving their victim behind. It was a barn-owl, bleeding heavily, backed up against the wall of a building. It opened its sharp beak, flexed its claws, and screamed at them.

Mr. Meyer was stammering, "We can't leave it here, poor thing, but what can we do?" Before he finished speaking, Nila flipped up her hem and began hauling off her half-slip, stepped out of it, swooped down on the injured bird and wrapped it in the cloth before it could bite or claw. "Now what do we do with it?" she panted.

They went charging into the front office with it. It was a wild scene, everyone circling around them. Finally, Mr. McMahon's secretary called the Humane Society and instantly had instructions on where to take avian victims of urban violence. "I never knew we had owls in the city. I've never even seen an owl except on a nature program on PBS," said young Mr. McMahon, the boss's son.

"There are more than you'd think," said Mrs. Springfield briskly. "There are even nests of hawks in the high-rises of the financial district." She gave Mr. Meyer the directions to the shelter, young Mr. McMahon volunteered his car-keys, and they were off.

It was not until they were on their way that Nila turned beet-red in embarrassment at the thought of stripping off her underwear right there on the sidewalk. But Mr. Meyer, hunched over the steering wheel in grim determination to steer young Mr. McMahon's car through all the dangerous traffic, never noticed her distress.

After the owl rescue, Nila began to notice the hawks. One came screaming down, scooping up something brown and wriggling, flying up past the windshield of the bus, as Nila was putting her fare in the box. "Oh, my God, what was THAT?" said the shaken bus driver. "A hawk. They nest in the high-rises," Nila said. "Oh." He took a closer look. "Hey, you're a Indian, right? You guys know all about that stuff, huh?"

"Actually. I heard about it from some Asian guy at the Humane Society," she told him, stepping smartly to her seat.

On TV, in the papers, there were stories about raccoons in the suburbs, possums among the road-kill in the fancy developments, every day a new reminder that the city was not exactly removed from all the things Nila grew up with.

One Sunday, two things happened. First, Mickey gave Nila a present for her birthday, a pair of beaded earrings sold at the Indian Center where Mickey sometimes tutored. Nila loved them. She was exclaiming over them when she read the tag. "Eeeeeee," she cried in a descending wail of distress, the earrings slipping from her hands.

"Don't you like them?" asked Mickey.

"Look at the card."

" 'Made by Nyla Dove.' You know, if we were home, I'd feel funny about this," said Mickey.

This is the second thing that happened. Mickey and Nila decided to go down by the river and walk along the trail the city had built there. They planned to walk until they reached a marina where they could get sodas and sandwiches for lunch. When they were halfway there, they sat on a log for a breather. They saw, coming toward them, a very small deer, not a fawn, a miniature adult. It came straight toward them, looked both of them in the eye, nodded its head twice, then turned, and slowly walked back to the thicket. It was by this odd behavior the girls became convinced that what they had seen was an apparition, the Little Deer, seen by their people in times of calamity and change.

"Egi, I have to go home," said Nila.

"You do," said her cousin. They packed, got together their cash, and put Nila on the afternoon bus. Two days later, she was standing in the cemetery by a grave marked only with a stake and a number. It was her father's.

As they say, there's a price you pay, and it will be paid. And this is the price that Nila paid, and this is also the price that Nila's father paid, that the words she had to say to him had to be said to her father's grave.

On the bus back to the city, Nila finally fell into an exhausted sleep. She dreamed, she dreamed many things, but the last dream was this: she was a little girl again, before all the trouble had started, when her mother was still alive and her father was not a drunk. She was sitting on his lap in the big old comfortable armchair that was his favorite, drowsily watching the wood burn down in the stove, loved, safe, and warm. He was telling her a story in the dream, and, when Nila woke up, just at dawn, it seemed to her that his voice was still ringing in her ears, and she found that she could remember every word.

Denise Sweet

Dancing the Rice

For Mr. Bill Sutton

The fall season enters the rhythms of our pace
leaves gather like whorls on a spindle of wind
twisting and coiling around our feet;

the old man sits in front of the fire stirring
and singing low in whispers to himself, tossing
the rice slowly in the bottom of the black pot;

the good grain, manomin, turns slowly from green
to darkened fibers in the heat, we watch it turn
small swirls of steam wisp away from the parching;

the helper, a young man, slowly slips into moccasins
recalls that they belonged to his grandmother, and once
were too small for his feet — but they grew with him;

when we dance, he says, we caress the earth
we carry power in the way we present ourselves
as dancers, as singers, bringing the rice home;

this power enters each stem of manomin
but it must be a gentle step, the padding of feet
against the good grain; they hold our dreams

and we must be slow and gentle when we dance the rice
or they can quickly turn to broken stems and then to dust
then we have nothing and the manomin will not return.

He lowers himself into the barrel of parched rice
placing his feet gently against the heated grain
slowly lifting one foot, and twisting the other

he shifts his hips side to side; hoisting his weight
on the sides of the barrel, he gently kneads the grain
pressing each step in a circle against the barrel's bottom

"Everything tries to go in a circle. Everything in nature.
You and me. Yuh." The old man watches while the rice is tossed
from the basket into the air — tiny whirlwinds of chaff spring

forth like dervishes released from a magic lamp. The wind
sails them away from the winnowed rice — the grain chinks against
the birchbark basket in cadence with the dropping wrists and

the young man's swaying black hair — it is a dance of sweet and
gentle love — warming hearts and pleasing the old man who watches
and sees in circles, our survival embodied in the winds of October.

To Know by Heart: Saulte St. Marie, October 1989

For Conrad

I

In Batchawana Bay, a slight womanrain
casts a pewter haze while houses disappear
in shadows of the mountainous strata
pale pink ribbons of light glide
slowly over the horizon. Here you need no maps,

One finds the way by heart, you say. While
Precambrian shields bear the scars of our absence
stories of how Anishinabe blood shored into stones,
of how the old man returned them to soft graves.
We were here. We're still here. This place.

II

The colors are different at Blind River, you say
there, your map is the canvas, your colors

the reflection of flint upon water and ridge
your unusual recall — a palette for heartbreak.

When you run to the petroglyphs, you leave behind
the poison of frustration — like the paintings
of the bushmen, the wind whirls away scorpion patterns
above your head, beneath your heart until the heart
can rise high above any pain of history
any pain of remembering.

III

The step into the trading post while a black dog removes
himself slowly from the entrance. He is tolerant
of the tourists and has grown sadly arthritic, this one
who could sleep for nights under a sky of ice and stars.
He belongs here and we do not.

We wander alone through aisles of mass production
of miniature canoes and other half-priced authenticities
until we fall silent at the sight of insane opulence:
a foxskin tossed amidst a display of carved pipes and katchinas
I felt stupid and shy about tears I could not show you

When you explained how the templehairs of moose are dyed
and trimmed close into the shapes of flowerbuds. Before
leaving, you hand me a gift — a small carved bear.
Makwa, my dodem rises, swelling with the warmth of wood,
and the fenugreek odor of hands carving away the difference.

Luci Tapahonso

Light a Candle

The other night thunder shook the house
and lightning slashed brilliant blue across the bed.
I slept in bits, my heart raced with each explosion of noise and rain.
And though he held me, my breathing was ragged and exhausted.
I may never sleep through these storms.

Hector, light a candle for me.

Last week we returned to our birth place
and as we drove through southern Colorado,
we were stunned by the beauty of autumn leaves,
the deep cool mountain canyons,
and twice, deer stood beside the road.
They watched as we passed through their land.
Their eyes glistened black softness.
Misty said, "Isn't it neat that we see them on our way home?"

Hector, light a candle for her.

In a small reservation town, a little boy shakes his mother.
She is passed out on the floor and he is hungry.
"Mama," he says, "can you make some potatoes?"
She stirs, "Leave me alone, damn it."
He climbs up on the counter, takes down a box of Cheerios
and sits back down to watch TV.
The noise he makes eating dry cereal is steady and quiet.

Hector, light a candle for him.

Some evenings Leona just wants to sit with her sisters and mother
around the kitchen table and talk of everything and nothing.
Instead, she sits in the quiet kitchen and outside,
leaves blow against the window — the wind is cold and damp.
In front of Leona, the table stretches out clean and shiny.

Hector, light a candle for her.

North of here, the Kaw rushes westward, a wide muted roar.
The trees alongside sway and brush against each other.
dry, thin leaves swirl in the cold wind.
The river smell and heavy wind settle into my hair,
absorbing the dull thundering water,
            the rolling waves of prairie wind.

This time I have walked among the holy people:
the river, the wind, the air swirling down from the hills,
the exhilaration of the biggest catch,
the smooth grace of eagles as they snatch their prey,
the silent pleas of those who drowned here.

Hector, light a candle for me.
            light a candle for me.

The Pacific Dawn

It is spring in Hilo, Hawaii,
and the Pacific dawn is brilliant with color.
Early on, it is bright pink, streaks of gold line the clouds.

        It awakens me,
        drawing me to the window
        to pull back drapes,
        fill the entire room with the dawn.

I lie back down to sleep again.
Birds outside the window talk noisily.

I am tired. My eyes ache
        and I want to sleep and sleep;

nurture my body and let my bones soak
in quiet breathing and soothing thoughts.

But it is this: the dawn and the pounding ocean below;
clouds rearranging themselves over and over.
I breathe this air, gentle with alive flowers
and cannot sleep.

Not far from here, Pele stirs, she sighs, and it is a thick stream of
hot steam atop the dry volcano. She sees him — the dark handsome one
with a moustache. His hat is new and fine. Pele sits up and takes
a deep breath — she likes nice things. His hat blows off and whirls
downward to the center of her home. He reaches after it,
but it is lifted away. "Oh Pele," he says, smiling, "it is for you
I wore the hat."

Just yesterday, I felt her strength,
brimming beneath the molten island.
I leaned over the rim of the black volcano,
and sprinkled corn pollen, whispered a prayer;
I recall First Man and First Woman.
I recall the first perfect ear of white corn.
I recall the first perfect ear of yellow corn.
I recall the dust of my desert home.
I left a Zuni bracelet; perfectly shaped turquoise stones
set in smooth white silver and earrings, long thick jaa tl'ool.
She loves the most beautiful of everything.

I understand that I was destined to see this dawn,
to say this prayer,
and I am helpless in this beauty:

The huge flowers I couldn't have imagined,
the lilting songs of the throaty chanters,
the nurturing stories of long ago,
and those who spread luau before us
as if we have just come home.
It is here that my dreams take on an unnameable restlessness,
and the heavy current of the Pacific forces itself into my memory.

Drew Hayden Taylor

Oh, Just Call Me an Indian

The other day, I, a reasonably well-educated man of the evermore-complex nineties, made a tremendous political and social faux pas; I referred to myself and other people of my ethnic background as "Indians."

Oh, the shame of it. You could hear the gasp echo across the room.

It was done, I assure you, with the most innocent intention, but nevertheless, I was soon castigated by both my brethren and, in my humble opinion, the overly politically sensitive members of other cultural groups. And the white people.

Needless to say, in these politically correct times, I was inundated by these same people with criticisms about my use of such an outdated term. "We're/You're no longer called Indians!" I was told over and over again.

Well, I'm evidently severely mistaken in having responded to that term for the past twenty-nine years. No doubt an oversight on my part and that of my entire family and reserve, not to mention the vast majority of the country.

While we were growing up, we were all proud to be "Indians." The word had a certain power to it that set us aside from the white kids. (Or should I say children of occidental descent?)

Somehow the cry of "Proud to be Indigenous Population" just doesn't have the same ring.

Or picture this: You arrive thirsty in some new town, and you ask the first 'skin you see, "Yo, neeches, where's the nearest First Nations Bar?" Sorry — just doesn't work for me.

I guess at 29 I'm out-of-date. Oh, I understand the reasoning behind the hubbub. Columbus, as a member of the European Caucasian nation, thought he found India and so on.

That's cool, but there's also another school of thought that says Columbus was so impressed by the generosity and gentle nature of the native population of the Caribbean that he wrote back to Spain saying these people were "of the body of God" — or, in Latin, "corpus in deo." *In deo* equals Indian. A pretty thin link, but who knows? I know some Indians with God-given bodies.

But a person in my position doesn't have time to defend himself with theoretical history. Since my faux pas, I've been too busy handling the deluge of politically correct terms I am permitted and urged to use.

It must be obvious to most people that in the past few years, native people in Canada have gone through an enormous political metamorphosis, similar to that of people of African descent. Years ago they used to be called niggers, then Negro, then colored, then black and finally, today, I believe the correct term is African-American or African-Canadian.

That's nothing to the selection of names and categories available to the original inhabitants of this country. And these names or classifications have nothing to do with any tribal affiliations — they're just generic terms used to describe us "Indians."

Grab some aspirin and let me give you some examples.

We'll start with the basics: status, nonstatus, Metis. So far, painless. I guess next would come the already mentioned Indian, followed by native, aboriginal, indigenous and First Nations. Pay attention, there's going to be a test afterward. From there we can go to "on-reserve," "off-reserve," urban, treaty.

Got a headache yet? How about the enfranchised Indians, the Bill C-31 or reinstated people, the traditional Indians, the assimilated Indian? I'm not finished yet.

There are the wannabes (the white variety), the apples (the red variety), the half-breeds, mixed bloods and, of course, the ever-popular full bloods.

My personal favorites are what I call the Descartes Indians: "I think Indian, therefore I am Indian."

Get the picture? Right — there are a couple of dozen separate names for our people. Where does it all stop? I want to know just who keeps changing all the rules.

Even I get confused sometimes. That's why I usually use the term "Indian." I'm just too busy or too lazy to find out which way the political wind is blowing, or to delve deeply into the cultural and government background of whomever I'm talking or writing about. By the time I go through all the categories, I've missed my deadline. Then I become an un-employed Indian.

But I know what you're thinking. Why should I listen to the guy? What the hell does he know? He's probably just some status, off-reserve, urban, native, aboriginal, treaty, half-breed Indian. Well, this week, any-way.

Earle Thompson

Norman, Oklahoma, 07:VII:92

I inhale. The freshly cut grass
reminds me of the pea harvest
and Cayuse, Oregon. I listen
to the evening leaves
they become words
                and I am smitten
with a woman
                slim elegance
and moon-curved lips.
I shall be closemouthed
and not destroy
this moment.

Again, I listen to the evening leaves.
I am writing this for her.
I remember the morning flight
among the sea of clouds
they rub against the mountains
and quilted landscapes
pass me by.
I toss my head and dark hair
Into place.
I long for a voice and the words.
I recall the stars dancing,
Dancing in her eyes.
Still, I listen to the evening leaves.

Genesis: Coyote Talks!

February sun bleeds orange
staining mountains
purple.
Coyote interprets, musing,
and transcribes telephone lines
that grow cold with chatterings
of the night.

Under the filigreed awning
of a tamarack, Coyote regally poses
his most prominent
and interesting feature
is his long, proud
nose.
Coyote grins, beginning
his soliloquy:

"Some label or call me
a cultural anomaly,"
he laughingly barks.
The outer rim of his face
and an eye were visible;
the other half was obscured
by a bough, then he continues
his spiel.

"We create our own
mythologies. I
may be nonlinear.
Well, pard! Better circle
the wagons . . ."

Telephone poles extend into the sky
reaching for the moon.
They pierce the dark
creating a fine web of stars
on his fur and Coyote
begins again:

"Being the people's
poet,
I count the syllables
and breaths — the rise and fall
of one's voice — trying to understand
and examine the rhythm
of the world. . . ."

07:I:92

Pow Wow

Under an arbor of stars,
swaying pine boughs brush the evening.

"Intertribal. Come on, everyone
Let's dance. Come on,
show them you're alive. Intertribal.
Drummers and Singers!"

In the distance, mountainside curves
like the universe; dancers appear
to be dancing on the rim of the world.

Women's swirling, brightly colored
shawls and men's bustles
made of earth-colored feathers
they dance and the costumes'
shiny cut beads reflect light.
Outskirts of the camp, women
clean and prepare salmon.

Crow rests on chokecherry branch
eyeing discarded fish bones
and dreams of stringing a necklace.

Coyote, the Trickster, laughs and gnaws
at these words. He dances a jig
and snags his grey fur on barbed wire.
And he howls lustfully at the moon.

"We must learn and create. I sing
to the moon for her beauty."

Coyote grins, and joins the dance.

And again, women's swirling, brightly
colored shawls and men's bustles
made of earth-colored feathers
They dance the costumes'
shiny cut beads reflect light.

"Drummers and Singers!
Give us another song . . ."

Laura Tohe

Blue Horses Running

New possibilities exist with you
　　where sagebrush dots the desertscape,
　　　　where a string of crows float like black beads on a turquoise sky
　　　　　and where mountains hold plants spread out like a blanket

We travel the colors of brilliant red rock cliffs
　　that form within ancestral space
　　we travel on the colors of the rainbow
　　　　and know what it means to come forth, to awaken

Here it's possible to know that you belong to the earth
　　in a language that names us,
　　　　that this place formed you,
　　　　　and carved the high bones in your face

Cedar and rock monoliths know the motion of wind,
　　the patience of waiting, the gathering of strength
　　here it's possible to know the world in the words of our ancestors
　　the simplistic beauty of blue horses running

Haunani-Kay Trask

Returning the Gift

For Linda Hogan

I

an ocean and half a continent away
from home, a drenching heat
stirs rivers within me:
a poet's voice crosses
red clay canyons "at the edge
of a savage country
of law and order."

hope in a time of genocide.

II

delicate fireflies circle
the heat. burnt Oklahoma
dust bears away bones
of Chiricahua Apache
Chickasaw, Comanche, Cherokee

immense tragedy in a land
of discovery.

III

at Fort Sill, old hollow monuments:
to Geronimo, imprisoned by conquest,
buried in exile; to Kiowa chiefs
singing their death songs into massacre;

to unsung warriors from disappeared nations
neither truth nor passion marking
their sacrifice.

IV
maple and oak flutter in the dusk
the slow threshing of leaves weaving
a dry hot wind

no scarlet mango or crusted
breadfruit for my Hawaiian
eyes, only a wet dark stain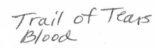
on Indian earth, returning
the gift of song and sorrow

He'eia, 1992

Hawai'i

I
The smell of the sea
at Hale'iwa, mixed with
early smoke, a fire
for fish and buttered clams

in a rapturous morning.
Vines of *naupaka*
leafy and stiff over

the puckered sand
and that ruddy face
coming from cold breakers

mesmerized by the sun.

They take our pleasures
thoughtlessly.

II

The *kōlea** stilts its way
through drooping ironwoods
thickened by the fat
of our land. It will eat

ravenous, depart rich,
return magnificent
in blacks and golds.

Haole plover
plundering the archipelagoes
of our world.

And we, gorging ourselves
on lost shells
blowing a tourist conch

into the wounds
of catastrophe.

III

The dancer's hem catches
a splintered stair. Descending
in a crash of couture

she winces over a broken
toe, hating the glittering
prison of Waikiki

but smiling stiffly
into the haze of white faces;
a spiteful whiteness

in the reef-ringed island
world of her people

now hawking adverts
in their lilting pidgin;
filthy asphalt feet

Pacific Golden Plover –
richly colored migratory bird

plover-shooting white man

unaccustomed to muddy
lo'i, kicking
cadillac tires

for a living.

IV
Green-toothed *mo'o* of Kaua'i   Wailua river
raises his *mo'o* tail
peaked in fury.

A rasping tongue hisses
in rivulets to the burning sea.

Near the estuary mouth
heiau[†] stones lie crushed   — sacred temples
beneath purple resort

toilets: Civilization's
fecal vision

in the native
heart of darkness.

V
Glint of life
in the graveyard's ghost
one yellowed eye

and a swell of heat:
two thousand bodies
exhumed for Japanese

money, developers' dreams,
and the archaeology
of *haole* knowledge.

Māui,** our own fierce — *ākua*   large Hawaiian
disemboweled   cemetery
by the golden shovel
of Empire.

VI

> E Pele e, fire-eater
> from Kahiki.

[handwritten: deity of the volcano]

Breath of *Papa's*[tt] life
miraculously becomes
Energy, stink with

[handwritten: earth mother]

sulfurous sores. *Hi'iaka*
wilting in her wild home:
black *lehua,* shriveled
pūkiawe, unborn *'a'ali'i.*

[handwritten: deity of the forest (sister)]

Far down her eastern flank
the gourd of Lono dries
broken on the temple wall.

Cracked lava stones
fresh with tears, sprout
thorny vines, thick
and foreign.

VII

From the frozen heavens
a dense vapor
colored like the skin

of burnt milk, descending
onto our fields, and
mountains and waters

into the recesses
of our poisoned
na'au.***

[handwritten: intestines / what the heart means to Westerners / home of emotions]

VIII

And what do we know
of them, these foreigners
these Americans?

Nothing. We know
nothing.

Except a foul stench
among our children

and a long hollow
of mourning
in our *ma'i.*†††

Hale'iwa, 1991

*In Part II, the *kōlea* or Pacific golden plover, is a richly colored migratory bird that arrives in Hawai'i about August and departs for Alaska in May. Usually, the *kōlea* appears as a thin, almost emaciated stilt but leaves fattened and beautiful. According to Mary Kawena Pukui, the expression *haole kī kōlea* refers to the "plover-shooting white man" and was said "in astonishment and horror at the white man's shooting of the plovers, contrasting with the laborious Hawaiian methods of catching plovers, a way of saying that white people are strange and different." Today, *haole* who exploit Hawai'i, especially developers and tourists, are referred to as *kolea* by many Hawaiians.

†Part IV. Along the Wailua river, Kaua'i, are found some of the oldest *heiau,* or sacred temples, in the Hawaiian archipelago. One of these *heiau* rests on the sand at the estuary of the Wailua River. A large hotel complex has been built adjacent to it, with guest restrooms.

**Part V. At Honokāhua, Māui, a large Hawaiian cemetery containing perhaps 2,000 or more ancient Hawaiian skeletons was threatened with destruction, including disinterment of the burials, to make way for a Ritz-Carlton mega-resort. The cemetery was on land owned by a missionary descendant whose hotel was to be funded by a silent Japanese investor. A huge outcry among Hawaiians stopped the disinterment and led the State of Hawai'i to purchase the land. While this episode ended well, the disinterment of Hawaiian burials for all manner of resort and residential development continues.

††Part VI. *Papa* — Earth Mother — and *Wākea* — Sky Father — are progenitors of the Hawaiian people. Geothermal energy development on Hawai'i island threatens the sanctity of *Pele,* Hawaiian deity of the volcano and her sister, *Hi'iaka,* deity of the forest. *Pele* and her family were originally from *Kahiki* in the South Pacific and migrated to the Big Island of Hawai'i after a long and dangerous journey across the Hawaiian archipelago. Today, *Pele* and her family continue to be worshiped by practitioners of the Hawaiian religion and members of *hula halau.*

***Part VII. *Na'au* means, literally, intestines. But metaphorically, *na'au* also represents what the heart means to Westerners, that is, the home of emotions, of understanding. *Na'au* can also refer, in a figurative sense, to a child.

†††Part VIII. Our Hawaiian *lāhui,* or nation, is now inundated by a foreign culture and people whose practices are antithetical to the Hawaiian cosmology in which the universe is a creation of familial relations. Therefore, family members (i.e., the earth, the people), must be cared for and protected. The *ma'i,* or genitals, are honored by our people (as in *mele ma'i,* or genital chants) as the source of our continuity. Thus the "hollow of mourning in our *ma'i*" refers to our dying out as a nation, that is, as a people.

i lament the abandoned
terraces, their shattered
waters, silent ears
of stone and light

>who comes trailing
>winds through
>*taro lo'i?*

i lament the wounded
skies, unnourished
desolate, fallen drunk
over the iron sea

>who chants
>the hollow *ipu**
>into the night?

i lament the black
and naked past, a million ghosts
laid out across the ocean floor

>who journeys from
>the rising to the setting
>of the sun?

i lament the flowers
a'ole pua, without
issue on the stained
and dying earth

>who parts the trembling
>legs, enters where
>*the god enters, not*
>*as a man but a god?*

i lament my own
long, furious lamentation
flung down
into the bitter stomachs

into the blood-filled streams
into the far
and scattered graves

who tells of those
disinterred, their
ground up bones their
poisoned eyes?

He'eia, 1988

*This poem is a lament for my ancestors, long dead, and for my land, scarred by American greed and cruelty. The *ipu* is a gourd that accompanies chant and dance. The phrase "from the rising to the setting of the sun" is a reference to a traditional time period from ancient chants; *a'ole pua* means, literally, without flowers. The flower is a metaphor denoting child and thus, in genealogies (our form of history) a bloodline listed as *a'ole pua* is a line without children. The phrase "the god enters, not as a man but as a god" is a traditional reference to our great creation chant, the *Kumulipo,* in which life is born of the divine presence of both the human and the godly. The "disinterred" refer to my ancestors as they are seen by developers and archaeologists who continue to dig for ancient bones to clear areas for hotels. The "ground up" reference is to osteological analysis, which archaeologists perform — every chance they get — on native bones.

Gail Tremblay

Owning Difference

Dominating strangers sense difference,
they stare trying to define the unacceptable
trait, the dusky gene that explains what is
so disturbing about the cut of an eye,
the length of an earlobe, the flatness
of the back of a head. Lack of experience
with genetic nuance makes this all a mystery,
the kindest adjective they find is exotic.
At least once a month someone looking
for an answer asks, "What are you anyway?"
They expect you to explain why you are
unacceptable, to incriminate yourself
by giving them the reason they reject you.
The answer, "Human," denies too much,
the sweet embrace of your parents, dark
and light, the mixing of eternal forces
across boundaries. How can one explain
complex migrations, the chemistry of passion,
the ability to risk ostracism that make
this life possible. I own difference
not because I chose it, but because love
made it inevitable. I grew conscious, knowing
life was full of contradictions, knowing
the stately dance around the drum was a gift
I earned by never denying the incredible richness

that others keep trying to obliterate. Refusing
to vanish, I can only answer with my dark name.

Nothing to Give

The woman was young, blond, beautiful
like the girls in slick magazines who model
jeans. She chose to wear a bone choker
with an ermine tail as though it is possible
to appropriate a culture by wearing its artifacts.
She read a poem in which she said that she was
the white girl who always wanted to be Indian
when she grew up. I sat feeling sick, recognizing
that strange phantom pain in the gut, listening
to her romantic distortions about Eagle Boy dancing
in her dreams, about cruel Indian men who undressed
her and then scolded her for being naked before
them when she was on her moon. She invented
unreality because she refused to witness the real
hard work of living in a world distorted by forced
assimilation, by faked authenticity, by loss
that beat in counter rhythm near the heart
and made the whole world seem out of balance.
She did not speak of struggle, stolen land,
the Earth raped so that strangers could reap
great profits no matter what the cost. Her desire
was for vision to fill an empty life. One more
taker, she invented ceremonies that mystified,
that made healing seem a hollow exercise untied
from the web of light that weaves things seamlessly
into being, untied from the people who for generations
shared a sense of what made things whole in a given
place. I sat and watched speechless, caught,
too paralyzed to walk away and make a scene,
aware how often revelation is impossible to explain.

An Onondaga Trades with a Woman
Who Sings with a Mayan Tongue

We trade in Spanish, but you with the rich
cloth, tell your son how to behave in Mayan,
a language so beautiful it sings in my ears.
I watch him sit straight on the sofa in the hotel
lobby; your words giving dignity to his face.
I long to speak to someone in Onondaga, wondering
if you would recognize it as an indigenous tongue
since your world is so full of foreign languages,
and my people live so far north, our sounds
cannot be familiar to your ears. Attracted
by my braids, you unwrap the fingerbraided,
tasseled band from your own and offer it for sale.
I feel hesitant because it is so outside
my own tradition, but in the end your insistence
and its beauty make it mine. I wish my Spanish
were better, so I could make you understand
why I may never wear it, but will always treasure
it because you were proud enough to keep the old ways
alive and to want to see my hair properly bound
according to your custom making me less a stranger
in this, your sacred and most magic place.

Georgiana Valoyce-Sanchez

The Dolphin Walking Stick

He says
sure you look for your Spirit
symbol   your totem
only it's more a waiting
watching
for its coming

You listen
You listen for the way it
feels   deep inside

Sometimes something comes
that feels   almost
right
the way that swordfish
kept cropping up with
its long nose

but no
and so   you wait
knowing it is getting
closer   knowing
it is coming

And when that dolphin
jumped out of the water
its silver blue sides all shiny

and glistening with rainbows
against the white cloud sky
and the ocean so big
and deep
it went on
forever
I knew it had come

My father rests his hand upon
the dolphin's back
the dolphin's gaze serene
above the rainbow band
wrapped around the walking stick

He leans upon his brother friend
and walks across the room

    As he walks
strings of seashells clack softly
as when ocean waves tumble
rocks and shells and
the gentle clacking song
follows each wave
as it pulls back into
the sea

    The sea

    So long ago
the Channel Islands filled
with Chumash People like
colonies of sea lions
along the shore   so many
people
it was time for some to
make the move
across the ocean to
the mainland

    Kakunupmawa   the sun
the Great Mystery
according to men's ideas

said   don't worry
I will make you a bridge
the rainbow
will be your bridge   only
don't look down
or you will fall

      Have faith

So the chosen ones began
the long walk across
the rainbow
they kept their eyes straight
toward where the mainland was
and all around them
was the ocean   sparkling
like a million scattered crystals
so blue-green and singing
lovely and cool
some looked down
and fell
into the
deep
to become
the dolphins
they too
the People

My father turns to look at me

Someone told me that story
long before I ever heard it
      It's those old ones
he says   pointing up to the ceiling
as if it were sky

They sent the dolphin to me

I always loved the sea

The Fox Paw and Coyote Blessing

You've heard of the Fox Paw
It's supposed to be that french phrase
faux pas
pronounced Fo pah
meaning social blunder
a false step
    but I know
that old fox
is a cousin
to coyote

The morning of my Giveaway
at the Sunrise Ceremony
sprinkling tobacco to the east
of the ceremonial ring
I prayed to my Papago Pima Gramma
who died a few years back but is
alive somewhere

Gramma   I said
I'm going to do this thing
in thanksgiving for my friends
and I want to do it right
Gramma   make sure
it comes out right

So the time came
for my Giveaway
last in line
the sun descending
the ceremonial ring
a ring of brown faces
rainbow-ribboned shirts
feathered bustles and buckskin
    and my special dance was called
my husband at my side
his Tarahumara blood resigned
my Chumash father with his

dolphin walking stick
my Papago Pima mama
shawled in black and turquoise
the family waiting
my friends waiting
the people waiting
        and the drum began
        the southern drum

Just then
in the hush before the dance
that old fox
placed his paw on my shoulder
and steered me north
to dance around the drum
in the wrong direction

Well
Fox and Coyote
led the dance
hopping and twirling around
like fancy dancers
all seriouslike as if
the world depended on it
and me
just grinning
as if I didn't know better
all my family and friends
behind me
dancing around the drum
in the wrong direction

Gramma   I said later
Gramma   how could you
let me go the wrong direction?
What was that Fox Paw doing there?
and why Coyote?
I've never danced the northern way
except when Alice Keshic's cousin died
and she is Winnebago from the north

By myself I asked her this

And this is what she told me

Never forget
Coyote helped to form the world
For all his trickster ways
Coyote helped to form the world
The world was made with Fox Paw
and all the seeming backward things
that make the world go forward

Fox and Coyote
travel to the Four Directions
but no matter where you stand
the Four Directions touch you

Still
though you are touched
by each direction
you are from a people of
the red-brown earth
of Sacaton and southern Arizona

Remember me

We are a plain and simple people
desert people
our way is not of Southern Plains
or Northern Plains

You called for Southern Drum
and honored all your friends
from Southern Plains

You danced the Northern way
and honored all your friends
from Northern Plains

Fox and Coyote
know
what they are doing

By dancing Northern
to the Southern drum
you told the people gathered
you were neither

You danced for O'odham
and Chumash
and all the ones
who have no Pow Wow
to their name

By dancing right   the wrong way
you remembered
who you were

That is a blessing

If it comes from Fox Paw
or Coyote
You remembered
who you were

According to Hopi prophecies we are now in the Fourth World, a world that is
Koyanisqatzi, out of balance. The prophecies strongly suggest that if we do not
learn to respect the earth and each other, this world will end in a terrible way,
perhaps in a nuclear holocaust.

From the Front of the Fourth World

For Robert Boissiere—in gratitude

The Iraqi soldiers
came up out of the earth
like the First People
came into the First World
born
of bubbling fire
the heat of creation a
fire-wind funneled

to order
to balance
to song
       and the power of the Song
created people of all races
and color
and every living thing
was related
       even rocks and sand
and the Song of Creation was given
to remind the people
of their relations
but most forgot
and the First World
was destroyed by fire

The Iraqi soldiers
came up out of the earth
brown faces blending with
bunkers of packed desert sand
their army fatigues dusty
from sandstorms and
bombs   blasting
the earth
       and in the distance
oil wells burned bright
black smoke trailing
against the gray sky
fossil fuel remnants
       from the Second World of
gigantic animals
giant flowers and ferns
       a time when people
became greedy
in a world of plenty
and the ones who remembered
the Song of Creation
were criticized
by the ones who forgot

the instructions
     and the Second World was
destroyed by ice
frozen
from pole to pole
the ones who remembered
hidden deep
in the womb
of the earth

The Iraqi soldiers
came up out of the earth
speaking in Arabic
telling about no food and
drinking only scarce rainwater
saying
     no more war
     no more war
like the people of the Third World
who grew to be many and
built big cities and civilizations
and some powerful ones
tried to change the course of
the Song they forgot
and built armies and war
machines to destroy
annihilate others
     and the ones who remembered
the Song of Creation
who wanted no war returned
to the earth deep
in the earth with a reed
to breathe through when
the flood was unleashed
to destroy the Third World

The Iraqi soldiers
came up out of the earth
thousands
with white flags fluttering

like dove's wings
a red sun behind them
flaring low on the horizon
like a distant atomic
detonation

       And in some desolate
circle of desert
       five Iraqis
came up out of the earth
their arms raised in surrender
eyes wide and frightened
cautiously making their way to
one blond U.S. soldier who held
a big black machine-gun
the conventional voice of the
Fourth World order
       and the Iraqi soldiers bowed
and kneeled
one soldier kissing
the hand   holding the gun
while the startled American struggled
to maintain
military order
motioning with the gun
      to move over
      get down
but as he looked into the eyes
of the kneeling Iraqis
he seemed to remember   something
that softened the set of his jaw
      You're all right
      You're all right   he said
and the desert sands
whispered in the wind
a song
      of remembering

Judith Mtn. Leaf Volborth

Ancient Rain

For Geary and Barbara Hobson

A leafy movement of small creatures,
a rush of wings.
sparrows hook the Sky
birdprints float to Earth
The sound of distant thunder.

a scrim of rain —
fluid charms of ancient ancestors
fall and weave for us
a shawl of white shell dreams.

Pollen-Old-Woman

Listen . . .
        Pollen-Old-Woman
slides her cane in a crescent moon motion,
in her fissured palm she breathes on tiny seeds,
sings poetry into life.
There is pollen beneath her tongue.

Chumash Country

It was a cold, frigid night in Topanga.
I saw Coyote —
Well, it was really his breath I saw.
Cold puffs of it
traveling up the hillside.

Ron Welburn

Sentinel Robins

From the trees at the Shinnecock homes
young robins scout the roads,
ready for dog soldier days,
ready for intruders and outside related
daring to sack the Res'.

The robins keep me in sight
on a morning walk to take in
the cove and the salted air.

Silently they edge just ahead of me,
tree to bush, tree to obscure fence post;
males young and tough and still
vaguely spotted.
Nesting is over
and they have come into seasoning
for stalwart duties older than memory.

These days strife still comes along
before, as in the old times,
a village could prepare for it.
Blood spills and war clubs
of the hand and mind raise;
legs broken.

Going onto the Res' late one night
I heard sentinel robins

call their resonant warning;
but we're here to celebrate
Labor Day's 39th, hoping
there'll be a 49th Pow Wow
and maybe a good-time 49.
We're redwing brothers
who've come in peace many times
to share in the fun and
be with our friends.
No one's looking for an ugly afternoon.

Canoe Circle

For Elliott, August 27, 1992

The great blue heron circles us.
Delayed at his fishing,
his flights curl around the pottery
of the creek.
Four times his great winged form
shapes our canoe, easing along the reeds
toward the bend and the bridge,
turning, easing back downstream.
The boy in the middle gains
the strength of paddling and seeing,
listening all around himself.
His eyes and heart find visitors in
the turtleheads and the loosestrife
and the basking turtle.
His godfather teaches with stories
and soft strokes, and at the canoe prow
his father learns the deft placement of wood
in the water, the motion of fathers and sons,
as they follow the great heron
curling back to origins.

Jordan Wheeler

Volcano and Kiwi

Lying on our backs staring up at the sky, we were trying to find the Southern Cross. Follow the seven sisters, we were told, through the pot, and it points straight to it. Her finger traced through the sky connecting blue clusters in a high arc. The pot, I noted, was Orion. "There," she said. I followed her finger and it pointed to half the sky. I saw three crosses.

"Which one?"

"The upside down one that's slightly askew."

"Slightly askew," I pondered, my neck getting sore. It took awhile to find one that fit the description. "Are you sure?"

"No."

The Southern Cross carried some clout in my understanding. I had read *Hawaii* and I was tired of Polaris (although I missed Bear). To lay eyes on the Southern Cross was not the purpose of my trip, but it made an interesting side bar.

I imagined ancient Polynesians navigating their huge canoes by the cross to tiny island specks in the sea. Their brevity was impressive. Seven canoes, according to the history that didn't have clout with some of the people, landed in Aotearoa (Land of the Long White Cloud) and they became Maori, the first people of what they now call New Zealand.

I was lying in the grass in a field of the town called Ngaruawahia with a Maori woman who didn't know where the Southern Cross was. A friend had pointed it out to her and still we couldn't find it. "I don't know a thing about stars," she admitted again.

Santa Claus came to mind. Not because it was mid-December and the yuletide season was near, despite the subtropical weather, but because all of us, at a certain age, realize Santa isn't real. I was feeling that way again. I sought solace in Orion.

"Do you have kids?" she asked.

I looked at her, curious about the question. Fiddling with a blade of grass between her fingers, she was not as taken by the sky as I was, despite the night's black brilliance. Reesa, I thought, wondering if her name meant anything. Perhaps it meant "one who cares not about the sky." I'm from the prairie.

"I have a little boy," I told her, turning back to Betelgeuse. She shivered and I gave her my PEACE VILLAGE sweat shirt.

"Aren't you cold?" she asked.

"I'm from Canada."

She laughed for a moment and I added, "His mother and I broke up eight months ago." She didn't respond and I didn't quite know why I told her.

Between Betelgeuse and Bellatrix a meteorite raced into a bright stream, then disappeared. It brought with it a wind — cold and biting as it swept past. I shivered, Reesa didn't.

"Did you feel that?" I asked, wondering if it happened often in Aotearoa.

"Feel what?"

I didn't answer her — I didn't even hear her. The meteorite had a trailer which flew in the same arc. It flew through the pot, but took a sudden left at Canopus. In awe, I watched it hurl toward me growing into the size of a basketball. It hit me in the face with enough force to knock my head into the wet grass. A twig scratched my right eyelid.

Reesa must not have heard the thump because when I awoke, she was gone. It was 4:00 A.M., according to my watch, and I was shaking like false teeth on a drum. I looked up and Orion wasn't where I'd left it.

Lake Taupu — the image hung above me, and then it was gone. I sauntered through the dark to the parking lot and climbed into the rented Nissan van. Lake Taupu — the name rattled on like a burr stuck in a goat's chin. I couldn't get rid of it.

Looking back, I didn't have the luxury of peripheral vision. I didn't see it coming. There were signs and I knew them, thanks to Cree and Irish folklore, but I didn't listen. Following our group from Vancouver to Aotearoa was a leprechaun — I was blind. I saw water twirl down the drain in a different direction than back home — I didn't anticipate the effect a different magnetic pull would have on the gremlins. Something had shifted, some kind of gear.

I found a highway map and located Lake Taupu, then cranked the motor and aimed the Nissan south. Bye, bye, Turangawaewae Merae.

The moon was full but it lay behind the rugged mountains terraced by millions of grazing sheep. All the sheep were asleep. There was little traffic on the windy, narrow road and I was beginning to have fun navigating the many turns. I checked my rear view mirror once in awhile and nearly lost control of the vehicle when I saw Reesa.

"We usually drive on the left hand side of the road here," she said. I changed lanes.

"How did you know I was leaving?" I asked.

"Do you think I'm following you?"

"You keep showing up."

"Where are we going?"

"Lake Taupo."

Like the wool, she went to sleep. I drove in silence and watched the sun's daily murder of the stars. I put on my 100 percent UV protection sunglasses and slipped on my warm diet Coke. Twice I had forgotten to drive on the left. Arriving in the town of Taupo at eight, I parked at a restaurant for some breakfast. Exhausted, I leaned across to the back seat where Reesa had stretched out. "Breakfast," I told her, shaking her gently.

"I'll water the plants tomorrow," she answered. Somehow it made sense, so I went inside by myself.

Two eggs over easy, sausages, buttered toast, a danish, coffee (one cream, one sugar), and new arteries coming right up. I read the menu for entertainment. Small towns in Aotearoa, I noted, were much like small towns along the Trans-Canada. It could have been Kenora. I never spent much time in Kenora — I didn't want to. And then I wondered what the hell I was doing in . . . it took a moment to remember the name. I slowly paid for the portions of animal I ate, then walked back to the van. Reesa was still asleep. Taupo — Lake Taupo.

I drove to a park and went for a walk. The crappy coffee swished in my belly.

"What the hell am I doing in Lake Taupo?" I asked myself. I watched the waters of a stream rushing beneath a stone bridge. The steep descent created the illusion of a waterfall. I climbed into the gully to soak in the water's spray and noticed how the few rays of sun able to penetrate the growth made small rainbows in the mist. Somehow, the spray gave me strength and resolved my determination. Positive ions, I concluded. Trekking back to the Nissan, I stared at the western sky dominated by Mt. Tongariro. I could make out several clouds joined at the edge which gave the land its name. I passed an American tourist complaining that he couldn't get a decent cup of coffee. Aotearoa — land of the wrong white crowd. Reesa, I noted, wasn't in the van when I got back. I climbed in and drove away.

Across the Pacific, past Fiji, Tahiti, Bora Bora, and Hawaii, something beckoned. Kanata, I whispered to myself, what do you want?

Lake Taupo emerged on my left and signs led me to a beach. It was an impressive lake — not like Lake Winnipeg, Great Slave Lake, Lakes Superior, Huron, Michigan, Erie or Ontario, but it was a grand lake for Aotearoa. As morning wind whipped the water I stripped to my underwear and waded in to my chest. Waiting for a revelation I noted that I was the only person around. Traffic began to wake up and the highway made the odd noise, but only the wind was master, and the rapidly moving clouds (reminiscent of Spielberg adventures). Thunder bubbled and exploded before me. There was a brilliant flash of blue followed by rainbows, then a bright but ugly light. I noticed my eyes were closed, so I opened them.

"How do you feel," a blurry face asked. I groaned, wondering why I felt hung over. "You'll be okay," the familiar voice repeated, "for someone who was struck by lightning . . . twice."

Two days, I learned later, I had been unconscious for two days. Not only did I miss the remainder of the conference at the Turangawaewae Merae in Ngaruawahia, but I was suddenly in Auckland. Tomorrow we were leaving for Vancouver. A sense of dread came over me, but I didn't know why. "How was the conference?" I asked.

"It rained."

The familiar voice, I remembered, belonged to Kathy Clark — the Canadian coordinator I had traveled with. "A Maori woman said you had been hit by ball lightning before you drove off to Taupo."

Ball lightning, I pondered. I thought it was the trailer of a meteorite. Sitting up I felt a wave of nausea sweep over me, then quickly pass. Doctors and nurses fussed about, but it was clear that the lightning strikes (both of them) had little effect on my system. Feigning hostility, I was released just after supper.

The air dripped. Inhaling the humidity I left Kathy and our Merae and wandered the hills of Auckland. Even the hills dripped. On closer scrutiny, I could see the hills weren't hills, but volcanos. Dark and brooding they loomed over the city lights, reminiscent of Polynesian gods. Maori God didn't come to mind because most of Maoridom had converted to Christianity. Hearing Kanata beckon once more I began to walk toward the closest volcano. It seemed dormant and close. It was dormant.

As I trekked through eternity, the volcano loomed persistently in the distance. Martin, South Dakota, came to mind. The prairies are truly eternal, vast sky over low land. Traveling toward the Pine Ridge Indian Reservation, the towns are few and the night is a lesson in highway hypnosis. When the distant glow of the town of Martin begins to loom, there is a sense of relief for parched throats, hungry tummies, and empty gas tanks. Martin, however, remains a distant glow for several more miles. An hour passes and the town seems closer, but by then the gas tank is empty. South Dakota is not the place for an Indian to run out of gas. I named the volcano Martin.

Later (how much later I don't know) I stood at the base of Martin. As I climbed I noted with some exasperation that the volcano was not as small as it appeared from a distance. Although I was still wondering what the hell I was doing in Lake Taupo in my underwear, I hadn't yet questioned why I was climbing a volcano in downtown Auckland. At least I had my pants on.

Panting, I contributed to the still mist that hung about the city on the isthmus. Unsettled by it, I stopped and stared at it for several moments. I hate stagnant air (and so I hated Utah), but I saw it fluctuate. Satisfied, I resumed the journey. The air and I both dripped.

Benevolent to time I arrived at the summit wondering which way was west. The magnetic gremlins played havoc with my orientation. In the high altitude the mist had thinned. Above me were stars, but no Orion to grant me comfort. Dizzy, I watched the sky spin, then found myself on the ground with my mouth full of dirt. A pair of sandals situated themselves close to my face. I looked up and it was Reesa. Taking off my overcoat, I laid it on the ground and she joined me.

"Have you found the Southern Cross?" she asked.

"No."

We lay there in silence. There was no wind, but I could hear Kanata's whisper.

"I am calling you," she said.

Her words echoed and reality became as benevolent as time. Reesa and I made love on my overcoat atop the volcano I had named Martin. The view of Auckland was splendid, and either the Earth moved or Martin wasn't dormant after all.

I woke in the morning and Reesa was gone. In her place, on my stained overcoat on top of the active volcano, was a kiwi fruit. I had it for breakfast and began the trek back to the merae. The gremlins were still at work, but Kanata led the way.

There was much commotion in our group when I returned. They were about to leave without me. Making it to the airport on time I said good-bye to the Leprechaun and the Gremlins. Gremlins and Leprechauns won't fly on DC-10s.

The Pacific seemed like a slough, and we passed over the international date line on my birthday — so I had two of them. The free booze made it easy to celebrate. I said good-bye to my traveling companions in Vancouver and boarded a 737 to Winnipeg. Winter had missed me, but the feeling was unrequited. I froze my balls waiting for a cab.

Rather than return to the one I left two weeks before, I went straight to the one I left eight months before. Her sister, not at all pleased to see me, said she was in the hospital. I jumped back in the cab and raced to Winnipeg General. The cab driver wouldn't take New Zealand dollars, but he settled on American. Tracy was in the maternity ward. The dread returned. Kanata was now silent.

"Tracy?" I said in her room. Bloated, her eyes were encased in dark circles and her hair clung to her face in clumps. She was beautiful. Slowly her eyes opened. "Why didn't you tell me?" I asked.

"Too messy," she mumbled. It had been. Spite, hate, antagonism, and fear marked our last days together. But time had removed them all but fear — fear for what was left. She held my hand and we wept.

"We have a daughter," she told me, "and she wants her father."

My daughter was named Reesa Kanata, and she knew how to play with lightning.

Roberta Hill Whiteman

Wherever in Winter

Wherever in winter you go, child,
I hope you hear our prayers with you in the wind.
The moon's not full tonight, but waxing toward a quarter,
with Venus shining to its east.
Together they'll travel this January night,
crossing each other at the horizon
in that cold moment before dawn. By that time, you may be
crossing for home.

I've asked each tree, each block,
each tower of steel and glass, each shrub along the alleys
if they've seen you passing by.
You left without a word, disappearing
quickly in these quaking cities.
I wake at four A.M.,
feeling a cold wind blowing
in every room. No one on earth has yet
helped me understand
this status, this bare sadness rushing
through dark halls. Is this what my father felt
in his bedroom, wondering where I'd gone
on those spring nights that churned
with an energy I could not deny?

I tell myself old stories about the prodigal,
or the youthful immortals of Asia,

or the restless coyote with his nose
sniffing a pile of snow or shit.
I say to myself that tomorrow you'll look
from a window where people rush to work,
and in that moment of sun, you'll find
the red road and a friend.

I have faith the stars recognize your spirit
as it catches the sun's last flame.
I keep faith that the spirits will keep you aware
that we are
related to everything here.

Reparations

I

I drove from Mazeppa
through hills that aged with every turn
where trees grew
denser than liquid dark.
I went up and over crests
down around ravines
without seeing another car.

When fog enveloped every view,
I peered into the windshield as I slowed,
knowing that in these hills
Traverse de Sioux was signed,
feeling that those who long ago
loved these green coulees
would have camped in this cloudland
to dream of deer.

Lost in my machinery,
I pushed on, even though in glowing clouds,
I lost all direction — hills swallowed me whole.
I drove over the tops of trees.
Risks like these kept me shaking.

You were alone on that same road
and if I had stopped,
we might have met
under the green drifts of that canopy.

So much of my life was like that road,
where I longed to stop,
but didn't dare,
urging myself to push on somewhere
unimportant,
unaware how close a friend
was passing by.

Reaching the clear air of the river after midnight,
I gunned the car around a curve.
Where only dark had been,
there from the reeds, a herd of twenty deer
bounded around the fenders.
The doe worked hard
to shift the young buck's elegant hurdling
away from my hard lights.

Red eyes and budding horns.
His hind hooves hit my right front fender.
I too have a son, passing
through this world's happenstance.
I stopped and searched for the young deer
whose ancient energy invests
the summer wood,
but all were gone.
I asked forgiveness,
but my voice plied the reeds
like a finger of wind.

II
All the long way home deer came out to graze
and graze me with their eyes.
I have maimed more than deer
with my impatience,
with my driving full tilt

on a curve where I could slow
and meld the motion of the night
with my own soul.
These words
are reparations for that deer.
I leave them in this bundle, filled
with rose and purple winter twilights,
and the feathered dark of trees
in hard-packed snow.
This bundle contains a healing sound—
the blast of wind that wakens trees.

Later you said you too
had hit an animal on that road.
We speak of it six years later,
a quiet circumstance,
unlike marriage or children leaving home,
but subtle all the same in how it helps us age.
Perhaps wisdom lives in such places
where we are forced to stop
with wind in our wet eyes.

Ramona Wilson

Driving North Poems

1

to my left the sun
reluctant to leave
caresses long fingers
over the backs of hills.
to my right the round moon
dances up all mystery
and newness, bringing the scent
of hay and quiet horses.
summer, time to go home.
happiness is mine, I am smiling
into the glowing air.

2

finally the road climbs
into the Siskiyou
the air sweetens
northern mountains, wild
our little people
our mountain people watch.
I have no offering
and I drive at night.
I have to trust I am recognized.
    It is only that woman
    from the north, going home.

3

golden coin moon
over Steptoe country
long fingers of light
in the coulee water.
Elvis singing
its now or never
and I laugh and say aloud
its always like that
moments deceptive as shadow
in their power
the moon balanced just so
above that point,
tomorrow already
in a different place.

4

near the end of the long climb
out of the Columbia gorge
coyote intends to cross the road
stops to glance at me
hey I say, hey brother
go on where you are going
and like that he takes his slim body
a slow trot, eyes straight ahead
until he gets to the other side
and stops again to look at me
over his shoulder
and I grin
thanks for coming over, I say
it makes it easier to go.
You know how it is, some of us
seem to be always traveling
seem to be always saying,
I'll be seeing you soon.

Elizabeth A. Woody

The Luminaries of the Humble

Stars of Solace

The adverse year was uncertain for the Salmon.
Four Snake River Sockeye jump the counting ladders.
Dear Chewana, the river of veracity, burned in the throat,
wordless. They flag as expression the impasse.
Millions of those who have traveled before
move in the celestial bone shapes of night.

Nightmares

As crosses burn, hate is not an outlaw.
In the thousand points of light there is not one bristle
of outrage, only when the American flag is burned.
Silence is camouflage. Blank fronts are innocuous.
The other self closes the window to traffic
and obsessive street. Unemployed in the brightness,
a subversive desires the inevitable collapse.
The night burns with inflamed crosses and swastikas.

Luster

I am a dress of vermilion, harvest of orange roses,
a Sunday visit, not a descendant today, strolling
to the petroglyph, Tsagaglallal. A family of five stare
at the Ghanian healer, his Belgian secretary, the Reiki healer,
the adopted relative of a Lakota man, and myself. They stumble
over the rocks, videocam in hand, screaming, "Mygod! Omygod!"

I am only a dress in the state of being true. They hope
to converse.

Exhibit
I lie on the illusion of verdant environment at Horse Thief Lake
Park surrounded by the vermeil of copper drought. Built over
the site of a nameless "Wishram Village." The illusion
is that there are no Wishram. I ponder with affection the sky
and poplar trees. The assurance and comfort move the tension
in my spine, slowly loosening to say I am where I most belong,
at the moment. Families move about my body in the usual manner.
Chatter, ignore my incongruous presence, distribute their food,
consume. The Village. This is my village of vicarious backgrounds,
the new River People, who are brown and white. In living diorama,
they are poor from the loss of land, hauled out piece by piece,
as lumber, salmon, and fruit. The children, all brown as potatoes,
round-tummied, with the dimple of their navels pointing ahead,
run into the shallows, twirl like fish lures, oblivious of
dispossession. Water skippers are quaint shadows at the edge
of calm water. Willows break for paths. Birds are busy
with delicate manners. Their feet are so bare, beaks, tiny bone
needles, their eyes rimmed with endearing vulnerability.

Wish-xam*

Rattle seedpods, shed skins, to translucent hulls.
Imagine diamonds,
ant-rocks tumbling in the gamble
of wind tonight. The song is Stick Game† and atonal.
The auditory texture of grass is shirred fabric.
A gilded shimmy dance toward the barrier of rocks.
The fence edges in the rim of sight for wild horses.

Breath in the tongues of flowers, small as beads in shells.
Fringe tendrils of toadflax, tip up jaws,
stretching in motions to point at rock cairns.

The dark lava is as human as inukshuks** in the tundra.
Vertebrae mark the broad skin of the volcano's back.

Old snakes drink with solemnity,
knowing the drought fractures only possibilities and the reckless.
This river glows in prime abstraction from the heat.
Rich with oils and segments of heartbeat in sturgeon,
the river like the snake rests its spine by dreaming.

*Wish-xam is a tribe, a branch of the lower Chinookan, as were the Wascos and
Watlala (Cascade) who lived along the middle to lower Columbia River.

†Stick Game, a gambling game prevalent in the Northwest, comprised of two teams
who sing and try to guess which hand holds the stick with marks of a set of two. This game
will go for days, with interchanging teams.

**Inukshuks are rock piles made into human shapes and were built by the people in
the circumpolar region on the tundra.

Warm Springs River

Daylight moves the wind while the river fastens
on a cloak of rippling tensions.
Through the reeds, sage blossoming,
skin shivers from the distance of heat in the pinto sky.
Bright with expectations.
Thirst has fingertips of grief over remnant scaffolds
of small flowers. As one markless palm of thunder
at the rimrock, the broad pulse of the body has been overwhelmed.
A filament of light wavers on the liquid turn over lichenous stone.
It sinks in its own gravity.
It is a quick fin and tail.
Our eventual blindness is the underside of leaves,
myopically stunning in the retinal flicker of signals.
Shallow desire is shadow cast from forms bent in embrace.
As Salmon smell, in a spectrum of seasons, their compulsion,
we no longer possess extravagance to throw between us as shells
of dentalium bridal veils* and belts.

Several loose sequins of scales fray into clouds,
beam over the hillsides, opal into swaying yellow bunchgrass.
Forgotten rivers fill their mouths with fragments from excess.
Zigzag basalt springs, green lush V's of moisture,
point to the feast of supple trout and the brief thrumming of flies.
The current floats into secretive arms of safety.
The burn of volcanic springs cools in depths of caution.

*"Dentalium bridal veils" refer to Wasco, Wishram, and Cascade headdresses that are made from the dentalium shells; for the wedding dress, the belts were loomed, intricate designs, and the entire attire of the bride was given to the groom's family, in the exchange of wealth. These tribes who lived from the middle to lower Columbia River now reside on the Yakima and Warm Springs Reservation. The Warm Springs River is a tributary of the Columbia River.

Carole Yazzie-Shaw

Back in Those Days

Grandma sat on the dirt floor of the hogan singing a morning song as she ground corn. Her strong hands were tightly wrapped around the mono as she rocked back and forth. The sound of grinding as the mono crushed corn woke her granddaughter, Desbah, from sleep. She sat up with a puzzled look, as she combed her fingers through her hair. She got up from her sheepskin bedding and folded her blanket. Yawning, Desbah rubbed sleep from her eyes and began to walk outside, when Grandma called out to her.

"Shi yazhi, on your way back in, bring some firewood with you."

"Yes Masani, I'll be back in a little while. You want me to get water too?" Desbah asked, scratching her back.

"I already got it while you were sleeping."

Desbah stood watching her grandmother's large hands as they gripped the mono. They looked like the hands of a man, and her fingernails were yellow with jagged edges. Desbah was still very sleepy. Grandma looked up to see why she hadn't left yet. The light from the kerosene lamp showed years in Grandma's once dark brown eyes. They were fading with age, causing them to have a light ring around the iris.

"What's the matter with you silly girl, are you sleepwalking?"

Desbah looked down embarrassed.

"You shouldn't stare at people. Now hurry up! You mustn't waste the morning! "

Closing the door behind her, Desbah looked out to the horizon and tied her shoestrings. It was a beautiful morning, and the birds had already begun to sing. The air was fresh and cool, and the stars were still shining. The morning shadows were dark on the bluish light from the white line of the horizon.

When Desbah started toward the East, she heard a coyote somewhere far away in the canyons howling as it made its kill. The sheep in the brush corral shuffled around because of the howling, so Desbah ran faster in fright, avoiding big sagebrush. The farther she ran, the more light dawned upon her. She felt as if she were running into the early morning.

Desbah was breathing fast when she stopped and could feel tiny beads of sweat forming around her face and dry lips. When she stood for a moment to catch her breath, the cool air burned her throat and warm streams of sweat ran down her neck. She looked past the hills covered with piñon trees and sagebrush and saw hints of yellow light as the sun began to come up. She reached into her pocket, took out a medicine pouch and made an offering to the Sun and to Mother Earth, the way Grandma taught her to do. She felt good and began to pray.

"Holy People of the early morning, it is I your granddaughter. I pray to you for a good day. Bring us health and happiness. Watch over my Masani and Mom and Dad, and all my people. May Mother Earth provide enough food for all living things — may all things be good."

Desbah felt a rush of happiness. She felt good all over while she listened to the birds and Mother Earth waking with life. She took a deep breath and headed for home. As she ran home, the sun began to rise, and the sagebrush smelled of early morning dew. When Desbah returned home, sunlight was hitting the tips of trees and bushes. She picked up some firewood before she entered the hogan. Her Masani was kneading dough from the corn.

"Shi yazhi, put some more wood in the fire."

"Masani, when will Mom and Dad come to see me?"

"I don't know. . . . Go let out the sheep. We have much to do."

Grandma did not know what to tell her granddaughter. She didn't know when the girl's mother or father would come back. Desbah's mother said she was going to find work in Gallup, but she was drunk when she said this. She said she would return to get Desbah when she found a place to stay, but that was months ago. Ester was with another man. She had tears in her eyes when she left with this man. Grandma wondered where her daughter was now. Many times she watched Desbah stand in the doorway listening and watching the road to the hogan, hoping to see her parents walking up the road. She often said, "They'll probably bring me something when they come. Maybe some candy."

Desbah walked to the brush corral she and Masani were always having to repair. The main support posts were made of juniper, but the rest was made of sticks and brush tied together with baling wire and pieces of rope. The odor from the sheep stung her nose while she removed the poles to let the sheep out. Desbah thought of her parents while the sheep ran out one at a time. She remembered their fights and the drinking. Her father would frighten her when he hit her mother. Both she and Mom would sit outside and cry while they hid from him. Mother was usually drunk, too, and she would start to say strange things. She often spoke of dying or killing father. Desbah felt a tightness inside of her. Mother told her she would come back soon when she left her with Grandma. Suddenly, Desbah heard Masani yelling and waving her arms.

"Come in, it's time to eat!"

"I'll be there in a little while," Desbah said as she waited for the last sheep to run out.

Summer was ending, and Desbah liked living with Grandma. They did many things together. Sometimes Masani would surprise her with a new clay animal she had made, and they would play with them together. While the sheep were grazing, they would make little hogans and brush corrals made of twigs, but Masani always quit playing too soon. Today she and Masani were to pick piñons while they herded sheep.

When Desbah went back into the hogan, Grandma had made breakfast — mutton, fried bread made of ground corn, and coffee. Everything smelled so good. The juices in Desbah's mouth began to stir.

"Wash your hands."

"Are we going to look for piñons today?" Desbah asked while she washed her face and hands in icy cold water.

"Yes, and what you pick, you can sell at the trading post and buy anything you want," Grandma said, putting out two metal cups and the salt shaker.

"I'll pick a lot so I can buy you a new shawl, the kind with a lot of different colors and long fringes. What's your favorite color, Masani, what color do you like? Mine is red — I like red," Desbah said while she tore a piece of fried bread and wrapped it around mutton. She jerked when she sipped her coffee too fast because it was too hot. Grandma laughed, covering her mouth with her hand to hide her missing teeth.

"I guess I like blue. But I don't think you'll make enough money to buy a shawl from picking piñons. Maybe you should buy yourself a doll."

"Yes, Masani, one with a real pretty red dress and little shoes. Let's hurry and eat. We need to start picking right away!" Desbah said, trying to imagine what the doll would look like. She wanted one with long black hair and shiny shoes — like the one she saw in an old catalog that someone had thrown away.

The door was open while Grandma and Desbah sat eating as sun threw light on their faces. Desbah noticed that in the light, her Masani's hair looked almost yellow instead of white. Then a small puppy came up to the doorway, wagging his tail begging for scraps. Desbah was going to give it a piece of bread, when she saw Masani glare at her.

"Shoooo!" Grandma threw a piece of wood at the puppy.

"The puppy eats too much, even if he doesn't help us much, does he Masani?"

"Yes but he's still learning — just like you. . . . You came back from running later than yesterday," Grandma said, picking her teeth with a splinter she broke off the firewood.

"Yes Masani, I ran farther today. The sun is making me strong like you said it would if I pray for strength," Desbah said in between bites.

"Yes, but you must run every day. Then you will be strong."

After breakfast, Desbah sat on a slab of rock outside by the door finishing her cup of coffee. She was watching the sheep far off in the field. It was a cool morning, but the sun felt warm on her skin.

"Masani, I'm afraid the sheep might get lost. There's nobody watching them."

"No, they won't go very far — they didn't eat all night so they won't have the energy," Grandma said, cleaning up after breakfast.

"But aren't you afraid that the coyotes will get them? I heard them crying this morning when I was running, and they kind of scared me."

"No, sheep dogs will take care of them. Besides they won't come out this far unless they are starving. You have much to learn."

"Well, what would you do if they came too close and started to kill the sheep, Masani? What would you do?"

"I'd use that to scare them!" Grandma said, pointing at an old Winchester hanging on the wall.

"Really? You would shoot a coyote?"

"Don't be silly. The gun is just for making noise. You just shoot up into the air several times — then the coyotes get scared and run off. Only certain people can kill them, not just anyone like you or me. It would be dangerous for just anyone to kill them."

"How come only certain people can kill them?"

"Because coyotes are like holy people. They give people messages — that's why they're special. One has to have a special ceremony before they have the right to harm the coyote."

"Gosh Masani, I didn't know that." But Desbah didn't ask anymore questions because she saw that Grandma was getting annoyed.

"Let's go before the sheep go too far," Masani said.

When Grandma and Desbah reached the sheep, they gathered them up and followed them toward the hills where the piñon trees were. They both carried flour sacks for the nuts, the kind with the blue bird on it.

Desbah could feel the tiny pine needles poking through her skirt while she knelt to pick the nuts, one at a time. She carefully picked each nut, for when she picked piñons the first time, she had been scolded for picking empty shells. Now she knew well enough to pick the fresh red ones and not the gray ones. A few feet away, Masani was hitting the trees with a long stick to make the cones fall to the ground. When they hit, the cones would burst and nuts would fall out. After a while, she stopped to rest.

"Shi yazhi, climb up there and shake the tree."

She lifted Desbah into the tree. Desbah started to shake the piñon tree as hard as she could. Desbah was laughing while she shook the tree, because the cones were hitting her Masani in the head.

"Ah Yah! Wait until I'm out of the way," Grandma scolded.

Desbah stopped for a moment to check on the sheep when she suddenly saw two men wearing white men's clothes walking toward them.

"Look Masani! Somebody's coming."

Grandma lifted her out of the tree and set her on the ground. Desbah was frightened so she ran behind her Masani's long skirt. When they came closer, the smaller man was a Navajo and the taller one was a white man with a mustache.

"Who are they, Masani? I wonder what they want," Desbah said in fright. She had never seen a white man this far out before.

"They must be Gáámaliis, missionaries from the Mormon Church. They usually come around here trying to make believers out of the Navajo," Grandma said.

Desbah wondered what believers were; she wondered what they believed in. As the two men approached, they both had smiles on their faces.

334

"Yah-ta-hey!" The white man said. He reached out to shake Grandma's hand.

"Yá'at'eeh, Hello," Grandma said and shook both men's hands. Grandma didn't know how to speak English so she looked at the Navajo questioningly.

"Old one, we have come to take the little girl. She must go to school."

Grandma was not surprised. She knew this would happen soon. She looked down and seemed to notice her worn-out shoes for the first time. Desbah was frightened. She couldn't understand why she had to go to school.

"Masani, am I a bad person? Why does the white man want to take me? What did I do?" Desbah asked almost crying.

"Shh! Don't ask so many questions," Grandma said, putting her finger to her lips.

Desbah tried to focus her sight, but the blur wouldn't go away. She had always been told that if she was a bad girl, the Bilagaana–white man would come and take her away. He is said to have hair all over his body. Desbah stared at the white man's mustache, and she could see glimpses of the hair on his chest sticking out of his shirt. He even had hair on his hands. She was shaking with fright.

"Masani, no! Please don't let the white man take me away. They might kill me!" Desbah was so frightened, she remembered her mother telling her that the Bilagaana kills bad children. "He'll carry you off in a bag and club you so you don't know where he's taking you, or what he does to you. Then he kills you," Mother used to say. She always had stories like that.

"Please Masani, I've been good. I even prayed to the sun like you told me to. I don't want to die." Tears were running down Desbah's cheeks. She was holding her grandma's hand tight. Grandma looked at her pitiful grandchild.

"What has your mother told you? You mustn't talk like that, it's wrong. No one is going to hurt you." She put her arms around Desbah and squeezed her.

"No!" she said, staring at both men.

"She has no parents. You cannot take her away. She'll be too lonely. T'ah yee' 'awee' 'at'eh, she's still a baby. She does not understand this thing called school."

"Please old one, it's the law. You know that. You could be sent to jail. Then who's going to take care of her?"

The white man began to speak.

"Tell her that the school is good. It has good food, and there are other Indian children there. We'll take good care of her."

The Navajo interpreted the message.

"She's old enough to be in school. The younger they are, the better," the white man said.

"Please, old one, we have to do this, you know that. She's old enough to start learning the white man's ways. She'll have a better chance of getting a job when she grows up. I know they will take good care of her. I've been to the school. They even give the children new clothes," the Navajo explained. He did not like doing this, but it was worse when the parents said no. Many were threatened with jail until they agreed to put their children in school. He just wanted to help these people. Many just did not understand.

"And what's wrong with being a sheep herder," the old woman said. But she knew there was no arguing with these men. She remembered hearing such stories before, and she knew that there was no way out. School ruined the children. They would come home like babies, not knowing how to care for the sheep and unable to fend for themselves. School made the children forget about their people, their language, and their religion. Many returned home only to laugh at the old ones. Grandma looked at her granddaughter with tears in her eyes. They were just getting to know one another, but there was no choice.

"My little one, I don't think we can say no. I have taught you that the sheep keep us strong and if I say no, then they will take you and me away. There will be no one to take care of the sheep. Without the sheep, we will surely lose our strength."

Desbah looked down at the ground because she didn't want to see the tears in her Masani's eyes.

"We have a new program. The little girl will come home several times a year. She will have a good place to live," the Navajo said.

"What else can I say. You know I have no choice. You've already made up your minds. There's nothing else to do. I'm sure you will take good care of her," Grandma said.

"We'll have a truck to pick her up tomorrow. There will be other Navajo children on the truck."

The White man smiled and reached out to Desbah.

"There, there little girl, everything's going to be okay. Tell the old woman to have her ready by morning."

Desbah jerked away from the white man. The Navajo interpreted the message and told them good-bye. Both Desbah and her Masani were very quiet the rest of the day. They didn't pick any more piñons. They just followed the sheep in silence.

Greg Young-Ing

X Mas 92

For Kat

They say a mysterious child
was born clean
under a glistening
perfect star
long long ago

before they ever knew
the same stars shimmer
off the back of a turtle shell
far far away

On the anniversary
of that white legend
(which might have been
the end of prehistory)
I was left wondering
if your soft feet
were caressing islands of turtles
or serpent volcanos that sleep
waiting to awaken
exploding upward
into endless ocean skies

Now it is five centuries
since the white legend came

following the wrong star
misleading to our turtle

And all I can do
is wish the best in the years
already beginning to stretch out ahead
though they will not be shared
except for precious laughter and words
sent across tables
whenever drifting paths cross

After the last time
I ran into the sharp sting
of the cold night
which held me tight
just like fire heat
that lingers on my skin
pulsing
while I leave the flame

And your presence
stays too
long after
the parting

But although every moment
that the world spins around us
passes like history
nothing really leaves

Ofelia Zepeda

Pulling Down the Clouds

Ñ-ku'ipadkaj 'ant 'an o 'ols g cewagĭ.
With my harvesting stick I will hook the clouds.
Nt o 'i-wannio k o 'i-hudiñ g cewagĭ.
With my harvesting stick I will pull down the clouds.
Ñ-ku'ipadkaj 'ant o 'i-siho g cewagĭ.
With my harvesting stick I will stir the clouds.

With dreams of a distant noise disturbing his sleep,
the smell of dirt, wet, for the first time in what seemed
like months.
The change in the molecules is sudden, they enter
the nasal cavity.
He contemplates the smell, what is that smell?
It is rain.
Rain somewhere out in the desert.
Comforted in this knowledge he turns over
and continues his sleep,
dreams of women with harvesting sticks
raised toward the sky.

WORDS CANNOT SPEAK YOUR POWER
WORDS CANNOT SPEAK YOUR BEAUTY

GROWN MEN WITH DRY FEAR IN THEIR THROATS

WATCHING THE WATER COME CLOSER AND CLOSER

THEIR DRIVER TELLS THEM "IT'S JUST THE OCEAN,
IT WON'T GET YOU, WATCH IT, IT WILL ROLL AWAY AGAIN"

MEN WHO HAD NEVER SEEN THE OCEAN
IT WAS HARD NOT TO HAVE THAT FEAR THAT SITS QUIETLY
AT THE PIT OF THE STOMACH

WHY DID THE DRIVER BRING US THIS WAY?
OTHER TIMES WE CROSSED ON THE DESERT FLOOR
THAT LAND WITH HOT DRY AIR
WHERE THE SKY ENDS AT THE MOUNTAINS
THAT LAND THAT WE KNOW
THAT LAND WHERE THE OCEAN HAS NOT TOUCHED FOR
    THOUSANDS OF YEARS

WE DO NOT BELONG HERE
THIS PLACE WITH A SKY TOO ENDLESS
THIS PLACE WITH THE WATER TOO ENDLESS
THIS PLACE WITH AIR TOO THICK AND HEAVY TO BREATHE

THIS PLACE WITH THE CONSTANT ROAR AND ROLL OF THUNDER
ALWAYS PLAYING TO YOUR EARS

WE ARE NOT READY TO BE HERE
WE ARE NOT PREPARED IN THE OLD WAY

WE HAVE NO MEDICINE
WE HAVE NOT SAT AND HAD OUR MINDS WALK
THROUGH THE IMAGE OF COMING TO THE OCEAN

WE ARE NOT READY
WE HAVE NOT PUT OUR MINDS TO WHAT IT IS
WE WANT TO GIVE TO THE OCEAN
WE HAVE NO CORNMEAL, FEATHERS, NOR DO WE HAVE SONGS
    OR PRAYERS READY

WE HAVE NOT THOUGHT WHAT GIFT WE WILL ASK FROM THE
    OCEAN
SHOULD WE ASK TO BE SONG CHASERS
SHOULD WE ASK TO BE RAIN MAKERS
SHOULD WE ASK TO BE GOOD RUNNERS
OR SHOULD WE ASK TO BE HEARTBREAKERS

NO, WE ARE NOT READY TO BE HERE AT THIS OCEAN.

About the Contributors

Sherman Alexie (Spokane/Coeur D'Alene) is an enrolled Spokane/Coeur D'Alene Indian from Wellpinit, Washington, on the Spokane Indian Reservation. His poetry and fiction have appeared in *Another Chicago Magazine, Beloit Poetry Journal, Caliban, Hanging Loose, Journal of Ethnic Studies, Red Dirt,* and others. He is the author of a book of poetry, *The Business of Fancydancing,* and a collection of short stories entitled *The Lone Ranger and Tonto Fistfight in Heaven.*

Annette Arkeketa (Otoe, Missouri/Creek) is currently living in Corpus Christi, Texas ("Come Visit!"). She is president of the American Indian Resource and Education Coalition, Inc., a statewide organization in Texas to help the state understand there are Indians in Texas! Some issues the coalition is currently addressing are repatriation and Indian education. Her other involvements include work as Human Rights Advocate! and Indian Issues Activist. She is also working on a documentary about AIDS. Her work has been published in *Markings* (Nimrod Publication, Tulsa Arts and Humanities Council, 1989) and *That's What She Said* (Indiana University Press, 1984).

Jeannette C. Armstrong (Okanagan) is author of the novel *Slash,* a poetry collection entitled *Breath Tracks,* and *The Narrative Creative Process: A Collaborative Discourse* with Douglas T. Cardinal, and she is director of the En'owkin International School of Writing and Visual Arts.

Gogisgi / Carroll Arnett (Cherokee) was born and reared in Oklahoma and the Marine Corps, the old one; she was transplanted to west-central Michigan in 1970. Her most recent book is *Night Perimeter: New and Selected Poems 1958–1990* (Greenfield Review Press, 1991). "I make money, spend money, and clean. I write, shoot all manner of small arms, and smoke. I pray to and for the Earth. All the time."

343

Marilou Awiakta fuses her Cherokee and Appalachian heritages with the experience of growing up on the atomic frontier in Oak Ridge, Tennessee. Her books *Abiding Appalachia: Where Mountain and Atom Meet* and *Rising Fawn and the Fire Mystery* were chosen by the U.S. Information Agency for its 1986 global tour of American writers. *Rising Fawn and the Fire Mystery* has been called "a classic in Native young readers' literature." *Selu: Seeking the Corn Mother's Wisdom* was published by Fulcrum in 1993. Awiakta now lives in Memphis, Tennessee. She received the Distinguished Tennessee Writer Award, 1989.

Lorenzo Baca (Isleta Pueblo/Mescalero Apache). "As a visual, performing, and literary artist I draw on traditional forms with the use of modern technology to express contemporary concepts." Currently, she is focusing on performance of poetry, storytelling, and song, with a new compact disk to be released soon.

Marie Annharte Baker (Anishinabe [Saulteaux]) lives in Winnipeg, Manitoba, the "roughest toughest" urban Indian capital of North America. She is a personal essay stylist published in *Semiotexte*, and she is working as an apprentice storyteller and hopes to form a "storytelling" theater. Performance pieces on which she is working include "Alter-Native: The Only Way Outta the Present Moment"; a chapbook, "Coyote Columbus Cafe"; and a new book of poetry, "Blueberry Canoe." Her first book is entitled *Being on the Moon* (Polestar Press, Vancouver, B.C.).

José Barreiro/Hatuey (Guajiro/Camagüey) is editor-in-chief of Akwe:kon Press, Cornell University. A native of Camaqüey, Cuba, Dr. Barreiro has authored numerous articles on Native issues. His novel, *The Indian Chronicles,* was published in 1993 by Arte Publico Press.

Diane E. ("Lxeis") Benson (Tlingit ['Tak'deintaan]). "I am originally of the sea, a Sitka girl, a fishing spirit. I live in Chugiak, running dog team for fun, handling them for my son who runs them competitively. I write for my sanity, and being published is just a delightful by-product. I am working on stage scripts again. I am an actress, but am seriously turned on by directing. I just directed the 'Ecstasy of Rita Joe' for University of Alaska Mainstage, a real honor. I do theater workshops with children as an Artist in the School under the Alaska State Arts Council. All I know is I am grabbing life with two sober hands. That's all there is to say. Gunalcheesh."

Duane Big Eagle (Osage) was born at the Indian Hospital in Claremore, Oklahoma, in May 1946. He has a B.A. degree from the University of California at Berkeley and has been writing and publishing poetry for twenty years. He has taught creative writing for sixteen years through the California Poets in the Schools program and is a past president of the Board of Directors of that organization. A lecturer in American Indian Studies at San Francisco State University, his new manuscript, "Birthplace: Poems and Paintings on the Modern World," is scheduled to be published by Clark City Press in Montana in 1994.

"As an American Indian youth," he writes, "I was taught to value a connection with the land which sustains our lives. I learned early that individuality, creativity, self-expression, and love of beauty are essential to the survival of a whole and healthy person. And I experienced the roles that art, music, and poetry play in the passing of culture from one generation to another. These lessons and values have formed the person I have become — writer, painter, artist in education, community organizer, and cultural activist."

Gloria Bird (Spokane) is co-winner of the Returning the Gift–Diane Decorah First Book Award for Poetry. Born in Sunnyside, Washington, in the Yakima Valley, she grew up on the Spokane Reservation and on the adjoining Colville Reservation where her mother now lives in Nespelem. A survivor of the reservation mission schools and BIA boarding schools, she has an M.A. in literature from the University of Arizona. Currently, she is working on a new manuscript of poetry and teaching creative writing and literature at the Institute of American Indian Arts in Santa Fe, New Mexico.

Kimberly M. Blaeser is of mixed ancestry, Anishinabe and German. She is an enrolled member of the Minnesota Chippewa Tribe and grew up on White Earth Reservation. She is currently an assistant professor at the University of Wisconsin, Milwaukee, where her teaching area includes Native American literature. Blaeser's own writing — poetry, short fiction, personal essays, journalism, reviews, and scholarly articles — has appeared in various journals and collections including *World Literature Today, Gatherings, Akiwetcon, American Indian Quarterly, Cream City Review, American Book Review,* and *Narrative Chance: Postmodern Discourse on Native American Indian Literature.*

Tracey Kim Bonneau (Okanagan). "I write only in my spare time. I'm hoping one day to write a script for a feature film. I was born and raised in the Okanagan Valley. I am an Okanagan from the Okanagan Tribe."

Beth Brant (Mohawk). "I am the editor of *A Gathering of Spirit,* an anthology of native women's writing and art. I'm the author of *Food & Spirits.* Am currently working on a book of essays about land and spirit. Have taught and lectured throughout North America. I'm a lesbian mother and grandmother, and divide my time between living in Michigan and Canada."

Charles Brashear (Cherokee). "I had stories recently in *Studies in American Indian Literatures, Fiction International, Four Quarters,* and other quarterlies. I'm working on a novel, 'Under the Dawn Star: A California Indian-Family Chronicle, 1832–1973.'"

William Bray (Muskogee [Creek] Kialegee Tribal Town). "I am from Wetumka, Oklahoma, and have attended Dartmouth College and Oklahoma City University. I am currently at Stanford University where I study and work for the Native American Program. I am greatly influenced by other Creek poets such as Joy Harjo, Louis Oliver, and my friend Annette Arkeketa, as well as the rhythms of our elders. Creek people sing when they speak and always have a good joke to tell. *Mvto.*"

Silvester J. Brito (Comanche/Tarascan). "My work as a poet comes from the lives of the people (Native Americans) I have lived with. Most of my poems are thus based on these learned experiences — reflecting either a metaphysical or a philosophical view on life. I am also very interested in the field of folk medicine, especially as practiced by the shamans in the New World."

Barney Bush (Shawnee/Cayuga). "Grandson of Clyde & Etta (Tyner) Vinyard, and Robert & Hattie (Reynolds) Bush, I was instilled by first memories with a belief in Native Nationalism. Traveling and surviving at the psychotic edge of colonial oppression, I am still alive by the spirit of language. I write and perform and am wearied by listing part publications. The current one is a two-volume compact disk, 'Remake of the American Dream,' from NATO Records in Paris, France, 1993."

Bobbie Louise Bush (Chehalis). "During my childhood and part of my adulthood I have survived physical, sexual, emotional, and spiritual abuse, and because I have survived, I possess the tenacity to continue my growth. I was born in San Rafael, California, and lived near there until April 1989, when I moved to Washington State. Raised in a state separate from my family and culture, I feel many of the challenges I faced are related to the separation from my culture. I returned to Washington to be closer to my family and to learn about my culture and traditions.

"I was sidetracked for a few years by drugs and alcohol. When I sobered up, I dreamed of working for a Native newspaper. I realized part of that dream when I began working for the Skokomish Tribe in August of 1989. I feel it is very important to provide a 'Voice' for my tribal community. There are so many things written in 'mainstream' media about us as Native people, I feel it is necessary to provide an accurate Native viewpoint.

"Currently, I am enrolled full-time at the Evergreen State College through the Native American Community Based/Community Determined Liberal Arts Degree Program. My friends and I have formed an Olympic Peninsula Native Writers Group. We learned at the 'Returning the Gift' experience that as indigenous people it is time to begin telling our own stories."

E. K. Caldwell (Tsalagi [Cherokee], Creek, Shawnee, Celtic and German). She currently lives and works in Depoe Bay, on the Central Oregon coast. She is the author and narrator of the dance piece, "When The Animals Danced," which is currently being performed as part of an international dance exchange program. Her work is included on the Harbinger NW Cassette Sampler "Lights." She also writes for *Perpetua*, a coastal magazine.

Jeanetta Calhoun is of mixed Lenápe and European ancestry. She is an activist for Native American rights and a freelance writer and poet. Her poetry has been published in *Piecework*, *SAIL*, and *Pig Iron Press* and accepted for publication in *Reinventing the Enemy's Language*. Other published work includes a book review for *Parabola*, critical essays, and lyrics for a song recorded by a rock group in Pisa, Italy. Ms. Calhoun is currently working on a play tentatively titled "Heroes."

Chrystos (Menominee) was born off-reservation in San Francisco on November 7, 1946. He is a land and treaty rights activist, also working toward freedom for Leonard Peltier and Norma Jean Croy. He is author of *Not Vanishing* and *Dream On*.

Robert J. Conley (Cherokee [UKB]) is author of *Mountain Windsong, Nickajack,* and *The Witch of Goingsnake and Other Stories* and lives in Tahlequah, Oklahoma, the historic capital of the Cherokee Nations, with his wife Evelyn, also Cherokee. Conley is writing full-time.

Elizabeth Cook-Lynn is a poet and fiction writer whose work focuses on a particular geography, the Northern Plains, and culture, the Lakota/Dakota Sioux of North and South Dakota. She is a member of the Crow Creek Sioux Tribe, born and raised at Ft. Thompson, South Dakota. She is a professor emeritus in Native studies and English at Eastern Washington State, Cheney, Washington, and a Visiting Professor at the University of California at Davis.

She comes from a family of Sioux politicians — her father and grandfather served on the Crow Creek Sioux Tribal Council for many years — and from Native scholars. Her grandmother was a bilingual writer for early Christian-oriented newspapers at Sisseton, South Dakota, and an elder grandfather, Gabriel Renville, was a Native linguist instrumental in developing early Dakotah language dictionaries.

In addition to teaching, she is a founding editor of *The Wicazo Sa Review,* a Native American Studies journal that has achieved a national reputation for excellence. Her poetry, fiction, and essays have appeared in scholarly journals. Her poetry collections include *Then Badger Said This* and *Seek the House of Relatives. The Power of Horses,* a collection of short fiction, and her 1991 summer-release novel, *From the River's Edge,* are both published by Arcade Publishing (Little, Brown & Co.), New York, New York.

Kateri Damm (Ojibway/Chippewas of Nawash Band). "I am a Band member of the Chippewas of Nawash, on the Cape Croker Reserve in southwestern Ontario. I was born in Toronto in 1965 and lived there until 1976 when my family moved to the Owen Sound area. I am currently living in Ottawa where I am completing my master's degree in English literature. My first chapbook was published in April 1993. I thank my grandmother O. Irene Akiwenzie for giving me words and the courage to voice them."

Nora Marks Dauenhauer (Tlingit) was born (1927) in Juneau, Alaska, and was raised in Juneau and Hoonah, as well as on the family fishing boat and in seasonal subsistence sites around Icy Straits, Glacier Bay, and Cape Spencer. Her first language is Tlingit; she began to learn English when entering school at the age of eight. She has a B.A. in anthropology (Alaska Methodist University, 1976) and is internationally recognized for her fieldwork, transcription, translation, and explication of Tlingit oral literature. Her poetry, prose, and drama have been widely published and anthologized. She is principal researcher in language and cultural studies at Sealaska Heritage Foundation in Juneau. She has four children and thirteen grandchildren.

Charlotte DeClue (Wa-zha-zhe [Osage]). "I am a 44-year-old Osage Indian woman who has survived the last several years of the Bush and Reagan administrations, which is an accomplishment in itself. I am 'from' the place where I, and my people, continue to 'make our stand': Indian Territory, despite concentrated efforts to annihilate us. For the last several years my work as a Native poet has appeared in numerous journals, anthologies, and magazines, in the United States and in Europe. My most recent work has appeared in 'Ten Good Horses,' in a book entitled *Stiletto 2: The Disinherited.* Since then I have been working on a series of fictional character sketches and short stories."

Ed Edmo (Shoshone/Bannock). His poetry has been published internationally in *A Nation Within* (New Zealand, 1983). He is a founding member of the Northwest Native American Writers Association. His plays have won awards in Oregon and he has written a movie script and wants to write movies and for the theater.

Melissa Fawcett (Mohegan) is the official historian for the Mohegan Nation in Uncasville, Connecticut. She is the winner of the 1992 Returning The Gift First Book Award in the category of Creative Nonfiction for her manuscript *The Lasting of the Mohegans.* Melissa lives in her homeland with her husband, Bart, an attorney, and three young children.

Connie Fife's (Cree) work has appeared in numerous journals including *Fireweed: A Feminist Quarterly* and *Gatherings.* Her book of poetry, *Beneath the Naked Sun,* was published in 1992.

Chris Fleet (Akwesasne Mohawk). "Age 23. Got a B.A. from Hamilton College in Creative Writing. Right now I'm trying to find a publisher for my first collection of stories and poems currently titled 'Love and Rattlesnakes.' In the spring of 1993 I had my first public poetry readings."

Jack D. Forbes (Renápe/Lenápe) is author of *Columbus and Other Cannibals* (1992), *Africans and Native Americans* (1988, 1993), *Tribes and Masses* (1978), and many other works. He is co-founder of D-Q University; director of Native American studies at the University of California at Davis; editor of *Warpath,* 1968–69; and coeditor and editor of *Attan-Akamik* (Powhatan-Renápe Nation).

Della Frank (Navajo). "I am of Navajo — Beside the Water Clan — origin. I now live near the Four Corners area of the World. I am in the process of getting ready for 'an artist show' in Cortez, Colorado. I will read my works and discuss 'origins of my life' as best as I know how. I also have a book coming out from Navajo Community College Press entitled *Duststorms: Poems from Two Navajo Women,* with another writer. I live and work on the Navajo Reservation. This year I am an administrator. I oversee a dormitory, the staff at this dormitory, and the Navajo-Ute students who reside at this dormitory. I would like to continue my writing, which gives me courage, identity, and strength — as a Native American in the hardships of America. I have three children. I am alone. I like solitude — it gives me time to think."

José L. Garza / Blue Heron (Coahuilteca/Lipan Apache). "I was born in San Antonio, Texas, but have lived most of my life in the northern United States. I started writing seriously in 1980 after being a visual artist for about eight years, although I have been doing both since age 12. I write mainly short stories/observations and poetry and limit my art to illustrations and graphics. I have been published in over thirty-five publications, including *The Great Lakes Review, New Rain Anthology, Black Bear Review, Akwekon, The Wooster Review, Poetry East, HIPology Anthology, The Wayne Review,* and *Triage.* I have published three books of poetry and short stories: *Masks, Folk Dances and a Whole Bunch More; Kamikaze;* and *Momentos.* Currently, I am involved with lecturing about writing and native culture and working on a new manuscript. I am a member of Casa De Unidad Community Arts Center, Kanto De La Tierra, Wordcraft Circle, and the Native Writers Circle of the Americas."

Robert Franklin Gish (Cherokee Nation of Oklahoma) is director of ethnic studies at California Polytechnic State University, San Luis Obispo. His most recent books are *First Horses: Stories of the New West* (University of Nevada Press, Reno) and *Songs of My Hunter Heart: A Western Kinship* (Iowa State University Press, Ames). He is a contributing editor to the *Bloomsbury Review* and on the editorial boards of the *American Indian Culture and Research Journal* and *Western American Literature.*

Diane Glancy (Cherokee) teaches Native American literature and creative writing at Macalester College in St. Paul, Minnesota. Her second collection of fiction, *Firesticks,* was just published by the University of Oklahoma Press, Native American Literature and Critical Studies Series.

Mary Goose (Mesquakie/Chippewa). "I have a card that my friends Dennis and Paula gave me years ago. I keep it, because it reminds me of me — my life, my writing, everything. On the front of the card is a herd of buffalo stampeding. One of the buffalo says to the one next to it, 'As if we all knew where we're going.'

"When I write that is how it usually turns out. One of my poems started out being the great idea that I would write the science fiction story that I have always wanted to do. Instead it ended up being a poem about a cornfield here on earth in Iowa that is near my family's home in Tama. The only thing I have learned to do is say 'Oh well, that's how it's supposed to be.' If I had learned to be this way or think that way twenty years ago, just think where I might be now. 'Oh well, that's how it's supposed to be.' "

Roxy Gordon is a writer and performer of Choctaw Indian descent who was, in July 1991, adopted into the Assiniboine tribe at the Fort Belknap Reservation in northern Montana. He was adopted by the John and Minerva Allen family in a traditional ceremony at the Assiniboine Sundance. His new name is *Toe Ga Juke Juke Gan Hok Sheena,* which means *First Coyote Boy.*

Roxy Gordon has released three record albums, the last two being released by Sunstorm Records of London, England. He is the author of six published books and approximately 200 published poems, short stories, articles, and essays. His work is used in several college Indian Studies courses and in the creative writing program at Schreiner College in Kerrville, Texas.

He has coauthored two plays, *Big Pow Wow* and *Indian Radio Days.* Both were written with Oklahoma Choctaw writer LeAnne Howe.

Janice Gould (Maidu/Konkow). "I was born in San Diego, and grew up in Berkeley, California. I attended U.C. Berkeley where I earned degrees in linguistics and English. I now live in Albuquerque, where I attend the University of New Mexico. I'm working on a Ph.D. in English, with an emphasis in American Indian literature. In 1988, I received a grant from the NEA, and in 1990 my first book of verse, *Beneath My Heart,* was published by Firebrand Books. Last year I was given a writing award from the ASTRAEA foundation."

Richard G. Green, a turtle clan Mohawk, was born on the Six Nations Reserve where he now lives. In 1973 he was an editor on the staff of *Indian Voice Magazine,* in Santa Clara, California, to which he contributed short stories. Other short stories appear in Indian publications and anthologies in the United States and Canada. His "Our Town" column has appeared since 1987 in the *Brantford Expositor.* He is Writer in Residence at the Mississaugas of the New Credit First Nation Library, where he is currently working on a screenplay.

Raven Hail of Mesa, Arizona, is a Cherokee Indian from Oklahoma and Texas. Her stories and poems have been widely published. Her books currently in print are *The Raven Speaks, Windsong, The Pleiades Stones, Native American Foods,* and *The Raven and the Redbird* (a play in three acts).

Joy Harjo (Creek) was born in Tulsa, Oklahoma, in 1951 and is an enrolled member of the Creek Tribe. She graduated in 1968 from the Institute of American Indian Arts and from the University of New Mexico in 1976. In 1978 she received an M.F. A. in Creative Writing from the Iowa Writer's Workshop at the University of Iowa. She also completed the film-making program at the Anthropology Film Center. She has published four books of poetry including *She Had Some Horses* (Thunder's Mouth Press) and the award-winning *In Mad Love and War* (Wesleyan University Press). *Secrets From the Center of the World* (University of Arizona Press, Tucson) is a collaboration with photographer/astronomer Stephen Strom. Currently professor of English in the creative writing program at the University of New Mexico, Joy has received numerous awards, including the William Carlos Williams Award from the Poetry Society of America, the American Book Award, and two National Endowment for the Arts Creative Writing Fellowships. Her forthcoming works include a children's book, *The Goodluck Cat,* (Harcourt Brace & Jovanovich), and an anthology of Native American women's writing, *Reinventing the Enemy's Language,* from the University of Arizona Press, Tucson. Joy gives poetry readings nationally and internationally, and she plays saxophone with her band, Poetic Justice.

Gordon Henry (White Earth Chippewa [Anishinabe]) has been published in *Earth Power Coming, Songs from This Earth,* and *North Dakota Quarterly,* among other journals. He has a novel scheduled for release by University of Oklahoma Press in 1994, and he is currently putting together a collection of poems as well as a second novel.

Lance Henson is a member of the Southern Cheyenne Nation, an accomplished poet, and an activist for Native American rights. He has published sixteen books of poetry both in the United States and Europe, and his work has been widely anthologized. He has written lyrics for an Italian rock music album and for *Winter Man,* a musical theater piece produced off-Broadway in 1991. Lance co-wrote *Coyote Road,* a play produced in 1992 by Mad River Theatre Works of West Liberty, Ohio. He is currently working on a new manuscript of poetry entitled "Between the Dark and the Light" and is collaborating on a play commissioned by a theater company in Indianapolis. He is also collaborating with Barbara Santoro of Long Island, New York, on a series of poem-paintings.

Geary Hobson (Cherokee-Quapaw/Chickasaw) is a professor of English, specializing in Native American literature, at the University of Oklahoma. He is the author of *Deer Hunting and Other Poems* (1990) and the editor of *The Remembered Earth: An Anthology of Contemporary Native American Literature* (1979). He has served since 1991 as the project historian of Returning the Gift, otherwise known as the Native Writers Circle of the Americas.

Linda Hogan's (Chickasaw) newest book of poems, *The Book of Medicines,* was published in 1993 by Coffee House Press. She is at work on a new novel and essays on environmental issues.

Andrew Hope (Sitka Tribe of Alaska [Tlingit]) is a member of the Sik'nax°ádi clan of the wolf moiety of the Tlingit. He currently serves as president of the Before Columbus Foundation.

LeAnne Howe, Choctaw, is an author, playwright, and poet. She has two collections of short fiction, and her work has been published in several American Indian anthologies, including *Spiderwoman's Granddaughters, American Indian Literature, Fiction International #20, Looking Glass, Reinventing the Enemy's Language, Earth Song, Sky Spirit: An Anthology of Native American Writers,* and various poetry journals. In 1991 she received an NEH grant to research a novel she is currently writing called "The Bone Picker."

Her first album, *Hawk in Hand,* is coproduced with musician Jarryd Lowder. She has collaborated on several projects with Choctaw poet Roxy Gordon. Their first play, *Big Pow Wow,* was produced in Fort Worth in 1987 by the African-American theater company, Sojourner Truth Players. Howe and Gordon also wrote *Indian Radio Days,* a theatrical radio program produced in the fall of 1993. She has collaborated on several nonfiction historical articles about her tribe with Choctaw attorney and author Scott Morrison.

"As a Choctaw, I grew up in a house of women. From my single mother, the other women in my family, my mother's friends: I was influenced by the way they managed their lives. These very strong Indian women were providers: mother, father, friend, and sometimes enemy. I learned to be my own woman from watching them. I can't imagine a life any other way."

Alex Jacobs (Mohawk). "I've been waiting the whole term of George Bush to have my 'latest' material published. It's titled *Loving...in the Reagan Era.*"

As of October 1992, Alex is a head writer and a lead vocalist-performer for a performance-band called Tribal Dada, a five-member group, four of whom are Native Americans. All are artists based in Santa Fe, New Mexico.

Lenore Keeshig-Tobias (Ojibway/Pottawatomi) is a writer, storyteller, and cultural worker residing part-time in Toronto and at Neyaashiinigmiing, her home reserve on the Bruce Peninsula. She has published articles, poetry, children's literature, and drama, and has helped develop curricular material for use in Native schools and in Canadian journals.

Keeshig-Tobias has been actively promoting the production and dissemination of Native literature in Canada, working in close connection with other authors and initiating and founding the influential COMMITTEE TO RE-ESTABLISH THE TRICKSTER (CRET). Keeshig-Tobias has come out strongly on several occasions against cultural appropriation. The wide attention this issue is receiving in the arts community across Canada is mainly due to her work on the issue. She has also been influential in the formation of an alliance between racial minority writers (First Nations, Asian-Canadian, South-Asian Canadian, and African Canadian) around the issues of cultural appropriation and racial inequity in the arts.

Maurice Kenny (Mohawk) was born in 1929 between the St. Lawrence and Black rivers. He has been poet-in-residence at North Country Community College in Saranac Lake, New York, and a visiting professor at Oklahoma State University in Norman, Oklahoma. One of the founding editors of the literary review magazine *Contact II,* he is editor and publisher of Strawberry Press. His books include *Between Two Rivers: Selected Poems, Rain and Other Fictions, The Mama Poems,* and the recently published *Tekonwatonti/Molly Brant (1735–1795): Poems of War.* The book is a collection of narrative poems that trace the life of the Mohawk woman Molly Brant, the wife of Sir William Johnson and the sister of Chief Joseph Brant, revealing the historical and spiritual reality of this heroic woman, who eventually led her people in a futile attempt to hold their ancestral lands.

Harold Littlebird (Laguna/Santo Domingo) is a poet, musician, storyteller, and potter, and his poems have appeared in many magazines and anthologies, including *Songs from This Earth on Turtle's Back* and *The Remembered Earth.* He is the author of a book of poetry, *On Mountain's Breath* (1982), and has two audio-cassette tapes of original poetry and music: *A Circle Begins* and *The Road Back In.*

Mary Lockwood (Inupiaq) is a native from Unalakleet, Alaska. In 1970, she attended the University of California at Santa Cruz, where she graduated in 1986 with a B.A. in community studies. She has two sons, Brook and Ben Wynn. Mary lives in Santa Cruz, writing for periodicals and compiling a fictionalized autobiography of her first decade. Her stories are published in *Raven Tells Stories* (Greenfield Review Press, 1991) and will be seen in *Daughters of the First People,* an anthology of Native women (1993) and *The Colour of Resistance* (Sister Vision Press, 1993).

Evelina Zuni Lucero (Isleta/San Juan Pueblo) is working on a novel, "Fancy Dancer," chapter excerpts of which have been published in *Blue Mesa Review* (Spring 1989) and *Northeast Indian Quarterly* (Winter 1991). She teaches composition and Native American literature at the University of New Mexico in Albuquerque and at UNM–Valencia campus.

Mazii / Rex Lee Jim (Diné [Navajo]). "I am of the Red House Clan. I am born for Red Streak Running Into Water Clan. My maternal grandfather is of the Towering House clan. My paternal grandfather is of the Wandering People. I am from Tsé Dildó'ii, eight miles southwest of Rock Point, Arizona. My grandfather's name was Hosteen Yellowman. He was a well-known medicine man. All the stories I tell belong to where I come from, who I am, and where I am going."

Daniel David Moses (Delaware), poet and playwright, lives and writes full-time in Toronto. His publications include the books of poems *Delicate Bodies* (Nightwood Edition, Harbour Publishing, 1992) and *The White Line* (Fifth House, 1990) and the plays *Coyote City* (1990) and *Almighty Voice and His Wife* (1992) (both from Williams-Wallace). He also coedited *An Anthology of Canadian Native Literature in English* with Terry Goldie for Oxford University Press, 1992.

Julie Moss is a Cherokee tribal member, born and raised in Cherokee settlements in northeast Oklahoma. Primarily a poet, she also writes interviews, articles, and essays and does some photography. In 1981, she co-founded a local Indian Writers' Group. As a result, *Echoes of Our Being,* a book of the group's poetry, was published by Indian University Press in 1982. In 1992, she founded and established an international journal of Indigenous worldview, *The Indigenous Eye.* Originally an experimental quarterly, it is being restructured as a biannual. She serves as the editor-in-chief. She serves on the Indigenous Peoples Task Force of Amnesty International and lives in the country near Stilwell, Oklahoma, with her husband and son.

Joe Dale Tate Nevaquaya (Yuchi/Comanche) is a visual artist as well as poetry maker. He is co-winner of the 1992 Returning the Gift–Diane Decorah Memorial Award for a First Book of Poetry entitled *Leaving Holes,* publication of which is pending with Contact II Publications. He is recently returned from France where he read and exhibited at several art institutes. Although he now resides in Bristow, Oklahoma, he was raised by a grandmother, Polly Long, who shaped his artistic and poetic sensibilities through the lesson that "What is shared will be returned." This remains the powerful mandate by which the poet makes his art.

Duane Niatum (Klallam [Jamestown band]) was born and still lives in Seattle, Washington. He has published poems, stories, and essays in over a hundred magazines and newspapers in the United States and Europe. Recently he published his fifth volume of poetry, *Drawings of the Song Animals: New and Selected Poems* (Holy Cow Press, Duluth, Minnesota, 1991). He has a collection of stories and essays now making the rounds of the publishers. He is an enrolled member of the Klallam tribe (Jamestown band) of Washington State.

Jim Northrup's (Chippewa [Anishinabe]) stories have been featured in such anthologies as *Touchwood: An Anthology of Ojibway Prose, Stillers Pond,* and *North Writers.* His poems have appeared in numerous literary magazines and his book of poems and fiction, *Walking the Rez Road,* was published by

Voyageur Press in 1993. He writes a syndicated column called "The Fond du Lac Follies" and works as a roster artist for the COMPAS Writer-in-the-Schools Program. Northrup, his wife Patricia, and their family live the traditional life of the Chippewa on the Fond du Lac Reservation in northern Minnesota.

nila northSun (Shoshone/Chippewa). "Living on my rez in Fallon, Nevada. I am the director of an emergency Teen Shelter. Since participating in the 'Gift' Conference in 1992, I've poked the smoldering writing coals and started writing and submitting again. A book of old and new poems will be published in 1994."

Simon J. Ortiz (Acoma). "I've been a poet, writer, and storyteller for over thirty years, mainly trying to demystify language and enhance its meaning for me and readers and listeners. My teaching experience as a university instructor is extensive and well-established; I've taught for varying periods of time at the Institute of American Indian Arts, University of New Mexico, Navajo Community College, Sinte Gleska College, San Diego State University, College of Marin, Lewis & Clark College, Colorado College, and others. Usually I've taught Native American literature and creative writing (poetry and fiction). I've done poetry readings, some lectures, and storytellings across most of the United States, as well as several countries in Europe. I have three children, Raho Nez, Rainy Dawn, and Sara Marie. In the late 1980s I held official tribal positions as Interpreter and 1st Lt. Governor of Acoma Pueblo, my native community, in New Mexico. Most of my cultural and literary work continues to focus on issues, concerns, and responsibilities we, as Native Americans, have for our land, culture, and community."

Juanita Pahdopony (Comanche) is included in "Directory of Native American Writers," Fulcrum Press, Boulder, Colorado, 1993. She is currently exhibiting a painting, "Peyote Women," in the Denver Art Museum's show "Native Peoples" with fourteen Native artists from Plains Tribes across the United States. She serves on the National Advisory Caucus for Wordcraft Circle of the Native American Mentor and Apprentice Writers, is a Title V tutor/counselor at the elementary school level, and a high-school art instructor at Geary Public Schools — working with Cheyenne and Arapaho Tribes.

Elise Paschen's (Osage) chapbook, *Houses: Coasts,* was published in England, 1985, by the Sycamore Press. Her poems have appeared in *Poetry* magazine, *Poetry Review* (England), *Poetry Ireland,* and *Oxford Magazine*. She attended the Returning the Gift Festival in her capacity as executive director of the Poetry Society of America.

Robert L. Perea (Ogala Lakota [Sioux]). "I am presently the Native American Student Adviser at Central Arizona College. I'm a Vietnam vet and a graduate of the University of New Mexico. I won the First Book Award — Short Fiction at the Returning the Gift Festival in 1992 for *Stacey's Story*. I also play a mean game of 'Old Timer's' Indian Basketball."

Suzanne S. Rancourt (Abenaki) was born and raised in the mountains of west-central Maine and currently resides in Stony Creek, New York. She has had extensive counseling experience as well as herbal training. Her occupational diversity and philosophy have taken her to schools, stages, and conferences nationwide. Currently, Suzanne is exploring certification in writing therapy (much like art therapy). Her work has appeared in various publications including *Mildred* and *Tamaqua*.

Carter Revard / Nompewathe (Osage) is from Oklahoma. He was born in Pawhuska and grew up in Buck Creek Community on Osage Reservation. He is part Osage, part Irish and Scotch-Irish, with Ponca relatives. He was given an Osage name in 1952. He has been published in *Greenfield Review, Nimrod, Massachusetts Review,* and *Denver Quarterly,* among others. His published collections include *Ponca War Dancers* and *Cowboys & Indians, Christmas Shopping,* both published by Point Riders Press (1980 and 1992 respectively). His latest book, *An Eagle Nation,* was published as Sun Tracks #24 by the University of Arizona Press, Tucson (1993).

Wendy Rose (Hopi/Miwok) is an award-winning poet whose books include *Lost Copper* (1980), *What Happened When the Hopi Hit New York* (1982), *The Halfbreed Chronicles* (1985), *Going to War with All My Relations* (1993), and *Bone Dance* (1994). She has held positions with the Women's Literature Project of Oxford University Press, the Smithsonian Native Writers' Series, the Modern Language Association Commission on Languages and Literature of the Americas and the Coordinating Council of Literary Magazines. She is currently the coordinator of American Indian Studies at Fresno City College, where she is also a full-time instructor.

Armand Garnet Ruffo was born and raised in northern Ontario, Canada, and draws upon his Ojibway heritage for his work. An alumnus of the writing program at the Banff Centre School of Fine Arts, he also holds an M.A. in literature and creative writing from the University of Windsor. He has had work published in *An Anthology of Native Canadian Literature in English* (Oxford University Press, 1992) and recently in *Absinthe* magazine's anthology, "The Skin on Our Tongues" (1993).

Ralph Salisbury (Cherokee). "My books of poems, *Going to the Water, Pointing at the Rainbow, Spirit Beast Chant,* and *A White Rainbow,* are available from Greenfield Review Literary Center. My book of short stories, *One Indian and Two Chiefs,* is available from Navajo Community College Press. I am continuing work on four interrelated novels. The first of these, *A Raven Mocker War,* is now completed, and I am now revising the second novel, *The Charity War.* I teach fiction writing at the University of Oregon in Eugene, where I live with my wife, poet Ingrid Wendt. I have two sons, one daughter, and two grandsons."

Carol Lee Sanchez (Laguna). "I was born into the Oak Clan of Laguna Pueblo in 1934 and left rural New Mexico for the big city of San Francisco in 1964 where I joined the 'North Beach Arts Scene' as a painter and poet. In 1976 I joined the American Indian Studies faculty at San Francisco State University and taught there until 1985. In 1987 my husband and I opened an American Indian Art Gallery — for Indian artists only — in Santa Barbara, California, and had to close it in 1989. Since then we have lived on a farm near Sedalia, Missouri. Currently, I am delighted to be conducting poetry workshops in our rural county elementary schools, teaching a class at Missouri University in Columbia, and working on a couple of essays, some new poems, and paintings."

Cheryl Savageau (Abenaki) is the author of *Home Country.* She has been awarded fellowships in poetry by the National Endowment for the Arts and the Massachusetts Artists Foundation. Her poetry has been anthologized in *An Ear to the Ground, Reinventing the Enemy's Language,* and *Two Worlds Walking,* and has appeared in several literary journals. She works as a writer-in-the-schools and as a storyteller. She lives in Worcester, Massachusetts, with her husband and son.

Michael W. Simpson (Cherokee/Yakima). "Most of my people have lived in the Northwest for a long time, both Anglo and Indian. My ancestors lived along the Columbia River and the coastal bays, and their descendants still do. I was educated in many schools and have A.A., B.G.S., M.F.A., and Ph.D. degrees. I worked as a journalist and cultural consultant on the Oregon coast for ten years, and have published more than a hundred articles and three books on Indian culture while also teaching at every level from elementary to university. I'm currently writing an Indian Studies text, several books of poetry, three novels, a couple of nonfiction books, and a collection of short stories."

Virginia Driving Hawk Sneve (Rosebud Sioux) is author of eight published children's books. She has also published historic nonfiction for adults. She is the

1992 recipient of the University of Nebraska Press's Native American Prose Award and works as a high school counselor and associate instructor in English at Oglala Lakota College.

Jean Starr (Cherokee). "I teach English and ethnic studies at American Legion High School in Sacramento, an inner-city alternative school. I've been published in *Nimrod, Tamaqua,* and *Poetry East,* and I'm going to be published in *The Eagle* and *Thema.* I also wrote *Tales from the Cherokee Hills* (John F. Blair, Publisher, Winston-Salem). I would never have written this short story without the inspiration of Returning the Gift."

Denise Sweet (White Earth Anishinabe) teaches creative writing and American Indian literature at the University of Wisconsin, Green Bay. She is working on a collection of poems, her second. Her first collection, entitled *Know by Heart,* was published in 1992. Her poems have appeared in *Calyx, Sinister Wisdom, Transactions, Wisconsin Academy Review, Wisconsin Poetry,* and other journals.

Luci Tapahonso (Navajo) is originally from Shiprock, New Mexico, on the Navajo Nation, and is an assistant professor at the University of Kansas in Lawrence. She is the author of three books of poetry, and her fourth, *Sáanii Dahataa,* was published by the University of Arizona Press in 1993.

Drew Hayden Taylor (Ojibway) is an award-winning playwright, scriptwriter, and journalist. Originally from the Curve Lake First nations, Drew considers himself a contemporary storyteller, who uses the various media to get his message across. He has just celebrated the publication of his fourth book.

Earle Thompson (Yakima) is author of *The Juniper Moon Pulls at My Bones* (1985), and his poems have appeared in *Songs From This Earth on Turtle's Back* (1983) and *Dancing on the Rim of the World* (1990).

Laura Tohe (Navajo) is Diné. She is the author of *Making Friends with Water.* She is currently writing a children's play for the Omaha Emmy Gifford Children's Theatre. In 1993 she graduated from the University of Nebraska with a Ph.D. in English literature. She is the mother of two boys.

Haunani-Kay Trask (Hawaiian) is descended of the Pi'ilani line of Maui and the Kahakumakaliua line of Kaua'i. She is a Hawaiian nationalist, a professor of Hawaiian Studies at the University of Hawai'i, and an author of scholarly and literary works. Her books include political theory, *Eros and Power* (1986), a collection of essays, *From a Native Daughter* (1993), and a book of poetry, *Light in the Crevice Never Seen,* forthcoming from Calyx Books, 1994.

Gail Tremblay (Onondaga/Micmac) has written three books of poetry. The most recent is *Indian Singing in 20th Century America* from Calyx Books (Corvallis, Oregon, 1990). She has also been published in *Denver Quarterly, Northwest Review,* and *Calyx,* and in numerous anthologies. In addition she is a widely exhibited visual artist.

Georgiana Valoyce-Sanchez (Tohono O'odham–Pima/Chumash). "I am the daughter of an O'odham mother and a Chumash father, both from a time when the world was very different. I was formed by the stories they told and by the land they loved. It is my responsibility to live the stories and to pass them on. As a teacher of American Indian literature and Native American women's literature at California State University, Long Beach, I am taught by some of the best writers in the world. My work has been published in *The Stories We Hold Secret* (Greenfield Review Press), *Invocation L.A.* (West End Press), and *The Sound of Rattles and Clappers* (University of Arizona Press, Tucson), to name a few. The Stories Live. I am grateful."

Judith Mtn. Leaf Volborth (Blackfoot/Comanche). "I am currently working on four collections of poetry which include a book of Coyote poems, free verse, haiku, and a collection of sensual poetry entitled 'Pollen-Leggings.' I am blessed with much beauty in my life. I love cats and adventure, and I am homesick for the Northeast."

Her work has been published in *Talking Leaf, Westwind: A Quarterly of the Arts, The Nishnawbe News, A: A Journal of Contemporary Literature, The Denver Quarterly, Shantih, Alcheringa, North Dakota Quarterly, Plainswoman, Calapooya Collage, Windchimes, Gatherings, The Third Woman: Minority Women Writers of the United States, Native American Renaissance, That's What She Said, Native American Literatures,* and *Reinventing the Enemy's Language,* and she has a collection of poetry entitled *Thunder-Root: Traditional and Contemporary Native American Verse,* published by the American Indian Studies Center, UCLA.

Ron Welburn (Cherokee/Conoy). "Though growing up in Philadelphia where I fell in love with jazz, I spent a lot of time in rural Berwyn where I started school. Both parents are of Cherokee ancestry; the Wests on Mom's side are listed in the 1851 Siler Roll. Other family branches come from the Delmarva and various parts of eastern Pennsylvania; and like many Natives here we are part African American. I've published other collections of poems but those in *Council Decisions* (American Native Press Archives, 1991) are my strongest. I teach a range of American literatures in the English department at the University of Massachusetts at Amherst, and my wife and I sell books for the Native American Authors Distribution Project at powwows throughout the Northeast. In the past few years my poems have appeared in *Gatherings, Pig Iron,* the *SAIL* poetry issue, and *Archeae.*"

Jordan Wheeler (Cree/Anishinabe/Assiniboine) writes stories for many media, including television and books. He lives in Winnipeg with his wife Tanis, children Kaya and Cam, and their two cats, Ovide and Phil.

Roberta Hill Whiteman (Oneida). "I am a poet, fiction writer, and scholar, currently working on completing my dissertation, a biography of Dr. L. Rosa Minoka-Hill, my grandmother. I recently completed a second collection of poems, titled *Philadelphia Flowers,* to be published by Holy Cow! Press. My fiction appears in *Talking Leaves,* edited by Craig Leslie."

Ramona C. Wilson (Colville [Pitt River]). "I grew up between two rivers and remember perfectly the smell and touch the land gives, in dry summer and brittle winter. This remains with me, here in the city where I now live. I work for my people, for our children as an educator. I do many kinds of writing, as well as poems. But the poems, the finished poems, give me a feeling of completion to moments in life, and help me keep them. I enjoy helping children write their poems and stories."

Elizabeth A. Woody (Navajo/Warm Springs, Yakima, Wasco). "These last few years have been productive. I have finished my second manuscript of poetry, *Luminaries of the Humble,* shown my artwork, and met many good people. As a poet, to find the pleasure in producing work has been an accomplishment. I am a founding member of N.W.N.A.W.A., and believe sharing work, and hearing others' writing, a gift."

Carole Yazzie-Shaw (Navajo). "Diné nishli—I am Navajo. I was born in a small Catholic mission at Tsénitsaa deez'áhí, Rock Point, Arizona. I went to school in Gallup and later received my bachelor's degree in sociology at the University of New Mexico. This was where I met my best friend, Curt Shaw, whom I married, and we now live in Albuquerque, New Mexico.

"I come from a verbal tradition, rich with stories that my parents and grandparents told me that I want to share.

"When I begin to write, it takes me home. I live in Albuquerque, but my heart and strength come from my family, my people, and my land on the top of Canyon de Chelly, called Lee tsoí, Yellow Clay. This is where I come from. I belong to the Tábhí, Water Edge clan. My father is Ta'neeszahnii, Tangle People. My grandfather on my mother's side is Tótsohnii, Big Water, and my father's father was Tódich'ii'nii, Bitter Water. . . . This is who I am."

Greg Young-Ing, a Cree from The Pas, Manitoba, works at the En'owkin Centre in Penticton, B.C., where he is managing editor of *Gatherings, The En'owkin Journal of First North American Peoples,* His poems have appeared in a number of magazines and in the anthology *Seventh Generation* (1989).

Ofelia Zepeda is a member of the Tohono O'odham Tribe (Papago) of Arizona. Born and raised in Stanfield, Arizona, a rural cotton farming community near the Tohono O'odham Reservation, her family is of Sonoran O'odham ancestry. She is a native speaker of the Tohono O'odham language and is completely literate in the language.

Her educational background includes an M.A. and Ph.D. in linguistics at the University of Arizona. Author of the first grammar of the Tohono O'odham language, *A Papago Grammar* (University of Arizona Press, Tucson), her teaching background includes courses on the O'odham language as well as a number of courses on American Indian linguistics, American Indian language education, and creative writing for native speakers of southwest Indian languages.

Involved in promoting literacy among native speakers of O'odham, she was a section editor and contributor to a volume of bilingual literature from the Southwest, *The South Corner of Time,* and editor and contributor to a collection of Pima and Papago poetry, *Mat Hekid o Ju:/When It Rains,* both from the University of Arizona Press.

She is currently an associate professor in the Department of Linguistics at the University of Arizona, Tucson, and is series editor of Sun Tracks.

Writers Attending the Returning the Gift Festival

Anne Acco, Cree
Humberto Ak'abal, K'iche Maya
Sherman J. Alexie, Jr., Spokane/Coeur d'Alene
Anne Anderson, Metis: Cree/Iroquois
Annette Arkeketa, Otoe, Missouri/Creek
Jacinto Arias Perez, Tzotzil Maya
Jeannette Armstrong, Okanagan
Bernice Armstrong, Navajo
Gogisgi/Carroll Arnett, Cherokee
Bernard Assiniwi, Cree/Algonquin
Marilou Awiakta, Cherokee
Lorenzo Baca, Isleta Pueblo/Mescalero Apache
Marie (Annharte) Baker, Anishinabe [Saulteaux]
Charles Ballard, Quapaw/Cherokee
José Barreiro, Guajiro/Camagüey
Russell Bates, Kiowa
Gail Bear, Cree
Betty Louise Bell, Cherokee
Kathryn Bell, Cheyenne
Diane Benson, Tlingit ['Tak'deintaan]
Duane Big Eagle, Osage
D. L. Birchfield, Choctaw
Gloria Bird, Spokane
Kimberly Blaeser, Anishinabe
Victor Blanchard (Singing Eagle), Pottawatomi
Columpa Bobb, Metis: Cree/Salish
Tracey Kim Bonneau, Okanagan
Beth Brant, Mohawk
Charles Brashear, Cherokee
Silvester J. Brito, Comanche/Tarascan

Vee F. Browne, Navajo
Joseph Bruchac, Abenaki
Helen Chalakee Burgess, Creek
Diane Burns, Chippewa/Chemehuevi
Barney Bush, Shawnee/Cayuga
Bobbie Louise Bush, Chehalis
Jeanetta Calhoun, Lenápe
Jose Balvino Camposeco Mateo, Jakalteko Maya
Gladys Cardiff, Cherokee
Helen Slwooko Carius, Siberian Yupik
Chrystos, Menominee
Robin Coffee (Cherokee-Creek/Sioux)
Hortensia Colorado, Chichimec
Elvira Colorado, Chichimec
Robert J. Conley, Cherokee [UKB]
Lynn Celeste Connor, Chiricahua Apache
Elizabeth Cook-Lynn, Lakota
Jackalene Crow-Hiendlmayr, Cherokee-Creek
Beatrice Culleton (Mosionier), Metis
Kateri Damm, Ojibway/Chippewa
Nora Marks Dauenhauer, Tlingit
Charlotte DeClue, Wa-zha-zhe [Osage]
Ed Edmo, Shoshone/Bannock
Melanie M. Ellis, Oneida
Anita Endrezze, Yaqui
Melissa Fawcett, Mohegan
Connie Fife, Cree
Jack D. Forbes, Renápe/Lenápe
Adam Fortunate Eagle, Chippewa
Lee Francis, Laguna Pueblo
Della Frank, Navajo
Marie Frawley-Henry, Ojibway
Alice French, Inuit
Forrest Funmaker, Winnebago
Eric Gansworth, Onondaga
José L. Garza, Coahuilteca/Lipan Apache
Karl E. Gilmont, Coharie
Robert F. Gish, Cherokee
Diane Glancy, Cherokee
Gasper Pedro Gonzales, Q'anjob'al Maya
Sister Goodwin, Inuit
Mary Goose, Mesquakie/Chippewa

Roxy Gordon, Choctaw
Janice Gould, Maidu/Konkow
Lana Grant, Sac/Fox-Shawnee
Rayna Green, Cherokee
Richard G. Green, Maidu/Konkow
Regina Hadley-Lynch, Navajo
Raven Hail, Cherokee
Duane K. Hale, Creek
Joy Harjo, Creek
Gordon Henry, White Earth Chippewa [Anishinabe]
Lance Henson, Cheyenne
Vi Hilbert, Upper Skagit
Geary Hobson, Cherokee–Quapaw/Chickasaw
Linda Hogan, Chickasaw
Andrew Hope, Sitka Tribe of Alaska [Tlingit]
LeAnne Howe, Choctaw
Rosa Howling Buffalo, Arapaho-Cheyenne
Alootook Ipellie, Inuit
Morris Isaac, Micmac
Roger Jack, Colville
Alex Jacobs, Mohawk
Rex Lee Jim, Diné [Navajo]
Basil H. Johnston, Ojibway
Ted Jojola, Isleta Pueblo
Moses Jumper, Jr., Seminole
Lenore Keeshig-Tobias, Ojibway/Pottawatomi
Maurice Kenny, Mohawk
Wayne Keon, Ojibway
Alice Lee, Metis: Cree
Harold Littlebird, Laguna/Santo Domingo
Mary Lockwood, Inupiaq
Ramson Lomatewama, Hopi
Evelina Zuni Lucero, Isleta/San Juan Pueblo
Lisa Mayo, Cuna-Rappahannock (with Gloria Miguel, Cuna-Rappahannock
and Muriel Miguel, Cuna-Rappahannock) as Spiderwoman Theatre
Brian Maracle, Mohawk
Lee Maracle, Metis: Cree-Salish
Duane Marchand, Okanagan
Rudy Martin, Tewa-Navajo/Apache
Glen McGuire, Pawnee
Gary McLain (Eagle Walking Turtle), Choctaw
Howard L. Meredith, Cherokee/Akokisa

Barry G. Milliken, Ojibway
Felipe Molina, Yaqui
N. Scott Momaday, Kiowa/Cherokee
Victor Montejo, Tzutihil Maya
Joel Monture, Mohawk
Kelly Morgan, Lakota
Lynn Moroney, Chickasaw
Daniel David Moses, Delaware
Julie Moss, Cherokee
Joe Dale Tate Nevaquaya, Yuchi/Comanche
Duane Niatum, Klallam
Linda Noel, Concow-Maidu
Jim Northrup, Chippewa [Anishinabe]
nila northSun, Shoshone/Chippewa
Jack Norton, Hupa/Cherokee
William Oandasan, Yuki
Lela Kiana Oman, Yupik
Simon J. Ortiz, Acoma
Jane Pachano (Willis), Cree
Juanita Pahdopony, Comanche
Gus Palmer, Jr., Kiowa
Camela Pappan, Seneca/Ponca
Elise Paschen, Osage
Robert L. Perea, Ogala Lakota [Sioux]
Robert J. Perry, Chickasaw
Russell M. Peters, Wampanoag
Boyd Pinto, Navajo
Linda Poolaw, Delaware/Kiowa
Vince E. Pratt, Yanktonnai Sioux
Ronald Burns Querry, Choctaw
Philip H. Red Eagle, Coast Salish/Klallam–Sisseton Lakota
Carter Revard, Osage
Fredy Amilcar Roncalla, Quechua
Wendy Rose, Hopi/Miwok
A. C. Ross, Sicangu-Santee/Sioux-Ponca
Gayle Ross, Cherokee
Armand Garnet Ruffo, Ojibway
Alyce Sadongei, Papago/Kiowa
Ralph Salisbury, Cherokee
Carol Lee Sanchez, Laguna
Cheryl Savageau, Abenaki
Diane Schenandoah, Oneida

Doris Seale, Santee Sioux/Cree
Vickie L. Sears, Cherokee
Leslie Marmon Silko, Laguna Pueblo
Glen Simpson, Tahltan/Kaska
Michael W. Simpson, Cherokee/Yakima
Eleanor Tecumseh Sioui, Huron
Grace Slwooko, Siberian Yupik
Virginia Driving Hawk Sneve, Rosebud Sioux
ssipsis, Penobscot
Jean Starr, Cherokee
Rennard Strickland, Osage/Cherokee
Denise Sweet, White Earth Anishinabe
Luci Tapahonso, Navajo
Drew Hayden Taylor, Ojibway
Mario Perfecto Tema Bautista, Sipakapa Maya
Earle Thompson, Yakima
Dorothy Thorsen, Metis
Laura Tohe, Navajo
Hanauni Kay Trask, Hawaiian
Gail Tremblay, Onondaga/Micmac
Lincoln Tritt, Gwichin
Joanne Trujillo (Sarah Snowgoose), Pojoaque Pueblo
Judith Mtn. Leaf Volborth, Blackfoot/Comanche
Anna Lee Walters, Pawnee-Otoe/Missouria
Vincent Wannassay, Umatilla
Barbara Warner, Ponca
Emma Lee Warrior, Piegan
Robert A. Warrior, Osage
Eddie Webb, Cherokee
Cora Weber-Pillwax, Metis:Cree
Ron Welburn, Cherokee/Conoy
Bernelda Wheeler, Metis: Cree-Saulteaux
Jordan Wheeler, Cree/Anishinabe/Assiniboine
Ellen White, Coast Salish
Roberta Hill Whiteman, Oneida
Don Whiteside, Creek
Richard (Ray) Whitman, Yuchi-Pawnee
Ted C. Williams, Tuscarora
Ramona C. Wilson, Colville [Pittville]
Shirlee Winder, Seneca/Oneida
Craig Womack, Creek
Elizabeth A. Woody, Navajo/Warm Springs, Yakima, Wasco

Miryam Yataco, Quechua
William S. Yellow Robe, Jr., Assiniboine
Greg Young-Ing, Cree
Ofelia Zepeda, Tohono O'odham

College Students

Gino Antonio, Navajo
Heather Ahtone, Choctaw/Chickasaw
Susan Arkeketa, Cree/Otoe
Shirley Brozzo, Chippewa
E. K. Caldwell, Tsalagi [Cherokee]/Creek/Shawnee
Annissa Dressler, Paiute/Washoe
Chris Fleet, Akwesasne Mohawk
Catron Grieves, Cherokee
Donna John, Athabascan
Hershman John, Navajo
Irwin Morris, Navajo
Ruth Mustus, Assiniboine/Sioux
Julia Salcido Nathanson, Navajo/Yaqui
Penny Olson, Chippewa
Michael Paul-Martin, Cree
Suzanne S. Rancourt, Abenaki
Lorne Simon, Micmac
Jason Smith, Yuki/Maidu
Tina Villalobos, Modoc
Carlson Vicenti, Jicarilla Apache
Georgiana Valoyce-Sanchez, Tohono O'odham–Pima/Chumash
Natasia K. Wahlberg, Yupik
Carole Yazzie-Shaw, Navajo

High School Students

Aaron Athey, Mohegan
Sonny A. Buffalo, Seneca
Brandon M. Clay, Choctaw
Ashlee Crow, Choctaw-Cherokee/Chickasaw
Cassandra Gollnick, Oneida
Ruth Hall, Hidatsa/Sioux
Ronda Hicks-Jimboy, Creek
Leah Lamont, tribe not given
M. Antonio Lopez, Pojoaque Pueblo
George (Gussie) Mills, Jr., Tlingit/Haida

Brian Pekah, Comanche
Kathy Peltier, Navajo-Chippewa/Sioux
Joshua Peter, Athabaskan
Evie Sunnyboy, Yupik
Dawn Toppah, Kiowa-Otoe/Missouria/Iowa
Ragan Traughber, Kiowa